Yale Publications in Religion, 15

JUDAISM AND
THE EARLY CHRISTIAN MIND

A Study of Cyril of Alexandria's
Exegesis and Theology

by Robert L. Wilken

NEW HAVEN AND LONDON

Yale University Press

1971

Published with assistance from the foundation
established in memory of William McKean Brown.

Library of Congress catalog card number: 74-140541
International standard book number: 0-300-01383-3

Designed by John O. C. McCrillis
and set in Granjon type.
Printed in the United States of America by
The Vail-Ballou Press, Binghamton, New York.

Distributed in Great Britain, Europe, and Africa by
Yale University Press, Ltd., London; in Canada by
McGill-Queen's University Press, Montreal; in Mexico
by Centro Interamericano de Libros Académicos,
Mexico City; in Central and South America by
Kaiman & Polon, Inc., New York City; in Australasia
by Australia and New Zealand Book Co., Pty., Ltd.,
Artarmon, New South Wales; in India by
UBS Publishers' Distributors Pvt., Ltd., Delhi; in Japan
by John Weatherhill, Inc., Tokyo.

To My Father and Mother

Louis and Mabel

In Remembrance of the Happy Days of My Youth

If He conquered as God, then it profits
us nothing; but if as man, we conquered
in Him. For He is to us the Second Adam
come from Heaven according to the Scriptures.

Cyril, *In Joannem* 16:33

Contents

Preface

His part in the Christological controversies of the fifth century has assured Cyril of Alexandria a prominent place in histories of Christian thought. But there is another Cyril who has been largely neglected. It is Cyril the exegete, a man whose mind and soul were shaped by the rhythms of biblical narrative and thought. The present work is a study in the relationship between exegesis and theology.

Not only was the Bible central to Cyril's thinking, but his exegesis was preoccupied by questions not directly related to the Christological controversies. Cyril was profoundly concerned with Judaism. To understand his concern it is necessary to examine carefully the nature of Jewish-Christian relations in the patristic era. In this light, Cyril's exegetical and theological work represents an important stage in the development of Christian thought as it was shaped by the polemic against Judaism.

Like most American Christian theologians I did not begin to think intensively about Judaism until the past few years. Of course, as a historian of the early Church, I realized that Judaism was an important factor at least in the first Christian century. But it was easy to assume that after the second century Christian thought can be understood with only incidental reference, at most, to Judaism. I no longer believe this to be the case. Another more personal development strengthened this convergence of my historical studies and theological interest. About the same time I was discovering the significance of Judaism for the early Church, I was becoming engaged in conversations between Jews and Christians in the United States. The more I talked with Jews and read Jewish thinkers, the more I discovered Jews in early Christian literature, and the more I discovered Jews in the writings of the fathers, the more I cherished conversation with Jews of our own time. This happy coalition of theological, historical, and personal discoveries has convinced me that the role of Judaism in shaping patristic thought must now become a primary area of investigation for both Christian and Jewish scholars.

The investigation is neither easy nor always pleasant. The patristic attitude toward Jews borders on the irrational. This is true of most of the fathers and particularly true of Cyril. Thus at the very time that my appreciation of Judaism was greatly heightened, I found myself writing a book about a Christian theologian who had little but contempt for the Jews. I have tried to write with a Jew looking over my shoulder, an attempt that is aided by living in New York City. But I know much of this book will be and should be offensive to the Jewish reader. As a historian I attempt to describe and interpret; I cannot change what Cyril wrote. Neither would it be honest to try to disentangle what Cyril says positively from his polemic against Judaism. Indeed, it is central to the thesis of this study that what Cyril says of Christ is inextricably related to what he thinks of Judaism.

Cyril is not a lonely exception. In the mainstream of Christian thought about Christ, there runs a current of presuppositions about the nature of Judaism. Sometimes the presuppositions are unacknowledged, at other times they are flaunted, but they are always there. Only a few Christian thinkers today seem sensitive to the fact that Christian beliefs were developed against the foil of Judaism. The Church has viewed the continuing phenomenon of Judaism as an instance of religio-cultural lag, a bothersome theological curiosity, or as a communal denial of the Truth to be extinguished or engaged in dialogue, depending upon the climate of the times. I hope this work contributes to historical awareness of the factors which have shaped the development of Christian thought. I have not attempted to deal directly with theological problems involved in Jewish-Christian relations. But the reader should not be surprised if they come to the surface in the course of the study. Cyril's writings do not permit us to evade them. The long-delayed task of confronting and resolving these problems has a claim upon the most creative minds of our era.

Many people have encouraged and assisted me in various stages of the writing of this book. I am especially grateful to Professor Jaroslav Pelikan of Yale University, who first interested me in

PREFACE

Cyril, and Professor Robert Grant of the University of Chicago, who guided my original research. Over the last several years a number of friends and colleagues have read parts or all of the manuscript. Among these are Professor E. R. Hardy of Jesus College, Cambridge University, Professor Wolfhart Pannenberg of the University of Munich, Cyril Richardson of Union Theological Seminary in New York, Professor Philip Hefner of the Lutheran School of Theology in Chicago, and Professor Herbert Musurillo of Fordham University. My close friend the Reverend Richard Neuhaus, pastor of St. John the Evangelist Church in Brooklyn, was of great help especially in the final stages of the writing. Professor Gershen Cohen of Columbia University aided me with some of the Jewish materials. Much of this manuscript was written while I was teaching at the Lutheran Theological Seminary in Gettysburg, Pennsylvania. The congenial atmosphere there—the interest and support of President Donald Heiges and the assistance of the library staff—contributed to the progress of the book. I am also grateful to Father Christopher Mooney, my department chairman at Fordham, who has supported my work, to Miss Eva Hoenig and Mrs. Peggy Honohan who typed the manuscript, and to Mrs. Jane Blanshard for a careful and thoughtful job of copyediting.

Finally I wish to acknowledge the unexpected and refreshing contributions of my wife Carol. She never could get interested in Cyril and she provided the needed diversion and distraction when the book seemed to enslave me.

R. L. W.

New York
July 1970

Abbreviations

Full bibliographical information on all works cited in the footnotes is given in the bibliography at the end of the book. I cite the Pusey and Schwartz editions of Cyril's works wherever possible; otherwise I cite the reprint of Aubert's edition in Migne. Abbreviations for Cyril's works are taken from the listing in G. W. H. Lampe, *A Patristic Greek Lexicon (PGL)*. I cite exegetical works according to the chapter and verse of the biblical book on which Cyril is commenting. Thus, *In Jo.* 1:3 (P 1:25) = *In Joannem* 1:3 (Pusey, vol. 1, p. 25); *In Is.* 25:26 (*PG* 70:84) = *In Isaiam* 25:26 (*Patrologia Graeca,* vol. 70, p. 84). Other abbreviations which appear frequently in the notes are as follows:

ACO: Acta Conciliorum Oecumenicorum. Edited by Eduard Schwartz.
Ador.: De adoratione in spiritu et veritate.
AH: Adversus haereses, St. Irenaeus. Edited by W. W. Harvey.
ANF: Ante-Nicene Fathers.
Arcad.: De recta fide ad Arcadium et Marinam.
Chr. un.: Quod Unus Christus sit.
CC: Corpus christianorum. Series latina.
CPJ: Corpus papyrorum judaicarum. Edited by Victor Tcherikover and Alexander Fuks.
CSEL: Corpus scriptorum ecclesiasticorum latinorum.
CT: Codex Theodosianus.
Glaph.: Glaphyra
GCS: Griechischen christlichen Schriftsteller.
H: Harvey, W. W., ed. *Adversus haereses.*
Inc. Unig.: De incarnatione unigenitii.
NEB: New English Bible.
Nest.: Adversus Nestorium
NPNF: Nicene and post-Nicene Fathers.
PG: Patrologiae cursus completus: ser. latina. Edited by J.-P. Migne.

PH: Paschal homily.
PL: Patrologiae cursus completus: ser. latina. Edited by J.-P.
   Migne.
Pulch.: De recta fide ad Pulcheriam et Eudociam.
RAC: Reallexicon fuer Antike und Christentum.
SC: Sources chrétiennes.
Thds: De recta fide ad Theodosium.
Thes.: Thesaurus.

The translations of Cyril are my own, except where I have
revised those of Pusey, e.g. the *Commentary on John.* In the case
of other writers I cite the standard translations, where available.
With a few exceptions, which usually occur within my translations
of Cyril, I quote from the Revised Standard Version of the Bible.

I use the designation Old Testament to refer to the ancient
Hebrew Bible (Tanach, Jewish Scriptures). Old Testament is, of
course, a Christian theological term unacceptable to the Jew, but
since it is the most familiar designation used by the Christian
writers discussed in this book, I have decided to use it as well.
Another term would, I believe, have been misleading.

Introduction

The Jews are the most deranged of all men. They have carried impiety to its limit, and their mania exceeds even that of the Greeks. They read the Scriptures and do not understand what they read. Although they had heavenly light from above, they preferred to walk in darkness. They are like people who had neither their mind nor their thinking faculty. Accordingly, they were seized by the darkness and live as in the night. They were deprived completely of the divine splendor and did not have the divine light. Jews keep the Sabbath according to the Law, keeping their bodies from any work and pursuing sloth in their bodily activities.

Cyril of Alexandria

Why should a bishop of the Christian Church living in Alexandria in the fifth century engage in such a vicious polemic against Judaism? Cyril's writings are filled page after page with attacks on Jewish beliefs, Jewish institutions, Jewish practices, Jewish interpretation of the Bible, and Jewish history. If these were simply random references to Judaism, they would not be exceptional. But Cyril's preoccupation with Judaism cannot be written off as peripheral; it dominates his work. Only John Chrysostom, the notorious Jew hater, rivals him in the bitterness of his attack against Jews.

To be sure, both Cyril and Chrysostom represent attitudes which developed in Christianity before the fourth and fifth centuries. When Christianity and Judaism were engaged in a life and death battle, it seemed as though the very existence of the one presupposed the demise of the other. Christians claimed that the Church was the new Israel. If that was so, it was surely embarrassing to be confronted daily with the presence of the old Israel.

But Cyril was consecrated bishop in 412 after the victory of Christianity over Judaism. Why should a Christian thinker be so preoccupied with Judaism after it had apparently ceased to

be a threat? Put in that fashion, the question raises the interesting possibility that Judaism may not have gone underground and
that its presence continued to confront Christianity. Is it possible
that Judaism played such a role vis-à-vis the Church in the fifth
century? We know from Chrysostom's *Homilies on the Jews*
that Judaism in Antioch did have a strong attraction for the
Christian population. Could this be the case in Alexandria as
well?

Scholars have grown so accustomed to interpreting the development of patristic theology in relation to Hellenism that they
may have overlooked the role of Judaism.[1] The chief influence—
both positively and negatively—is generally thought to be Greek.
Indeed, the one motif which is regularly used to interpret the
whole patristic epoch is Hellenism. While historians are willing
to recognize the importance of Judaism for the development of
Christianity during the first two centuries, they have generally
dismissed its influence in assessing the later period. But many
of the most violent anti-Jewish polemics come from the fourth
and fifth centuries.

The statements of Cyril of Alexandria—reprehensible as they
are—are striking. They may represent nothing more than blind
rhetoric, beholden simply to the exegetical tradition and blithely
ignorant of Judaism. But they may indicate a more deepseated
aspect of early Christianity. In any case, they bear further investigation and bid us consider whether Cyril's theology was shaped
by a polemic against Judaism.

Another concern also shapes my approach to Cyril. Although he
was first and foremost an interpreter of the Holy Scriptures, the
exegetical writings have seldom been employed in assessing him.
No other Greek father, save Origen and Chrysostom, has passed
on such a body of biblical commentaries, and from time to time
historians of exegesis have studied Cyril's works. For example,
J. G. Rosenmueller, who wrote a history of the interpretation of
the Bible at the end of the eighteenth century, seems to have

1. On the interaction between Jews and Christians in the early Church see
Marcel Simon, *Verus Israel: Étude sur les relations entre chrétiens et juifs
dans l'empire romain, 135–425;* also Robert L. Wilken, "Judaism in Roman
and Christian Society."

read Cyril's commentaries with some care. And in more recent years Alexander Kerrigan devoted an extensive monograph to Cyril's interpretation of the Old Testament. But the standard histories of biblical interpretation pay little attention to Cyril and give him only passing mention.[2]

Furthermore, the discussion of Cyril's theology has gone on almost without reference to his interpretation of the Scriptures.[3] In this book I intend to show that his interpretations of the Bible play a crucial part in his theological work. I shall do so by singling out certain exegetical themes which run throughout Cyril's writings. These are the Johannine idea of "worship in spirit and in truth," the Pauline view of Christ as the "second Adam" or "heavenly man," and the Pauline idea of new creation derived from 2 Corinthians 5: "If anyone is in Christ, he is a new creation." I believe that I can show that these themes arise out of the Christian polemic against Judaism. The chief task will be to demonstrate how the sociohistorical situation in which Cyril wrote influenced his exegesis of the Bible and how his exegesis influenced his theology.

At first glance Cyril of Alexandria is an unlikely candidate for such a study. In the history of theology he has been viewed

2. J. G. Rosenmueller, *Historia interpretationis librorum sacrorum in ecclesia christiana,* is still the most perceptive and complete history of the interpretation of the Bible. The very thorough discussion of Cyril (4:142 ff.) recognizes how markedly he differs from other Alexandrians. Rosenmueller also recognizes, rightly I believe, that Cyril has no clear exegetical principle guiding his work and often appears highly arbitrary. His concluding comment is worth citing: "Disputationes contra Hereticos, subtilitates dialecticas et somnia mystica, quibus hic Commentarius refertus est, commemorare, non est operae pretium" (pp. 179–80). Alexander Kerrigan, *St. Cyril of Alexandria: Interpreter of the Old Testament;* see also his article, "The Objects of the Literal and Spiritual Senses of the New Testament According to St. Cyril of Alexandria." Frederic Farrar's *History of Interpretation* mentions Cyril once—in a footnote. L. Diestel, *Geschichte des Alten Testaments in der christlichen Kirche,* and Robert M. Grant, *The Bible in the Church,* do not discuss him, nor does Wolfgang E. Gerber, in his recent article, "Exegese."

3. An exception is Luis M. Armendariz, *El Nuevo Moisés. Dinámica christocéntrica en la tipología de Cirilo Alejandrino.* See also the articles: Augustin Dupré la Tour, "La Doxa du Christ dans les oeuvres exégétiques de saint Cyrille d'Alexandrie"; J.-C. Dhôtel, "La 'sanctification' du Christ d'après Hébreux II, 11."

almost solely as a Christological thinker.[4] Hence he was interpreted within the somewhat narrow bounds of the traditional Christological questions. He is of course the chief exponent of the Alexandrian theological tradition and the most illustrious representative of this tradition in the Christological controversies of the fifth century. As the one towering figure in the fifth century in the East, he did crush his opponent Nestorius, and his ideas and language permeate the later Christological discussions. One cannot write the history of the period without granting a large space to Alexandria and to its prominent bishop. Cyril's letters are almost wholly preoccupied with the Christological controversy, and the majority of his dogmatic and polemical writings after 428—the outbreak of the controversy with Nestorius—deal explicitly with Christological themes. These writings, which comprise approximately one-fourth of Cyril's extant works, contain little to indicate that he was engaged in a polemic against Judaism. Most of them are treatises directed against Nestorius and other Antiochene theologians. Some are tracts to justify his belief and behavior to the emperor and his court. All arose out of the course of events leading up to and following the Council of Ephesus in 431.[5]

The Christological writings, however, are only a small part of Cyril's total corpus. Between his consecration as bishop in 412 and the outbreak of the controversy with Nestorius in 428, he wrote several other dogmatic works on the Trinity, including the *Thesaurus de sancta et consubstantiali Trinitate* and the *De sancta et consubstantiali Trinitate*. There is some dispute about the precise dating of these works, but they certainly antedate the Christological writings and show Cyril at work on a somewhat

4. The most recent full-scale study of Cyril's Christology is Jacques Liébaert, *La Doctrine christologique de Saint Cyrille d'Alexandrie avant la querelle nestorienne*. Aloys Grillmeier devotes a large section of his history of Christology to Cyril; see *Christ in Christian Tradition*, pp. 329–33, 401–17.

5. The treatise *Adversus Nestorium*, for example, was written in direct response to a number of homilies preached by Nestorius in 428. For the chronology of Cyril's writings see especially G. Jouassard, "L'activité littéraire de saint Cyrille d'Alexandrie jusqu'à 428. Essai de chronologie et de synthèse"; J. Mahé, "La date du Commentaire de saint Cyrille d'Alexandrie sur l'Evangile selon S. Jean"; Liébaert, *La Doctrine de S. Cyrille*, pp. 11–17.

different polemical front. Apparently Arianism, and such latter-day forms as Eunomianism, did not die after the condemnation at Constantinople in 381. At the beginning of the fifth century Arianism was still very much on the scene. Nor was it limited to a few scattered individuals or communities. It comprised organized groups with resourceful leaders capable of commanding the attention of the bishops and disturbing the life of the churches. The early works of Cyril arise out of the conflict with Arianism.[6] The *Thesaurus,* for example, is a kind of compendium of Arian objections to the orthodox view of the Trinity. In this work as well as in his other Trinitarian writing, Cyril is heavily dependent on Athanasius.

But before 428 the largest body of Cyril's writings by all standards is exegetical. We are not certain how many biblical books Cyril expounded because some of his works have been lost, but we still possess the following: two major commentaries on the Pentateuch, *De adoratione et cultu in spiritu et veritate* and the *Glaphyra* (Elegant Comments); a massive commentary on Isaiah in five books; an equally large commentary on the minor prophets; a commentary on John in twelve books; 160 homilies on the Gospel of Luke preserved in Syriac; numerous fragments on both the Old and New Testaments; and a series of paschal homilies which frequently include exegetical discussions. In the present edition of Cyril's works in J.-P. Migne, seven out of ten volumes are devoted entirely to exegetical works. Add to this the lost commentaries and it is apparent that the overwhelming majority of Cyril's writings were exegetical.[7]

Moreover, although we know the background and setting of

6. See Robert L. Wilken, "Tradition, Exegesis and the Christological Controversies," pp. 125–27; Liébaert shows how Cyril's earlier work was shaped by a polemic against Arianism. This is not to say that Christological questions had not been raised and discussed, but that they had not moved to the center of the stage. Witness, for example, the discussion surrounding Apollinaris, or more recently the interest in the problem of the "soul of Christ" in the *Psalm Commentaries* from Toura; see Adolphe Gesché, "L'Âme humain de Jésus dans la christologie du IVᵉ s., Le témoignage du *Commentaire sur les Psaumes* découvert à Toura," pp. 385–425.

7. For a listing of Cyril's exegetical works, see Johannes Quasten, *Patrology,* 3:120 ff.

Cyril's works on the Trinity and his Christological treatises, few of the exegetical works fit into those two categories. Of course, there is no need to explain why a bishop in ancient times devoted his literary efforts to an exposition of the Holy Scriptures.[8] The exposition of the Bible was one of the chief responsibilities of the bishop, and most fathers have left commentaries, sermons and homilies, and other works of an exegetical sort. But can anything more specific be said about the setting of Cyril's exegetical works? We do know that the *Commentary on John* arose, at least in part, out of the Trinitarian controversy, but this is not the case with the two works on the Pentateuch, nor the commentaries on Isaiah and the minor prophets.

In recent years a number of scholars have suggested in passing that Cyril's relation to Judaism may have had a bearing on his exegetical work. Alexander Kerrigan, for example, has called attention to the importance of Judaism in Cyril's day and intimated that this may have shaped his approach to the Bible. G. Jouassard suggested that the polemic against Judaism gave Cyril's exegesis some of its unique characteristics. For example, he called attention to Cyril's interest in the "historical sense" in the commentaries on the minor prophets and Isaiah, his widespread use of typology, and his concern for the relationship between the Old and New Testaments. Luis Armendariz reiterated the point in his study of the "new Moses" in Cyril.[9]

In spite of these suggestions, no one has actually taken up the historical question of the relations between Jews and Christians in Alexandria at the time Cyril was bishop. The suggestions are

8. This is, however, an interesting question and should be explored. For whom were commentaries written in antiquity, and what determined their "literary form"? We know that many commentaries were homilies, either preached on Sunday or during the week; others were more "scientific," e.g., Origen's on John; others were written for dogmatic or polemical purposes, e.g., Cyril's on John. Did the fathers follow the practice of the *grammatikos* who expounded Virgil or Homer, the model of Jewish commentators, or what? One of the few discussions of this question can be found in Henry-Irenée Marrou, *Saint Augustin et la fin de la culture antique* pp. 422–67. See also Robert M. Grant, *The Earliest Lives of Jesus.*

9. Kerrigan, *Old Testament*, pp. 2–3; G. Jouassard, "Cyrill von Alexandrien," 3:507–8; Armendariz, *El Nuevo Moisés*, pp. 17–18.

provocative, but they are primarily deductions based on Cyril's statements. No one has yet inquired whether there were significant numbers of Jews in Alexandria at that time and whether Christians and Jews had contact with one another. Therefore, my study takes the following form. In the first two chapters I discuss Christian-Jewish relations in the later Roman empire in general and in Alexandria in particular. I try to show that Christians and Jews did continue to interact and what kind of questions they discussed. Chapters 3 and 4 attempt to show how one of these questions, the relationship between the Old and New Testaments, informs Cyril's interpretation of the Scriptures. Chapters 5 through 8 discuss the exegetical-theological themes suggested by Chapter 4. In Chapters 9 and 10 I discuss these motifs in relation to Cyril's Christology and the controversy with Nestorius. In this fashion I hope to show the interrelation between exegesis and theology in his thought.[10]

10. On theology and exegesis in Cyril, see the comments of Jean Daniélou, "Bulletin d'histoire des origines chrétiennes," p. 272; also G. Jouassard, "Saint Cyrille d'Alexandrie et le schéma de l'incarnation verbe chair," p. 235. For a general discussion of the place of exegesis in the history of theology, see the chapter, "Exegesis and the History of Theology," in Jaroslav J. Pelikan, *Luther the Expositor.*

1 Jewish-Christian Relations in the Roman Empire

Judaism occupied a unique and special place in the Roman world. Ever a subject of interest and fascination, the Jews were approached with a mixture of curiosity, admiration, and wonder. Judaism appealed strongly to the religious instincts of the Hellenistic Age and made great gains in the Mediterranean world during the early empire. "As a general rule," wrote Philo, "men have an aversion for foreign institutions, but this is not so with ours. They attract and win the attention of all, of barbarians, of Greeks, of dwellers on the mainland and islands, of nations of the east and the west, of Europe and Asia, of the whole inhabited world from end to end." [1] There were Jews in most of the Roman provinces adjoining the Mediterranean as well as in Mesopotamia and Babylonia and the areas around the Black Sea. The greatest number were in Egypt, Syria, Asia Minor, and Rome. The exact number of Jews scattered throughout the Roman world is not known, but the figure has been estimated to be between four and five million. If the total population of the empire is estimated at fifty to sixty million, the Jews may have represented at least 7 percent of the total population. [2]

During the first and second centuries the Jews suffered greatly at the hands of the Romans, and their numbers were significantly depleted, especially in the eastern provinces. A large portion of the population fled to Babylonia and Mesopotamia, and it is there that many of the Jewish writings of the period originated. But Judaism did not disappear. Indeed, after a time it apparently recovered from the wars with the Romans and gained renewed vigor and vitality. The extensive legislation concerning Judaism

1. Philo, *Vita Moysis* 2. 20–25, in *Philo,* trans. F. H. Colson, Loeb Classical Library (Cambridge, 1958), 6:458–61.
2. Adolf von Harnack, *The Mission and Expansion of Christianity in the First Three Centuries,* pp. 4–9; Jean Juster, *Les Juifs dans l'empire romain,* 1:209–12 (see n. 4).

during the fourth and fifth centuries is only one testimony to
the continued presence of a lively Jewish community within the
empire.[3]

Rather than examining the history of Judaism during the later
Roman Empire, my comments in this chapter will be limited to
the evidence from Christian and Jewish sources concerning relations between Jews and Christians, especially during the fourth
and fifth centuries. Eight types of sources will be used:

Literary works of Christians.[4] Included among these are the
treatises *adversus judaeos* written from the middle of the second
century to the Middle Ages. References to Jews also occur in
sermons, commentaries, letters, dogmatic treatises, and almost
every other literary work written by Christians during this period.
The historical value of these works is difficult to assess, both
because they are so bitterly polemical and because Christians
frequently do not distinguish Jews of their own day from the
Jews of the Bible. Consequently, it is not always clear whether
they are providing concrete information about their contemporaries or simply reiterating the words of the Bible.

Jewish writings.[5] Here the problem is almost the reverse, because Jews seldom refer to Christians in a fashion which fully

3. See Robert L. Wilken, "Judaism in Roman and Christian Society."

4. See A. Lukyn Williams, *Adversus Judaeos. A Bird's Eye View of Chrisi-
tian Apologiae until the Renaissance;* A. B. Hulen, "The 'Dialogues with the
Jews' as source for the Early Jewish Argument against Christianity," pp.
58–70; Marcel Simon, *Verus Israel;* Juster, *Les Juifs;* James Parkes, *The Con-
flict of the Church and the Synagogue;* L. Lucas, *Zur Geschichte der Juden
im vierten Jahrhundert;* Robert Wilde, *The Treatment of the Jews in the
Greek Christian Writers of the First Three Centuries;* Bernhard Blumenkranz,
Die Judenpredigt Augustins; Adolf von Harnack, *Die Altercatio Simonis
Judaei et Theophili Christiani, nebst Untersuchungen ueber die anti-juedische
Polemik in der alten Kirche;* G. F. Moore, "Christian Writers on Judaism."

5. See Salo Wittmayer Baron, *A Social and Religious History of the Jews,*
2: chaps. 12–15; also Michael Avi-Yonah, *Geschichte der Juden im Zeitalter
des Talmud;* Judah Goldin, "The Period of the Talmud." For Judaism outside of the Roman empire see the recent work of Jacob Neusner, *A History
of the Jews in Babylonia.* For the use of rabbinic materials as historical
sources as well as for the light they throw on Christianity and Judaism
during our period, see the articles by Saul Lieberman, "The Martyrs of
Caesarea," and "Palestine in the Third and Fourth Centuries."

identifies them as such. The sheer complexity of the talmudic
literature is an almost insurmountable barrier for the nonspecial-
ist, and this makes it difficult to bring Jewish sources and Christian sources into conjunction. The Church historian with no
special training can hardly venture on this terrain without a sure
guide.

Ecclesiastical historians. The works of Socrates Scholasticus,
Sozomen, Thedoret, and others must be used only after careful
and critical examination. They are badly distorted by the Christian
bias against Judaism. To illustrate: Socrates reports that the Jews
attempted to rebuild the temple under Julian and that an earthquake foiled their efforts. The earthquake was sent by God, says
Socrates, as punishment for the Jews. They had no right to
rebuild their temple for they were living in disobedience to God.[6]

Laws. These include the canons of ecclesiastical councils as well
as the large collection of laws on Jews in the Codex Theodosianus
from the late fourth and early fifth century.[7]

Papyri. Thanks to the superb work of Tcherikover and Fuks,[8]
we now have some idea of the economic and social changes in
Jewish life in Egypt from Hellenistic times to the invasion of
the Muslims. Unfortunately, the papyri are frequently of little
value for cultural and intellectual history.

Inscriptions.[9] Here the yield is also meager for my purpose.

Archaeological finds.[10] In recent years a number of synagogues
which flourished during the period or shortly before have been
excavated. The most famous is the synagogue at Dura-Europos.
More recently a synagogue has been excavated at Sardis in Asia
Minor.

6. Socrates, *Historia Ecclesiastica* 3.20.

7. For ecclesiastical councils, see the material in Parkes, *Conflict of Church
and Synagogue,* pp. 174–77. For imperial legislation, see especially *Codex
Theodosianus* 16.8, 9. I quote from Clyde Pharr, *The Theodosian Code and
Novels and the Sirmondian Constitutions.*

8. Victor Tcherikover and Alexander Fuks, ed., *Corpus papyrorum judaicarum.* Hereafter abbreviated *CPJ.*

9. J. B. Frey, ed., *Corpus inscriptionum judaicarum.*

10. On Dura-Europos, see Carl Kraeling, *The Excavations at Dura-
Europos,* 8:322–39; also Erwin Goodenough, *Jewish Symbols in the Graeco-
Roman Period,* pp. ix–xi. On the synagogue at Sardis, see below, n. 59.

General histories of the period. Not much can be learned from these documents, but there are pertinent statements in Ammianus Marcellinus. The *Excerpta Valesiana* (sometimes edited with Marcellinus) gives an account of Jewish-Christian strife in Ravenna. The works of Julian, especially his *Against the Galilaeans,* give an impression of the kind of questions discussed by Jews and Christians.[11]

In assessing these materials, I shall focus on three questions: What were the questions Jews and Christians discussed with one another and how did the questions raised by Jews differ from questions raised by "Greeks"? Do the discussions of "Jewish questions" represent real or imaginary debates between Jews and Christians? Did Christians and Jews continue to have relations into the fifth century?

Turning first to the writings of the church fathers against the Jews, the earliest writing outside of the New Testament which deals at length with "Jewish questions" is the second-century Epistle of Barnabas, written early in the century—perhaps but not certainly at Alexandria. This epistle is not an apologetic work in the strict sense, for it does not attempt to persuade Jews or convert them to Christianity. Barnabas is concerned with the danger for Christians of reading the Old Testament in Jewish fashion and tries to meet this danger by developing another interpretation of the Scriptures. The epistle is devoted primarily to a discussion of passages from the Old Testament because "wretched men" (16:1) do not understand it.[12] Thus Barnabas argues that God is not really pleased with sacrifices (2:4–10), that he is opposed to fasting (3:1–5), that circumcision was only a temporary institution and is replaced by baptism (9:4; 11:1), that dietary laws are no longer in effect (10:1–12), that the sabbath has been replaced by Sunday (15), that God is present not in the old physical temple but in the spiritual temple among

11. *Ammianus Marcellinus,* ed. John Rolfe. For the *Excerpta Valesiana,* pt. 2, Item ex libris chronicorum inter cetera, see vol. 3. See also the material collected by A. J. M. Jones, *The Later Roman Empire, A Social, Economic and Administrative Survey,* pp. 944–50; for Julian, see William Cave Wright, *The Works of Julian.*

12. *Barnabas and Didache,* trans. Robert A. Kraft, pp. 84–85.

believers (16). He also devotes part of his letter to a discussion of passages from the Old Testament which he considers "types" of Christ, such as the bronze serpent. (12:6).

Like most Christian writers who deal with Judaism, Barnabas tries to show that his way of interpreting the Scriptures has roots in the Old Testament itself. Thus he regularly cites passages from the prophets which deplore Israel's lack of understanding and God's impatience with the religious practices of Israel. For example, quoting Isaiah, "What good is the multitude of your sacrifices to me? says the Lord. I am satiated with burnt offerings of rams and the fat of lambs," he uses the text to argue that the Lord no longer requires sacrifices or offerings. The external ritual is of no value. "Therefore he sets these things aside, so that the new law of our Lord Jesus Christ, which is not tied to a yoke of necessity, might have its own offering which is not man-made" (2:4–3:6). Similarly, he argues that the Lord set aside circumcision of the flesh and replaced it with a circumcision of the heart (9:5, citing Jeremiah 9:26).

Barnabas' extensive scriptural argument attempts to show that the covenant of ancient Israel has now become the covenant of the Church: "But let us see if this people is the heir or the former people, and if the covenant is for us or for them" (13:1). The Jews, because of their hardness of heart and their sins, were not worthy to receive the covenant; now it has been transferred to the Christians, for they keep the true Sabbath, understand the prescriptions of the ancient covenant, and are the new spiritual temple of God (16).

In some respects this early Christian writing is typical of the later apologetic treatises in answer to the Jews (*adversus judaeos*). It is extensively preoccupied with the interpretation of the Scriptures, particularly the Old Testament, and attempts to construct an alternative interpretation of the Old Testament which legitimizes Christian practice and belief. For this very reason, Christian writings dealing with Judaism regularly take the form of exegetical debates along the lines sketched out in Barnabas. Though the Scriptures were employed in works directed to the Greeks, they are not nearly so central to the argument and are handled in a considerably different manner.

The importance of exegetical questions can also be seen in Justin Martyr's *Dialogue with Trypho*. Here, as in Barnabas, the argument revolves around exegetical questions, and many of the same passages cited by Barnabas come up for discussion. Trypho had charged Christians with claiming to worship God but failing to keep his commandments; for Christians, he said, do not keep the Sabbath or the feasts, do not circumcise, and in general live very much like the heathen. "You have directly despised this covenant . . . and as persons who know God you attempt to persuade us, though you practice none of these things which they who fear God do." If you have a defense, wrote Trypho, "even though you do not keep the law," we would be happy to hear from you (10.4). Taking the offensive, he demanded that the Christians defend their use of the Old Testament.

In reply, Christians had to give a scriptural basis for their claims, and this meant a basis in the Old Testament. Because their interpretation conflicted with the Jewish interpretation, Christians were led to the conclusion that the Jews were spiritually blind, for they did not understand what the Scriptures were saying. "Jews do not understand the Scriptures," says Justin (9.1; p. 19). And elsewhere he writes about prophecies from David, Isaiah, and Zechariah:

> They are contained in your Scriptures, or rather not yours, but ours. For we believe them; but you, though you read them, do not catch the spirit that is in them. Be not offended at, or reproach us with, the bodily uncircumcision with which God has created us; and think it not strange that we drink hot water on the Sabbaths, since God directs the government of the universe on this day equally as on all others; and the priests, as on other days, so on this, are ordered to offer sacrifices; and there are so many righteous men who have performed none of these legal ceremonies, and yet are witnessed to by God himself. [29.2] [13]

Taken as a whole, Justin's apology to the Jews covers a wide range of topics: circumcision, Sabbath, the descent of the Spirit

13. Trans. *ANF* 1:209.

on Jesus, Christ's death and resurrection, specific passages from the Old Testament (e.g. Proverbs 8, Psalm 110, Psalm 72), the relationship between the old covenant and the new, the rejection of Jesus by the Jews, and others. The overriding question is the relationship between the old and new covenant, or, in more strictly exegetical terms, the relationship between the Jewish scriptures and the revelation in the New Testament.

> If the law were able to enlighten the nations and those who possess it, what need is there of a new covenant? But since God announced beforehand that he would send a new covenant, and an everlasting law and commandment, we will not understand this of the old law and its proselytes, but of Christ and his proselytes, namely us Gentiles, whom he has illumined. [122.3; *ANF* 1:260]

As Marcel Simon has pointed out, this larger question usually includes at least three specific areas: Christology, ritual prescriptions of the Old Testament, and the rejection of Judaism and the calling of the Gentiles.[14] These topics provide the basis for Christian-Jewish discussions and the themes of works directed against the Jews.

These questions regularly took the form of exegetical discussions and were influential in shaping the Christian interpretation of the Old Testament. During the third century Origen, in his fourth book of the *De principiis,* attempted an explanation and defense of Christian exegesis of the Bible. Among the reasons given he mentioned questions raised by Jews:

> The hard-hearted and ignorant members of the circumcision have refused to believe in our Saviour because they think that they are keeping closely to the language of the prophecies that relate to him, and they see that he did not literally "proclaim release to captives" or build what they consider to be a real "city of God" or "cut off the chariots from Ephraim and the horse from Jerusalem" or "eat butter and honey, and choose the good before he knew or preferred the evil."

14. Simon, *Verus Israel,* pp. 189–213.

Since Christians assumed the Messiah had in fact come, they had to answer the obvious question of why the messianic prophecies had not been fulfilled. For example, the Jews contended that the wolf had not lain down with the lamb because the Messiah had not come; but the Christians, who were not ready to debate that point, answered by interpreting the passages from the Old Testament in some other fashion. Origen, like Barnabas and Justin and most Christian writers, took this to mean that the Old Testament prophecies must be interpreted "spiritually." Origen wrote, "Now the reason why all those we have mentioned hold false opinions and make impious or ignorant assertions about God appears to be nothing else but this, that scripture is not understood in its spiritual sense, but is interpreted according to the bare letter." [15]

During the first three centuries Christian thinkers were forced to develop a systematic and thoroughgoing interpretation of the Old Testament. Christian tradition made clear that the Old Testament was to be kept in the church. Marcion's attempt to discard it was never widely accepted. Christians claimed that they were rightful inheritors of the patrimony of Israel and believed that they were faithful to this inheritance. At the same time, Christians knew they were not the same as Jews and had to demonstrate not only their faithfulness to the Old Testament but also the new import of their teaching, since, in Barnabas's words, we follow the "new law of the Lord Jesus Christ." [16] In short, Christian interpreters had to show what was *old* and what was *new* about the Christian revelation and interpretation of the Bible.

The same themes appear in a treatise against the Jews written at the beginning of the third century by Tertullian. The work, supposedly occasioned by a debate between a Christian and a Jewish proselyte which lasted all day into the evening, argues that, since Israel rejected the Lord and turned its back on God, it can no longer lay claim to the Old Testament. The Jews no longer understand the Scriptures correctly. They do not realize that the regulations of the Old Testament governing such matters as circumcision, the sabbath, and sacrifices have been shown to be

15. 4.2; trans. G. W. Butterworth, pp. 267–72.   16. Barnabas 2:6.

temporary and have been replaced by something else. Christians must read the Old Testament spiritually and not in the literal fashion of the Jews.[17]

Not too many years later another writer in North Africa, Cyprian, composed a book of a somewhat different character than Tertullian's but avowedly with a similar purpose. Cyprian writes in his preface:

> I have comprised in my undertaking two books of equally moderate length; one wherein I have endeavored to show that the Jews, according to what had before been foretold, had departed from God, and had lost God's favor, which had been given them in past time, and had been promised them for the future; while the Christians had succeeded to their place, deserving well of the Lord by faith, and coming out of all nations and from the whole world. The second book likewise contains the mystery of Christ, that He has come who was announced according to the Scriptures, and has done and perfected all those things whereby He was foretold as being able to be perceived and known.[18]

Cyprian's work is not really a treatise at all, for it simply gathers a great number of "testimonies" from the Scriptures touching on Jewish questions. The first part (1–7) treats the Jews

17. *Adversus Judaeos* in *Tertulliani Opera*, 2:1339–96. See especially chaps. 1–15. See the recent edition by Herman Traenkle, *Q. S. F. Tertulliani Adversus Iudaeos*. Traenkle believes that Tertullian is engaged simply in a "Scheinpolemik" (68–74). Traenkle may be correct in his claim that Tertullian's treatise is not addressed directly to Jews, but this does not make the work a "Scheinpolemik." As Simon, Blumenkranz, and others have shown, the works of the fathers on Judaism are sometimes prompted by the attraction of members of the Christian community to Judaism. The evidence from North Africa from the time of Tertullian to Augustine suggests that Jews were always present and did have an effect on the Christians. See P. Monceaux, "Les Colonies juives dans l'Afrique romaine," pp. 1 ff. Traenkle is aware of the evidence against his position, but he dismisses it on the assumption, it seems, that there *could* not be an *Auseinandersetzung* between Jews and Christians and therefore there *was* none. He dismisses the work of Simon in a footnote. Since this entire chapter is directed to the question raised by Traenkle, we will return to this matter at the end of it.

18. *Ad Quirinium testimoniorum libri iii,* preface (*CSEL* 3:1, 36); trans. *ANF* 5:507.

themselves, their sins, spiritual blindness and inability to understand the Scriptures, and their loss of their city Jerusalem for
their blindness. The second (8–18) treats Jewish ceremonies and
institutions: circumcision, old and new law, temple, sacrifice,
priesthood. Part three has testimonies on the new people and their
character; and the work concludes with what is in effect a plea
for conversion: Jews can only be pardoned for their sins by turning to Christ (24). In the second book Cyprian turns to matters
of Christology and discusses the incarnation and life and death
of Christ, the outcome of his work, how he was crucified by
the Jews, and his ultimate victory in the resurrection.

At a later date but still in North Africa Augustine wrote a
little work—perhaps a sermon—entitled *Adversus Judaeos*. It too
is largely concerned with exegetical questions concerning the
interpretation of the Old Testament. Augustine says that the Jews
ask, Why do you read the law but not follow its precepts?
"They base their complaint on the fact that we do not circumcise
the foreskin of the male, and we eat the flesh of animals which
the law declares unclean, and we do not observe the sabbath, new
moons and their festival days in a purely human way." Augustine
answers that the things of the law were types and shadows and
now that the thing itself has appeared we have given up the
types.[19] To establish his point, he turns to a number of texts from
the Old Testament, chiefly Psalms, and offers what he considers
to be their true interpretation.

Now we cannot claim more about these books in answer to
the Jews than they allow. The mere fact that Christians wrote
books of this sort is not sure proof that they were responding to
actual Jews. They may represent simply a literary tradition whose
raison d'être had lost its significance. On the other hand we
know that there were Jews living in North Africa, for example,
throughout these centuries (see n. 17), and it seems possible that
the continuous tradition of works against Jews in the patristic
Church reflected actual contact with Jews.[20]

19. *Tractatus adversus Judaeos* 1–5; on Augustine, see Blumenkranz,
Judenpredigt. See also, Augustine, *Epistle 196 Ad Asellicum*.
20. For other works in the West against Judaism see Blumenkranz, *Judenpredigt*, pp. 13–58.

To suggest that Christian works in answer to the Jews have real opponents in mind does not imply that the works were necessarily written directly to the Jews. In some cases it seems that the audience is clearly Christian and that the writer attempts to provide his hearers with the information and arguments necessary to engage in discussion with the Jews. This may be the case with Augustine's *Adversus Judaeos.* In the same way some of these works may be designed to attack Judaizers within the Church who either imported Jewish practices—for example, keeping of the Sabbath—into Christianity or participated in Jewish rites and festivals. Therefore, even if the works against the Jews are not themselves addressed to the Jewish community, they seem to give evidence that Christians had to contend with Jews during the period under discussion.

In the East Eusebius wrote two massive apologetic works, one, the *Demonstratio Evangelica,* addressed to the Jews, and the other, the *Preparatio Evangelica* addressed to the Gentiles. In the former work Eusebius sets out to explain why Christians have a right to read the books of the Jews and why they nevertheless reject the prescriptions of the Old Testament.[21] Like other writers Eusebius claims that the Mosaic law was only a temporary dispensation which served to prepare for the more permanent dispensation revealed in Christ. The work is largely exegetical and seeks to demonstrate by reference to the Jewish scriptures that the prophets foresaw the downfall of the state of Israel, as well as the coming of the Messiah, and even the call of the Gentiles. The later books are primarily devoted to Christology.

The most vituperative and vindictive attack on the Jews from Christian antiquity is in the famous homilies of John Chrysostom delivered to Christians in Antioch in 386 or 387.[22] The purpose of these homilies was to warn of the dangers of association with the Jews. Apparently Christians found Jewish rites and practices very attractive and had begun to observe some Jewish customs in their homes or in the synagogue. Chrysostom was appalled.

21. *Demonstratio Evangelica* 1.1.
22. *PG* 48:843–942; see Marcel Simon, "La polemique anti-juive de S. Jean-Chrysostome et le mouvement judaïsant d'Antioche," pp. 403–29; also *Verus Israel,* pp. 256–63.

What greater and more heinous apostasy than for Christians to take up some marks of a way of life which has been rejected by God? Even Jewish history, says Chrysostom, shows what fate befell the Jews because they refused to accept the Christ sent from God. It was not the emperors of Rome who devastated Jerusalem, but God who punished the Jews because they rejected Christ. In one passage Chrysostom cites Luke 21:24, "Jerusalem will be trodden down by the Gentiles," and interprets the text as follows. "This testimony has surely been discounted by you, nor have you accepted the things which were spoken. . . . This is the wonder, O Jews, that he whom you crucified afterwards destroyed your city, scattered your people, and dispersed your nation everywhere, teaching that he rose and lives and is now in the heavens. . . . But you do not yet believe, nor think him God and ruler of the world, but simply one man among men." [23] Why should Christians, says Chrysostom, frequent the synagogues of the Jews?

From approximately the same period we have a long series of homilies by Aphrahat, the Syrian theologian, which shed an interesting light on the relationship of Jews to Christians. Aphrahat, who of course was not writing within the Roman empire but in Persia, responded to the familiar charges found in other writers: e.g. ritual prescriptions of the law, the relationship between the two testaments, Christology. But in addition to these questions he was forced to answer attacks on the peculiar traits of Syriac Christianity, as for example its excessive asceticism. In *Homily* 18 he says that he will speak of something dear to his heart, "namely concerning this holy covenant and the virginal life and holiness in which we stand, at which the people of the Jews on account of their material nature and carnal desires take offense." The Jews say that the creator commanded men to be fruitful and multiply. Christians who practice celibacy are said to promote unfruitfulness and place themselves against the law. Aphrahat replies that a man can do the will of God and be blessed even if he lives without wife and children.[24] These

23. PG 48:884.
24. *Demonstration* 18.1 (*Patrologia Syriaca* 1:1, 817); also *Demon.* 18.11 (PS 1:1, 841–44), *Demon.* 22.25 (PS 1:1, 1043). On Aphrahat, see Frank

homilies underline the fact that Christian response to Judaism did not follow simply a literary tradition. What Aphrahat says about asceticism is not characteristic of most of the other writers we have examined. But we do know that this type of asceticism marked Syriac Christianity and was the subject of attack by the Jews. The debate between Jews and Christians in this instance was based on genuine acquaintance with one another and not solely on caricature or misunderstanding.

Writings such as these against the Jews are only a small segment of the literature devoted to this topic. There are many other works, as for example Novatian's *Epistula de cibis judaicis,* a technical discussion of the food laws of the Old Testament. Novatian offers a theological argument against the idea of "clean" and "unclean" animals, suggesting that God, after making everything good, would not declare certain things unclean.[25] In another vein altogether Jerome's commentaries give extensive evidence of continued contact between Jews and Christians.[26] There are a number of lost works on the Jews preserved only in fragments, as, for example Theodoret of Cyrus's work in answer to the Jews.[27] This impressive body of literature indicates the degree to which Christians addressed themselves to Jewish questions and devoted a significant part of their literary efforts to a defense of Christianity against Judaism. In most cases the same questions arise: the relationship of the Jewish scriptures to the New Testament, the role of the ritual prescriptions of the Old Testament, and Christology. And in all cases the debate centers primarily on exegetical questions.

Let us now turn to another area. We noted in the introduction that the patristic period is generally interpreted in relation to

Gavin, "Aphrates and the Jews." Gustav Richter, "Ueber die aelteste Auseinandersetzung der syrischen Christen mit den Juden." On the distinctive marks of Syriac Christianity, see Arthur Voobus, *History of Asceticism in the Syrian Orient.*

25. *Epistula de cibis judaicis,* ed. Gustav Landgraf and C. Weyman.

26. See, for example, G. Bardy, "S. Jérome et ses Maîtres hébreux"; also David S. Wiesen, *St. Jerome as a Satirist,* pp. 188–93.

27. On Theodoret, see M. Brok, "Un soi-disant fragment du traité *Contre les Juifs* de Théodoret de Cyr."

Hellenism. The influence of Hellenism on patristic theology is of course indisputable, and there is abundant evidence to show that Christian writers self-consciously directed their arguments to "Greek" questions. This is clear in patristic discussions of the doctrine of God and cosmology, to name only two instances. What is seldom recognized is that the same writers frequently make the point that a different set of questions arises from the Jewish side and that in dealing with these questions one should use a different set of arguments. The rules differ, say the fathers, and one should be sensitive to the peculiarities of each opponent. The best illustrations of the practice of placing Judaism and Hellenism side by side come from the catechetical literature of the fourth and fifth centuries.[28] In the Address on Religious Instruction, Gregory of Nyssa writes: "We must adapt religious instruction to the diversities of teaching; we cannot use the same arguments in each case." We must, he says, distinguish several classes. "A man of the Jewish faith has certain presuppositions; a man reared in Hellenism, others. The Anomoean, the Manichaean, the followers of Marcion . . . have their preconceptions and make it necessary for us to attack their underlying ideas in each case." [29] It does no good, says Gregory to "heal the polytheism of the Greek in the same way as the Jew's disbelief about the only begotten God." [30]

Cyril of Jerusalem, whose catechetical work also survives, makes similar observations. In questions of faith, he writes, we should "silence the Jews from the prophets, and the Greeks from the myths promulgated by them." "The Greeks plunder you with their smooth tongues . . . while those of the circumcision lead you astray by means of the Holy Scriptures, which they pervert if you go to them. They study Scripture from childhood to old age, only to end their days in gross ignorance." In his exposition of the creed at the phrase about the Virgin Birth he says, "Both Greeks and Jews harass us and say that it was impossible for the Christ to be born of a virgin." To Greek we can answer by reminding them of several ancient myths, as that of Dionysius

28. On Judaism in the catechetical literature see Juster, *Les Juifs*, 1:297 ff.
29. *Oratio catechetica magna*, preface (*PG* 45:9a).
30. *PG* 45:9b; see also pp. 17d, 20a,d.

who was born of the thigh of Zeus. "But those of the circumcision meet with this question: Whether it is harder, for an
aged woman [Sarah], barren and past age, to bear, or for a
virgin in the prime of youth to conceive." [31]

In his catechetical work Theodore of Mopsuestia frequently
refers to Judaism, particularly in contexts where he lists the
enemies of Christianity. Thus he attacks Apollinaris, whom he
calls an "angel of Satan," for false doctrine, but also in the same
passage says that those who try to persuade men to observe the
law in the fashion of the Jews are also the angels of Satan. "It is
the service of Satan that one should indulge in the observances
of Judaism." [32]

This pattern of addressing the Greek and the Jew was widespread in the ancient Church. Already we have noted the
apologetic works of Eusebius of Caesarea to both Jews and
Greeks. In the *Preparatio Evangelica* Eusebius writes, "With good
reason, therefore, in setting down this treatise on the demonstration of the gospel, I think that I ought, as a preparation for the
whole subject, to give brief explanations beforehand concerning
the questions which may reasonably be put to us both by
Greeks and by those of the circumcision, and by every one who
searches with exact inquiry into the opinions among us." The
Greeks ask questions concerning the strangeness of this new
life, about apostasy from the ancestral gods, about accepting new
doctrines without rational investigation, and they cannot understand why Christians claim to be faithful to the Jewish heritage
but do not follow the Jewish rites. On the other hand the Jews
find fault with us "that being strangers and aliens we misuse
their books which do not belong to us at all." [33] In the conclusion to the work Eusebius reiterates this point in anticipation
of his second apologetic work, the *Demonstratio Evangelica,*
directed against the Jews. "It remains, therefore, to make answer
to those of the circumcision who find fault with us, as to why

31. *Catechetical Lectures* 13.37; 4.2; 12.27–29; also 10.2; 7.8.

32. A. Mingana, ed., *Commentary of Theodore of Mopsuestia on the Lord's
Prayer,* pp. 40–42.

33. *Praeparatio Evangelica,* preface; trans. E. H. Gifford, *Eusebii pamphili
evangelicae praeparationis libri XV,* pp. 3, 5.

we, being foreigners and aliens, make use of their books, which, as they would say, do not belong to us at all; or why, if we gladly accept their oracles, we do not also render our life conformable to their law." [34]

About the same time Athanasius in his work *De incarnatione* also divided the objections to his argument into two classes, Jewish and Greek objections. "Let us put to rebuke both the disbelief of the Jews and the scoffing of the Gentiles." In sections 33–40 of the work he gives his reply to the Jews and here he relies almost wholly on arguments drawn from the Scriptures. "Jews in their incredulity may be refuted from the Scriptures which even they themselves read." [35] Basil of Caesarea, writing a generation later than Athanasius and Eusebius, also divides his opponents in the same way. "After having enlightened the Jews, it dissipates the error of the Gentiles . . . to make you understand that the son is with the father and yet guard you from the danger of polytheism." [36]

The same twofold approach appears in Cyril. In his paschal homilies he frequently complains on the one hand of the "blasphemy" of the Jews and on the other of the "mania" of the Greeks. The Jews are more demented than the Greeks for they possess the Scriptures and still do not understand them. "For one is not amazed that someone who has not read the Scripture is so deluded about divine teaching, as in the case of the Greeks, but when those nurtured in the law and prophets do not understand there is no excuse." The Greek should be met with reason and logic, but the Jew can be persuaded only if he sees that Christianity is the inheritor of the tradition of Israel. "How long will you continue in unbelief, O Jew? When will you listen to the voices of the holy ones? Perhaps you will say: Paul belongs to you, not to me. Spoken fairly and justly. But Paul whom you deny, is a Hebrew." [37]

We see then that Christian writers, especially in catechetical

34. Ibid. 14.52 (p. 856).

35. *De incarnatione* 33. Of the Greeks, Athanasius says, "Let us put them also to shame on reasonable grounds—mainly from what we ourselves see." (*De incarn.* 41).

36. *Hexameron* 9.6; See also *Epistle* 45 and PG 31:600.

37. *Paschal Homily* 4.4 (PG 77:460d–461a); 4.6 (PG 465b–c).

literature, but also elsewhere, continued to address their arguments to two different audiences even in the fourth and fifth centuries. This evidence along with the works written *adversus judaeos* suggests that we may be dealing with more than a literary tradition. James Parkes writes:

> During the period of the catechumenate a pagan was being for the first time introduced to the doctrines of the Church, and perhaps also was making his first acquaintance with the Scriptures common to both Jews and Christians. It was an obvious opportunity for Jews to put forward rival interpretations, and in actual fact we find considerable evidence that they did so in the frequent warnings against Jewish interpretations contained in the catechetical addresses of different readers.[38]

The literary works dealing with Judaism, however, are not sufficient evidence for the interaction of Jews and Christians during the period. We must look now at other evidence. During the fourth and fifth centuries the impressive number of canonical regulations of ecclesiastical councils attest to the presence of Jews and Judaizing influences throughout the empire. In Spain, the Council of Elvira (A.D. 306) leaves the impression that Jews and Christians must have had intimate social relations. Thus, Canon 16 prohibits marriage between a Jew and a Christian unless the Jew is willing to be converted to Christianity, "for there can be no fellowship between the believer and unbeliever." Neither laity nor clergy were allowed to accept any hospitality from Jews. Christians were also forbidden to have their fields blessed by Jews, a strange prohibition, but one which shows how deeply Christians were impressed by Judaism even to the point of employing Jewish ritual. The Council of Elvira also had several regulations on adultery between Christians, but added a further law which expressly prohibited adultery between Jews and Christians. Jews were very numerous in Spain and apparently grew in importance during the Christian era; in this period some Christians of high rank in Spain became Jews.[39]

---

38. Parkes, *Conflict of Church and Synagogue*, p. 172; see also p. 163.
39. Synod of Elvira, *Canons* 16, 49, 50, 78, ed. F. Lauchert, pp. 16, 21, 25–26.

In the Canons of Laodicea, a fourth-century collection of
ecclesiastical regulations, similar prohibitions against Judaizing
tendencies are found. In Canon 29 we read, "Christians shall not
Judaize and be idle on Saturday, but shall work on that day;
but the Lord's day they shall especially honor, and, as being
Christian, shall if possible, do no work on that day. If, however,
they are found Judaizing, they shall be shut out from Christ."
Canon 16 may hint at the same thing: "On Saturday, the
Gospels and other portions of the Scripture shall be read aloud."
This may simply mean that services shall be held on Saturday
as well as Sunday. But it may be directed against Christians who
read the Old Testament on Saturday but not sections from the
Gospels. A typical example of how this kind of evidence has
been dismissed occurs in Charles Hefele's work on the councils.
He simply writes off the possibility that this refers to Judaizing
by assuming that such could not have been the case in the fourth
century. "I may add that about the middle, or at least in the
last half of the fourth century, Judaizing no longer flourished,
and probably no single Christian congregation held such Ebionite,
un-Evangelical views." [40] An astounding conclusion in light of
Chrysostom's *Homilies on the Jews*—delivered in the latter half
of the fourth century!

We also learn of other legislation, such as the canon which
forbids Christians to carry oil to a synagogue or light lamps in
Jewish festivals. A synagogue was not even to be entered. "See
that you never leave the Church of God; if one overlooks this,
and goes either into a polluted temple of the heathens, or a
synagogue of the Jews or heretics, what apology will such a one
make to God in the day of judgment, one who has forsaken the
living God?" [41]

Turning from ecclesiastical to civil legislation the overwhelming impression is that Judaism was a vital and significant force
in the empire. There is extensive legislation extending across
the late fourth and early fifth centuries. The laws, preserved in
the *Codex Theodosianus,* are not directed against Judaizers but

40. Synod of Laodicea, *Canons* 16, 29, 37 (ed. Lauchert, pp. 74–76). See
Charles J. Hefele, *A History of the Councils of the Church,* 2:311.
41. *Apostolic Canons* 62, 65, 70, 71.

against Jews and give evidence of the necessity of regulating Jewish life. From these laws we get the impression of a Jewish community which is numerically large, geographically widespread, a force to be reckoned with in society. Most of the laws occur in a section especially devoted to Jews, Samaritans, and the obscure sect Caelicolists. But throughout the Code there are other types of laws touching on various aspects of the social life of the empire—questions of marriage between Jews and Christians, slaveholding on the part of Jews, economic matters concerned with prices of Jewish wares, etc., as well as statutes protecting the rights of the Jews (long the Roman policy) and laws extending their privileges to worship in their synagogues undisturbed.[42]

In a number of sections we get a glimpse of outright hostility between Jews and Christians, as in the statement that Jews burned a "simulated holy cross," [43] but largely we can only conjecture what the day-to-day intercourse between Jews and Christians actually was. Christians were apparently as guilty as Jews of committing outrages, for in a rescript sent to the Count of the Oriens in 393 we read, "We are gravely disturbed that their assemblies have been forbidden in certain places. Your sublime Magnitude will, therefore, after receiving this order, restrain with proper severity the excesses of those persons who, in the name of the Christian religion, presume to commit certain unlawful acts and attempt to destroy and despoil the synagogues." [44] Several other laws refer to burnings and destruction of synagogues, and the very fact that the government had to restrain such activity may be an indication of how widespread the conflict was between Jews and Christians and how Christians, exploiting their new status, harassed the Jews.[45] What impresses the reader, however, is the sheer volume of legislation from the late fourth and early fifth century touching on Jewish matters.

42. See Wilken, "Judaism," pp. 322–26; James Everett Seaver, *Persecution of the Jews in the Roman Empire;* Juster, *Les Juifs,* 1:168–72.

43. *Codex Theodosianus* 16.8.18; hereafter cited *CT.*

44. *CT* 16.8.9 (Pharr, p. 468).

45. *CT* 16.8.21,25; 16.9,1–5; 3.1.5; 16.8.24,8.6; 9.7.5,45.2; 16.5.44,7.3.

Beginning in the early part of the fourth century and continuing into the fifth century a number of laws were passed regulating slavery: prohibiting Jews from circumcising a Christian slave, from coercing a Christian slave to practice Judaism, and (in 417) from acquiring new Christian slaves. In 423 Jews were prohibited from building new synagogues. They were forbidden to contract marriages with Christian women, and any such union was considered adulterous. Apparently some Jews tried to pass as Christians or even join the Church in the hope of getting free of debts, for in 397 a law was passed outlawing this maneuver. In 408 the "audacity" of Jews, Donatists, and heretics had grown so great, said the law, that penalties were inflicted on those who did anything contrary to the Catholic Church. And as corroboration of Chrysostom's homilies against Judaizers, a law from almost the same time (383) calls attention to apostate Christians who have taken up the "contagions of the Jews." [46] These few examples should serve to illustrate the point.

Were the only contacts between Judaism and Christianity through riots, the torch, and persecution? Is there any evidence of actual discussions and debates with Jews on exegetical and theological matters?

In the *Contra Celsum* Origen mentions debates with Jews: "I remember that once in a discussion with some Jews, who were alleged to be wise, when many people were present to judge what was said, I used the following argument. . . ." Frequently Origen counters Celsus by pointing out that a real Jew would never say the things that Celsus has him say, thereby suggesting that Origen had some awareness of what real Jews were like. Thus he writes: "A Jew introduced as an imaginary character would not have said . . ."; "I remember once in a discussion with some whom the Jews regard as learned I used these prophecies. At this the Jew said that these prophecies referred to the whole people." Further, he observes that in disputes with Jews certain matters are held in common: "Whether we are disputing with Jews or are among ourselves, we acknowledge one and the same God." [47]

46. *CT* 16.21.25.
47. *Contra Celsum* 1.45, 49, 55; 6.29 (trans. H. Chadwick), also 2.32;

In one of his letters Origen recommends the study of the Scriptures as an aid in responding to Jews in discussions.

> And I try not to be ignorant of their various readings, lest in my controversies with the Jews I should quote to them what is not found in their copies, and that I may make some use of what is found there, even though it should not be in our Scriptures. For if we are so prepared for them in our discussion, they will not, as is their manner, scornfully laugh at Gentile believers for their ignorance of the true readings as they have them.[48]

In the fourth century Epiphanius is reported to have had a discussion with a certain Rabbi Isaac of Constantia (Salaminia).[49] From Jerome we learn that Jews studied the New Testament for the purpose of refuting Christians and that their knowledge of the Scriptures sometimes enabled them to locate a text more quickly than Christians could.[50] Jerome reports on a bishop Sophronius who was ridiculed by the Jews for his lack of knowledge of the Bible. And in the commentary on Titus he describes in vivid language a lively discussion with a Jew, portrayed by Jerome as having large lips, a twisted tongue, and deep guttural speech.[51] Theodoret of Cyrus tells of debates he had with Jews "in most cities of the East."[52] From Chrysostom we learn that Christian clergy were expected to be able to debate with Jews.[53] Manes, the founder of Manichaeism, seems to have engaged in debates with them;[54] and Cyril of Jerusalem says that "Jews are always prepared for controversy."[55] Isidore of Pelusium, a contemporary of Cyril of Alexandria and a bishop

---

4.2; on discussions between Jews and Christians, see Juster, *Les Juifs*, 1:53–54; Parkes, *Conflict of Church and Synagogue*, 112–15; Blumenkranz, *Judenpredigt*, pp. 85 ff.

48. *Epistle to Africanus* 5 (PL 24:144).   49. *Vita s. Epiphani* 1. 52.

50. "Illud quod in Evangelio Matthaei omnes quaerunt Ecclesiastici, et non inveniunt ubi scriptum sit . . . eruditi Hebraeorum de hoc loco assumptum putant." *In Is.* 11:1 (PL 24:561).

51. *Ad Tit.* 3:9 (PL 26:595–96).   52. *Epistle* 113; ep. 145.

53. *De Sacerdotio* 4.4.   54. Juster, *Les Juifs*, 1:53–54.

55. *Catechetical Lectures* 13.7.

of a town in Egypt, tells of debates between Jews and Christians in Egypt and even mentions what passages of the Jewish scriptures were disputed.[56] A number of fathers wrote works entitled *Quaestiones Veteris et Novi Testamenti,* in which some of the questions seem to arise out of Jewish-Christian discussions.[57]

Liturgical materials—prayers and hymns, the ordering of the calendar, the celebration of festivals—contain a wealth of material pointing to continued contact between Jews and Christians even into the later patristic period. One finds the persistent claim that the Christian cult is the only legitimate cult, as well as reproaches against the Jews in paschal homilies and prayers for the unbelief of the Jews. Juster is inclined to see much of the material on Jews in the liturgy as directed against Jewish proselytism.[58]

Testimony to the strength and vitality of Judaism during the period has come, somewhat unexpectedly, from archaeological discoveries, the most dramatic of which was the excavation at Dura-Europos on the Euphrates. The paintings on the synagogue wall have occasioned much discussion among scholars, and their interpretation is still a matter of dispute. But whatever the type of Judaism represented by this synagogue, it gives us an unusual glimpse of the creativity of the Jewish community during this time. Even more recently—and at a site within the empire—a building identified by archaeologists as a Jewish synagogue has been excavated at Sardis. Excavation of the site is not yet complete, and any thorough interpretation must await publication of the details of the find, but we do know from inscriptions that the synagogue was first built between A.D. 175 and 210 and was rebuilt toward the end of the fourth century. It is an immense building, some 300 feet long, and floored with mosaic. It includes a basilican hall and an apse with several tiered benches. Toward the western (apse) end stood a large marble table flanked by two pairs of lions. Reporting on the history of the synagogue David Mitten writes:

> The disrupted mosaic floors, the worn thresholds, and the evidences of remodeling throughout the building testify to

56. Chap. 2, below, has a discussion of these passages.
57. Simon, *Verus Israel*, pp. 212–13.   58. Juster, *Les Juifs*, 1:304–37.

a complex history throughout the fourth, fifth, and sixth centuries A.D., with a major remodeling in the fourth century, followed by increasing neglect. The synagogue appears to have been destroyed, along with most of the other major buildings in this part of Sardis, by the Sassanian raid under Chosroes II ca. 615 A.D.[59]

Interaction between Jews and Christians can be traced in the Christian writings of the period, as I have shown, but the evidence in Jewish literary sources is meager and difficult to evaluate. If there are references in Jewish writings to debates with Christians they are even more veiled and obscure than most Christian statements. However, critical study of rabbinic materials has uncovered passages that shed light on various aspects of Christianity during the patristic period. For example, Saul Lieberman's study of the Martyrs of Caesarea shows that rabbinic sources of the time corroborate and supplement Eusebius's work. He writes, "When we analyze the information supplied by the Rabbinic sources of the time and compare it with the records of Eusebius we see how remarkably they supplement one another." [60] It must be admitted, however, that most writers, both Jew and Christian, seem to have been reluctant to say anything concrete about their religious adversaries. Both Christians and Jews are like the contemporary politician who never names his opponent, while cutting him to pieces. But the question must be asked, Do we learn anything from Jewish sources that illuminates the topic before us?

When we go to the Jewish sources we immediately place ourselves squarely before the scholarly debate concerning the Minim, the "heretics" of Judaism, a matter of great complexity and one which is much beyond the scope of this book.[61] But it may

59. See the report by David G. Mitten, pp. 38–48; George M. A. Hanfman, News Letter from Sardis published by ASOR, August 10, 1965; *Archaeology* 19 (1966):96–7; Erwin Goodenough, *Jewish Symbols,* 12:191–97. A more detailed study of the synagogue at Sardis by Alf Thomas Kraabel, "Judaism in Western Asia Minor under the Roman Empire" (Ph.D. diss., Harvard, 1968), shows how important the Jewish community in Sardis was ca. A.D. 100–300.

60. Saul Lieberman, *The Martyrs of Caesarea,* pp. 396–97.

61. See Simon, *Verus Israel,* pp. 215–38; as well as pp. 500–3 in the *postscriptum* of the 1964 edition. For the older view that the Minim are

be helpful to adduce some of the passages from the Talmud
which touch on the kinds of questions discussed by Christians
in their works against the Jews. Marcel Simon went through
much of the material anew and argued that some of the passages
in the Talmud indicate that the term *Minim* is not reserved
solely for Jewish Christians or sectarian groups among the Jews.
Other scholars have come to similar conclusions with respect to
certain texts. No less an authority than Saul Lieberman, commenting on *'Abodah Zarah,* 4a, argues that "the simple meaning
of the text is that the Minim were Gentile Christians." [62] It is
unlikely that the term could have referred to Gentile Christians
at an earlier period, but by the fourth or fifth century it may
have been extended to include them.

Among the talmudic passages noted by Simon is the following:
"He who defiles the sacred food, despises the festivals, abolishes
the covenant of our father Abraham, gives an interpretation of
the Torah not according to the *halachah* and publicly shames
his neighbor . . . has no portion in the future world." [63] This
statement can be paralleled by passages in the fathers. Justin
says, "Is there any other fault you find with us, my friends, save
this, that we do not live in accordance with the Law, and do
not circumcise the flesh as did your forefathers, and do not keep
the sabbath as you do?" And to this Trypho replies that Christians "despise this covenant" and "neglect the commands" and
practice none of the things which men do who fear God.[64] Almost three centuries later Augustine echoed the same kind of
criticism of Christianity when he wrote:

> For they [Jews] say to us: "What is the reading of the Law
> and the Prophets doing among you who do not want to
> follow the precepts contained in them?" They base their

Jewish Christians, see R. Travers Herford, *Christianity in the Talmud and
Midrash.* Recently K. G. Kuhn came to the same conclusion as Simon, though
independently. See his "Se Siljonim und sifre minim" in *Judentum, Urchristentum, Kirche. Festschrift fuer Joachim Jeremias,* pp. 24–61.

62. Lieberman, *Martyrs,* p. 398.

63. Sanhedrin 99a. References to the Talmud and Midrash from the
Soncino edition: *The Babylonian Talmud* and *Midrash Rabbah.*

64. *Dialogue* 10.1–3.

complaint on the fact that we do not circumcise the foreskin of the male, and we eat the flesh of animals which the Law declares unclean, and we do not observe the Sabbath, new moons and their festival days in a purely human way, nor do we offer sacrifice to God with victims of cattle, nor do we celebrate the Pasch as they do with sheep and unleavened bread.[65]

At the same place (99a) of the tractate *Sanhedrin,* two lines above the passage cited at the beginning of this paragraph, there is a statement against "those who abolish the covenant of the flesh," which may be a reference to circumcision. It appears that one area of dispute between Jews and Christians was Jewish practice and that Christians responded by an exegesis which accented the spiritual significance of the ancient rites and practices. Augustine writes:

All of those things mentioned above [circumcision, Sabbath, etc.] the Apostle classified under the general expression of shadows of things to come, since at their time they signified events to be revealed which we have accepted and recognized as already revealed, so that with the shadows removed we are enjoying their uncovered light. It would take too long, however, to dispute these charges one by one; how we are circumcised by putting off the old man and not in despoiling our natural body; how their abstinence from certain foods of animals corresponds to our mortification in habits and morals.[66]

The question of the resurrection may also have been a matter of dispute, though the resurrection was also disputed within Judaism itself. The Minim asked Rabban Gamaliel, "Whence do we know that the Holy one . . . will resurrect the dead? He answered them from the Torah, the Prophets, and the Hagiographa, yet they did not accept it." [67] In this connection Gamaliel

65. *Tractatus adversus Judaeos* 3; trans. Marie Liguori, "In Answer to the Jews," p. 393.
66. Ibid.
67. Sanhedrin, 90b; Herford, *Christianity,* pp. 231 ff.

cites Deuteronomy 31:16, Isaiah 26:19, Song of Solomon 7:9—all
interpreted as referring to the resurrection. The biblical citations
support belief in the resurrection. If resurrection is already in the
Torah, Christians cannot claim that it is based on the resurrection of Christ. By showing the Old Testament roots of Jewish
beliefs, Jews were able to undercut the Christian claims.

The rabbis underline with particular insistence that the love of
God continues to be shown to Israel and that the apparent demise
of Israel in the destruction of Jerusalem is only temporary. Moses
is sometimes claimed as author of the Mishnah, and it is emphasized that the true people of God stem from Moses and possess
the Mishnah. Circumcision is traced back to the days before
Moses, a point of dispute in Christian commentators who claimed
that circumcision was a relatively late innovation which is not
part of the original covenant. There are passages in the Mishnah
which reflect Christian disregard for the sabbath, and some Christian writers (e.g. Aphrahat) go to pains to defend the Christian
practice. Elsewhere it is said of the Minim that they only follow
the Ten Commandments as given by God and do not observe
the other commands in the Old Testament. In all this the Minim
appear as the enemy par excellence, for they have some access to
the truth but totally misunderstand God's purpose.[68] The same
charge was leveled at Jews by Christians. It is as though two
brothers were contending in a bitter feud, each aware that they
share the same blood and came from the same womb—and because they can neither understand their differences nor reject their
past they ruthlessly pursue each other's extinction. One rabbi says
in the Mishnah, "Pagans have false ideas about God, because they
do not recognize him; the minim recognize him and have false
ideas." [69]

The term *Minim* may once have been applicable only to members of the synagogue, but as the years passed it was extended to
include Christians as well. Simon argues that the term came to
be used for Christianity as an immense apostasy from Judaism.
If this interpretation is correct it provides another bit of evidence
—now from the Jewish side—of the continuation of debates

68. See Simon, *Verus Israel*, p. 226 ff.   69. Tractate *Schabbat*, 13.5.

between Jews and Christians even during the later empire. This leads Simon to conclude that "we are justified in recognizing the reality of the doctrinal controversies. The Christian works, though their manner is perhaps stilted, have an echo of this." [70]

Now that we have surveyed some of the evidence concerning Jewish-Christian relations in the patristic Church we can return to the question posed at the beginning of this chapter. Do the many treatises against the Jews written by Christians from the early part of the second century through the fifth century reflect a genuine attempt to deal with real objections or are these writings simply part of a literary tradition which had lost its significance long before the fourth or fifth century? Adolf von Harnack, in a study of the Jewish-Christian dialogue *Altercatio Simonis et Theophili,* argued that such treatises do not represent actual controversies or discussion between Jews and Christians. Christians, claimed Harnack, constructed objections and conventions of reply, and they opposed Judaism not as it is, but as they imagined it to be. The objections made by Jews were actually constructed by Christians themselves on the basis of pagan objections to Christianity. After the time of Domitian, relations between Christians and Jews were an insignificant part of the religious life of the empire.[71]

Harnack's argument can marshall a significant body of evidence in its favor, and it has been the prevailing opinion in the study of the early Church. It rests on two pillars: (1) The works written in answer to the Jews are very similar in their argumentation and in their use of the Scriptures. This similarity between works written over a period of several hundred years raises the suspicion that Christian writers were dependent on a literary tradition divorced from the historical and social situation of the early Church. When Christians wrote about Judaism they had no idea what Judaism was like. They constructed a caricature and then developed their arguments to meet it. (2) "Jewish objections" to Christianity, that is, questions of the type a Jew might

70. Simon, *Verus Israel,* p. 233.

71. Harnack, *Altercatio,* pp. 75 ff. For a recent defense of this position see Traenkle, *Adversus Iudaeos,* pp. 68–88.

raise to Christians, are part of the standard repertoire of pagan critics of the Church. This suggests that Christians are really replying to Gentile criticism of Christianity even though the discussion takes the literary form of a debate with Jews.

There is no question that the fathers created a caricature of Judaism, and most early Christian critics of the Jews did little to familiarize themselves with what they actually believed. It is also true that Greek critics of Christianity, as for example Celsus and Julian, use "Jewish" arguments in their works. Celsus tries to show that there are obvious contradictions between Moses and Jesus. In the books of Moses, argues Celsus, God commanded the people of Israel to fill the earth and become rich. But Jesus said that no one may come to God if he is rich, loves power, or is too wise. "Who is wrong, Moses or Jesus?" asks Celsus. "When the Father sent Jesus had he forgotten what commands he gave to Moses? Or did he condemn his own laws and change his mind, and send his messenger for quite the opposite purpose?" Two centuries later Julian, in his *Against the Galilaeans,* tries to show that Christians are unfaithful to Moses and have established a new religion which is inferior to that of either the Greeks or the Jews. On the basis of this type of evidence some scholars have concluded that Christian literature on the Jews during the first four or five centuries does not reflect real controversies between Jews and Christians. But the evidence permits another interpretation.

The material presented in this chapter makes it apparent that Christians and Jews continued to have contact with each other well into the fifth century, and that Christians devoted a good part of their exegetical, theological, and catechetical endeavors to dealing with questions raised by the continuing presence of Jews.[72] Five points may be made in summarizing the argument

72. See the works of Williams, Parkes, Lucas, Hulen, and Simon cited in n. 4. Contra Harnack, L. Lucas writes: "Im Gegenteil wage ich die Behauptung dass ebenso wie im zweiten Jahrhundert auch spaeter die Propaganda fortgesetzt wurde, und dass sich vielfach die geschichtlichen Dokumente auch des vierten Jahrhunderts nur bei der Annahme einer Propaganda verstehen lassen" (*Geschichte,* p. 41).

thus far: (1) The anti-Jewish literature is more diverse than we have supposed. The topics discussed by Christians do not simply reflect traditional questions between Jews and Christians as they have been handed on in literary works; the discussion varied from place to place and author to author. Aphrahat reflects the peculiar experience of Syriac Christianity with the Jews, and Origen's discussion of the Jews in *Contra Celsum* demonstrates a degree of sophistication about Judaism that is hard to reconcile with the claim that Christians worked simply with a caricature. (2) The appearance of "Jewish" questions in pagan attacks on Christianity does not prove that Christian writings against the Jews were really directed at Greeks. Indeed this evidence proves just the reverse, namely that the claim "Christianity is unfaithful to the inheritance of Israel," when spoken by a pagan presupposes the presence of Judaism. Such an argument would lose its effectiveness if Judaism had passed from the scene. Further, the habit of distinguishing Jewish and Greek questions in catechetical literature and elsewhere indicates that Christians were actually forced to offer two different types of argument determined by two differing kinds of criticism. (3) We can document the fact that discussions between Jews and Christians took place throughout the whole patristic era and in most parts of the Christian world. This evidence is supported by legislation from councils, imperial legislation, and other sources. We also know that Judaism continued to build large and impressive synagogues during the period, and this suggests that Judaism continued to flourish. (4) In some areas of the Church Judaizers were a continuing cause of concern to Christian leaders. Judaizing at this time was not, as it has been in later times, represented by a so-called "Jewish attitude," that is, a kind of legalism. In antiquity Christian comments about Judaizing referred to actual borrowing of Jewish practices and to involvement in Jewish worship, festivals, and ceremonies. This kind of Judaizing assumes the presence of a Jewish community which was attractive to Christians. (5) The impressive array of works by Christians directed to "Jewish" questions cannot be dismissed out of hand. Why does this literature continue after it has supposedly lost its raison d'être? In the early medieval period the tradition of anti-Jewish literature stayed alive particularly in lands populated by Jews, such as Spain.[73]

73. Williams, *Adversus Judaeos,* pp. 206–92; see also L. Augustine Grady, S.J., "The History of the Exegesis of Matthew 27:25," who shows that among medieval commentators those who had firsthand acquaintance with Jews tended to give a more hostile interpretation of the text from Matthew (pp. 100–1).

2 Judaism in Alexandria

Jews settled in Alexandria with the founding of the city in 332
B.C. by Alexander the Great. According to Josephus, Alexander
gave the Jews a place to live in Alexandria and granted them
privileges on a par with the Macedonians.[1] From the very outset
the number of Jews was considerable, comprising a significant
percentage of the population of the metropolis. They were allotted
a special section of the city which Josephus called the finest
residential area because it bordered the sea in the northeastern
section.[2] By the time of Philo, in the first century A.D., the Jews
occupied two of the five sections of the city and may have numbered close to a million. There is every indication that they played
a prominent and influential role in Alexandria, especially during
the early Roman period. They enjoyed independence in governing their own affairs, they possessed large and numerous synagogues, and were by far the most creative writers and thinkers
of diaspora Judaism. "It is, perhaps, worth noting," wrote Tcherikover, "that they were the only group of foreigners from the
East who created an original branch of Greek literature."[3] In
Alexandria the splendor of ancient Judaism flowered in the work
of the philosopher-exegetes Aristobulus and Philo and the Hellenistic poet Ezechiel.

Judaism in Alexandria has rightly attracted the attention of
historians. However, most discussions of it are devoted almost
wholly to the first centuries B.C. and A.D.[4] No doubt this is partly
due to the abundance of sources from this period as well as the

1. Josephus, *Contra Apion* 2. 35; *De bello Judaico* 2.18.7; see also *Antiquities* 19.5.2. Some scholars have doubted this claim of Josephus, but H. I.
Bell, *Jews and Christians*, p. 10, argues that their views are not supported by
the papyri.

2. See *Antiquities* 14.7.2, where he cites Strabo, and *Contra Apionem* 2.4.

3. Victor A. Tcherikover and Alexander Fuks, *Corpus papyrorum judaicarum*, 1:61.

4. See for example the works of Bell, Shuerer, Milne, and Schubart listed
in the bibliography.

magnitude of the political issues between Jews and Romans at this time. We must not, however, let the significance of this epoch blind us to the presence of Jews in Alexandria after the time of Philo and the wars with the Romans. During the first and second centuries A.D. Alexandrian Judaism underwent serious persecution at the hands of the Gentiles in Alexandria; many Jews were cruelly murdered, their homes destroyed, synagogues demolished, and their leaders tortured. During this period the extent and influence of Judaism rapidly diminished, and it is something of a miracle that it emerged with any life whatsoever after the time of Hadrian. But the Jews did remain, though in drastically reduced numbers, and continued to dwell in Alexandria throughout the patristic era. H. I. Bell writes: "It [Judaism] continued nevertheless to play a not inconsiderable part in the life of the city until the year A.D. 415 when the patriarch Cyril . . . incited the mob to drive the Jews out of the city." [5]

The history of Judaism in Alexandria during the Christian era, however, has seldom been the subject of extensive research. The most thorough study is that of Tcherikover and Fuks on the basis of papyrological materials, but this work concentrates primarily on the Jews in upper Egypt where papyri are available. But by inference Tcherikover does draw parallels between Egyptian and Alexandrian Jewry. The purpose of this chapter is not to survey the history of Judaism in Egypt or Alexandria, but to discuss relations between Christians and Jews during the early centuries of the Christian era in Alexandria. I shall try to show that there were significant numbers of Jews in Alexandria up to the time of Cyril in the fifth century, that Christians and Jews had contacts with one another, though these were marked by increasing animosity, and that their contacts also included disputes over exegetical and theological matters.

The war of 115–17 destroyed Jewish social and cultural life. In towns where Jewish communities once flourished, the papyri give the impression of total breakdown; in other towns the Jews disappear almost entirely except for one or two solitary individuals who were spared. For example, in one village in the Fayyum,

5. H. I. Bell, *Cults and Creeds*, p. 41.

a town of 1000 males, there is record of only one Jew in the village in the middle of the second century.[6] The fact that so few literary sources remain from this period is itself a testimony to the devastation of Jewish life. Apparently the great synagogue of Alexandria was also destroyed and the activity of the Jewish court in Alexandria suspended.[7] Other than these few bits of evidence we are at a loss to say very much about Judaism in Alexandria during the second century of the Christian era. Unfortunately we are just as much in the dark concerning Christianity in Alexandria during this period. What evidence we do have of Christianity there at this time is difficult to interpret and it does not shed any light on relations between Jews and Christians. It may be that some form of Gnosticism was current in Alexandria during the second century and only toward the end of the century did Christianity assume there the form it was taking elsewhere in the Graeco-Roman world.[8]

By the end of the second century the fog begins to lift and we have a clearer view. In the writings of Clement of Alexandria we have the first sure evidence of relations between Christians and Jews.[9] Clement was apparently familiar with a "Jewish way of interpretation"[10] and this may be a reference to Jewish exegesis as contrasted with Christian exegesis. He sometimes refers to customs such as "Jewish washings."[11] He knows of controversies between Jews and Christians and in several places he supports his views with the phrase "a Jew told me so."[12] Clement is also familiar with the writings of Philo and other writers of Hellenistic Judaism who lived before his time.[13] In the main, however,

6. *CPJ*, Papyrus no. 460 (3:17–18).   7. Ibid., 1:93 ff.

8. See Walter Bauer, *Rechtglaeubigkeit und Ketzerei im aeltesten Christentum*, 49–64. For a more recent discussion of Christianity in Alexandria during the first two centuries see Manfred Hornschuh, *Studien zur Epistula Apostolorum*.

9. On Clement, see Robert Wilde, *The Treatment of the Jews in the Greek Christian Writers of the First Three Centuries*, pp. 169–80.

10. Clement of Alexandria, *Instructor* 1.34.3 (*GCS* 1:110, 29); see also Clement's reference to a possible rabbinic interpretation of Jer. 50:51 (*Strom.* 3.70.2; *GCS* 2:227, 30).

11. *Stromata* 4. 142.3 (*GCS* 2:311,7).   12. *Frag.* vii (*GCS* 3:225).

13. See Claude Mondésert, *Clément d'Alexandrie*, pp. 163–83.

he does not give us a great deal of information about Judaism in Alexandria and does not seem to have had extensive contacts with Jews. The situation is quite different with Origen in the next generation.

Origen, whose life spanned the first half of the third century, had extensive contacts with Jews and frequently commented on discussions between Jews and Christians. As noted in the previous chapter, he used his knowledge of Judaism to assist him in refuting his opponent Celsus. For example, in one place Origen, replying to Celsus's Jew, argues that Christian beliefs about Jesus are rooted in the prophecies of the Jewish scriptures. Origen sarcastically remarks that if Celsus had really wanted to give the Christians a good argument he should have cited those prophecies which they accept as referring to Jesus but Jews do not. "If he wanted with any show of logical argument to refute the belief in the prophecies, whether the coming of Christ is regarded as in the future or in the past, he ought to have quoted the prophecies used by Christians and Jews in disputing with one another."[14]

We also know that Origen makes use of Jewish exegesis in his own exegetical works. Gustave Bardy has gathered together the material from Origen's commentaries and it is impressive evidence indeed of Origen's familiarity with the Judaism of his time.[15] Other scholars have pointed out that Origen's work on the *Hexapla* presupposes close and intimate contacts with Jews in the establishment of the Hebrew text.[16] Some have tried to identify statements in the Talmud with conversations between Rabbi Hoshaya and Origen, though, if such conversations actually did

14. *Contra Celsum* 4.2 (Chadwick, p. 185). In one place Origen says that Jews press us on exegetical matters which we cannot avoid discussing (*Commentary on John* in GCS 4:199, 36–200, 1); see also chap. 1, n. 47. On Origen and the Jews see Robert Wilde, *Treatment of the Jews,* pp. 181–209; Adolf von Harnack, *Der kirchengeschichtliche Ertrag der exegetischen Arbeiten des Origenes,* 1:47–52; 2:81–87; M. Freimann, "Die Wortfuehrer des Judentums in den aeltesten Kontroversen zwischen Juden und Christen," 55 (1911): 554–85; 56 (1912): 49–64; 164–80.

15. Gustav Bardy, "Les Traditions juives dans l'oeuvre d'Origène."

16. P. E. Kahle, *The Cairo Geniza,* p. 162.

take place, they were probably in Palestine and not in Alexandria.[17] In his exegetical writings there are references to contemporary practices and customs of the Jews, to the *magistri et doctores synagogae,* to the hopes and disappointments of the Jews and their longing for the temple and the sacrifices of ancient times.[18] And what is most extraordinary for a Christian writer, Origen has something to say in praise of the Jews. Against Celsus he defends the Jews as a people whose life is worthy of admiration. They do not have gymnastic contests or shows or horse racing; their women do not sell their beauty. They still keep many of the ancient laws. Frequently they have greater wisdom than the philosophers; they have learned about the immortality of the soul and believe that a good life will be rewarded. Their only serious flaw is that they do not realize that their "novel doctrine" needs change in some respects so that it will be suitable for all men.[19]

From Origen and Clement, then, we have definite evidence of the presence of Jews in Alexandria and of contacts between Jews and Christians to discuss exegetical and theological matters. We are less well informed about the type of Judaism which existed in Alexandria at this time. Alexandria was the most creative center of Hellenistic Judaism and we would expect this type of Judaism to have continued into the Christian era. But it did not, largely because the bond between Judaism and Graeco-Roman culture was torn asunder by the Roman-Jewish wars. "The epoch of Philo was the last in which the ideals of a brotherhood between Greeks and Jews could still be seriously envisaged. The events of A.D. 66–70, fatal for the Jews of Palestine, decided also the fate of Egyptian Jewry: they put an end to any attempt at a reconciliation between the two nations." [20]

Christian writers sometimes distinguished between different types of Judaism, and Celsus seems to have known Hellenistic Jews. Eusebius, for example, said:

17. W. Bacher, "The Church Father Origen and Rabbi Hoshaya," pp. 357–60.

18. Harnack, *Der Kirchengeschichtliche Ertrag,* 1:47 ff.

19. *Contra Celsum* 5.42.   20. *CPJ* 1:78.

The whole Jewish nation is divided into two sections; the
Logos was forcing the majority to accept the prescriptions
of the laws according to their literal sense, but the other class
he exempted from this . . . that they might pay heed to a
philosophy which was more divine and too elevated for the
multitude, and that they might be able to grasp those things
which are signified spiritually in the laws.[21]

Origen, however, does not make such a distinction and seems
genuinely puzzled when Celsus cites statements by Jews which
could not have been made by the Jews that Origen knows. Celsus
had quoted a Jew as saying that the Logos is the "son of God."
To this Origen replies: "Although I have met with many Jews
who were alleged to be wise, I have not heard any who approved
of the opinion that the Son of God is the Logos, as Celsus has
said when he attributes this to the Jew, representing him as saying: 'Now if the Logos in your view is Son of God, we too
approve of that.' " [22]

In his study of controversies between Jews and Christians
M. Freimann argues that the leaders of the Jews who disputed
with Christians were Hellenistic Jews.[23] As evidence he cites the
Altercatio Jasonis et Papisci, the *Dialogue with Trypho, Contra
Celsum,* and other works. What he says concerning the *Dialogue*
may well be the case, but it is doubtful if it can be applied to
the other two works. So little of the *Altercatio* is preserved that it
is difficult to use it as evidence; Friemann attempted to deduce
the contents from the later work entitled *Altercatio Simonis et
Theophili,* but this is not a reworking of the earlier *Altercatio
Jasonis et Papisci* as he supposed.[24] And the evidence in Origen
seems to prove just the reverse, for he does not recognize the
Jew who speaks in Hellenistic terms.

Was Hellenistic Judaism widespread in the Roman empire
during the Christian era? Erwin Goodenough claimed that it
did continue well into the Christian period and he believed that
the discovery of the synagogue at Dura-Europos illustrated this.

21. Eusebius, *Praeparatio Evangelii* 8.10.18.
22. *Contra Celsum* 2.31 (trans. Chadwick, p. 93); see also 1.49.
23. M. Freimann, "Die Wortfuehrer."
24. A. L. Williams, *Adversus Judaeos,* p. 308.

In the last volume of his *Jewish Symbols* he also pointed to the newly discovered synagogue at Sardis as another instance of Hellenistic Judaism. Goodenough suggested, for example, that the immense table in the center of the synagogue at Sardis was the locus of a sacramental rite practiced among Hellenistic Jews.[25] Carl Kraeling has given a more balanced interpretation of the evidence from Dura and has been reluctant to draw such far-reaching conclusions about the character of Judaism at this time. He believed that it is possible to interpret the paintings at Dura in somewhat more traditional terms.[26] However, even if Goodenough is correct in his interpretation of Dura, this is an exceptional case and does not give us a basis for generalizations about Judaism in the empire. Furthermore, for the question of Jewish-Christian relations I do not think that the *type* of Judaism is the most significant factor. Hellenized or not, to the Christian a Jew was a Jew.

We can illustrate this point by reference to Christian exegesis of the Bible. Christians claimed that the Jews took the text of the Bible literally and because they saw only the outward meaning of the text they missed its true significance. But we know from Jewish exegesis of the period that many Jews used non-literal exegetical methods such as allegory and typology.[27] Not all Jewish exegesis was literal in the sense that it shunned allegory. When a Christian says that the Jews interpreted the Bible literally, it hardly means that Jewish exegesis read only the "literal" sense of the text. Christians mean rather that the Jews do not interpret the Bible Christologically.[28] The crux of the difference between

25. Erwin Goodenough, *Jewish Symbols in the Graeco-Roman Period,* 4:24 ff; 12:184–99.

26. Carl Kraeling, *The Synagogue,* pp. 340–63.

27. See for example Jacob Neusner, "The Religious Uses of History; Judaism in First Century A.D. Palestine and Third Century Babylonia"; also Géza Vermes, *Scripture and Tradition in Judaism.*

28. See *De princ.* 4.21; also *Contra Celsum* 5.60. "In fact, the reason why we do not live like the Jews is that we think the literal interpretation of the laws does not contain the meaning of the legislation. We maintain that when Moses is read, a veil lies upon their heart because the meaning of the Mosaic law has been hidden from those who have not eagerly followed the way through Jesus Christ. We know that 'if anyone shall turn

Jewish and Christian interpretations lay not in the methods they employed but in the different valuation each gave to the person of Christ. The Jews could read their own Scriptures without Christ; Christians thought this impossible. Whether a Jew was Hellenized or not, Christians would have found his exegesis objectionable and they would have had much to dispute with him about.[29]

In the fourth century the evidence for relations between Christians and Jews is meager, but what we do know suggests that relations were growing increasingly hostile. There was nothing like Origen's positive attitude toward and genuine interest in Judaism. Now the conflict, so deeply rooted in their separate histories, assumed wider significance as Christianity became the religion of the empire. Christians and Jews were engaged in a vicious struggle and one's success seemed to foreshadow the other's demise.[30] Christians now became associated with the ruling class. "Jews became openly hostile to the new rulers," writes Tcherikover, "and proffered assistance to any group of persons or to any social or religious movement in opposition to the official Church. Thus they certainly supported the Arians, and the Fathers of the Church classed Jews and Arians together as the fiercest enemies of orthodoxy. The Jewry of the Roman empire, though dispersed and lacking a national center in a state of its own, was nevertheless a considerable force, not to be overlooked by the Christian Church." [31]

During the episcopate of Athanasius, Jews and Christians clashed over the appointment of bishops to the see of Alexandria. The Arian bishop Gregory was appointed to take Athanasius'

---

to the Lord . . . the veil is taken away' and 'with unveiled face he reflects' as it were 'the glory of the Lord' which is in the thoughts hidden in the text." (Chadwick, pp. 310–11). See R. P. C. Hanson, *Allegory and Event*, pp. 237 ff; J. Daniélou, L'unité des deux testaments dans l'oeuvre d'Origène."

29. As the years went by, contacts between Palestine and Egypt increased considerably. Hebrew begins to appear in the papyri. For example we have the remains of a correspondence carried on by two Jewish leaders in Hebrew. At the time of Philo some Jewish leaders may not have even had a knowledge of Hebrew (*CPJ* 1:101–2).

30. See L. Lucas, *Zur Geschichte der Juden*, pp. 75 ff; 113 ff.

31. *CPJ* 1:97.

place. When the time came for his entrance into Alexandria, Catholics tried to prevent him from being consecrated, but Philagrius, the prefect of Alexandria, was an Arian supporter. According to Athanasius this prefect gathered together a large mob of heathens and Jews and set them against the Catholics with swords and clubs. They broke into the churches and desecrated holy objects, seized the virgins and monks, and burned the Scriptures.[32] The historian Theodoret reports a similar occurrence at the end of Athanasius' reign, when Peter was consecrated bishop. As soon as Peter was enthroned, the governor "assembled a mob of Greeks and Jews, surrounded the walls of the church, and bade Peter come forth, threatening him with exile if he refused." [33] Athanasius and Theodoret are, of course, hardly objective reporters; they no doubt exaggerate the extent of the attacks and cast the Jews in a foul light. But they do indicate the continuing presence of Jews in Alexandria and the growing animosity which was to culminate at the time of Cyril.

Athanasius makes special reference to Judaism in his Easter letters, and here he is interested in the exegetical differences between Jews and Christians.[34] In a recent study of these paschal homilies Merendino has shown that one of Athanasius' primary concerns is to show that the history of salvation as presented in the Old Testament is continued after the time of Christ in the Church.[35] The Jews continue to keep the passover feast because they do not understand that it was a type of the paschal mystery of Christ. "Even to this day they eat the lamb, erring in that they are outside of the city and the truth. As long as Judaea and the city existed, they were a type and a shadow, since the law commanded it," but when the city came to an end those things that were figurative were done away with. In another letter he makes a similar point: We should not be like the Jews "erring in the

32. Athanasius, *Encyclical Epistle* 3 (*PG* 25, 228 ff); see also *Apologia contra Arianos* 82 for the attitude of the Jews toward Athanasius.

33. Theodoret, *Historia Ecclesiastica* 4.18.

34. We have already called attention to his comments in *De incarnatione* 33 ff.; see chap. 1, n. 35.

35. Pius Merendino, *Paschale Sacramentum. Eine Untersuchung ueber die Osterkatechese des hl. Athanasius von Alexandrien in ihrer Beziehung zu den fruehchristlichen exegetisch-theologischen Ueberlieferungen.*

type and shadow and think that this is still sufficient, for though they have been illumined with the light of truth, they have chosen to reject it." [36] From these and other passages we get the impression that Athanasius' involvement with the Jews was not limited to riots and fighting over control of the churches, but must also have included debate over the correct interpretation of the Scriptures.[37] In these letters he returns regularly to the problem of the relation of Christianity to the Old Testament and attempts to justify the claims of Christians against those of the Jews. Merendino writes: "The situation of Athanasius was different [from that of Irenaeus]. He did not have to deal with Gnostics, but with Jews who were still very active and belligerent in Alexandria. For this reason his letters are not only catecheses for Christians; they also set before the Jews a challenge which frequently took the form of an intense *Auseinandersetzung*. He shows how the Old Testament is ordained to find fulfilment in the New Testament in Christ; the God, who works today in the Church and brings salvation, is the God of Abraham, God the father." [38]

Between the end of Athanasius' life (d. 373) and the beginning of Cyril's episcopate the evidence for relations between Jews and Christians is sketchy. We learn nothing from the few remaining fragments of the writings of Bishop Theophilus of Alexandria (385–412), the uncle and immediate predecessor of Cyril.[39] Nor does Didymus the blind exegete, the only other ecclesiastical figure of stature during this period, shed much new light on our subject. In his commentaries, especially the newly discovered commentary on Zachariah, he frequently refers to Jews, but he does so almost wholly in exegetical and theological terms. For example, he observes that the Jews celebrate the feast of tabernacles historically and literally and not spiritually; he refers to the day of atonement on which the Jews fast and which is preceded by days of purification.[40] But we have the same old

36. *Festal Letter* 1.7; 6.4.

37. See, for example, *Festal Letters* 5.4; 6.2–3.12; 11.13–14.

38. Merendino, *Paschale Sacramentum*, p. 16.

39. Agostina Favale, *Teofilo d'Alessandria. Scritti, Vita et Dottrina.*

40. There are a few passages in Didymus which seem to suggest that he was familiar with Jewish practices and perhaps with Jewish exegesis; see

problem of deciding whether he is speaking of the Jews in the Bible or the Jews of his own day.

We do possess an interesting law, dating from the end of the fourth century, which throws some light on the Jewish community in Alexandria at that time. It has to do with Jewish shipbuilders who lived there. Given in A.D. 390 it reads as follows:

> The group of Jews and Samaritans is recognized as not lawfully summoned to the compulsory public service of ship-masters. For if any assessment is clearly levied upon an entire group, it can obligate no specific person. Whence, just as poverty-stricken persons and those occupied as petty trades-men must not undergo the compulsory public service of transportation as shipmasters, so those persons suitable be-cause of their property, who could be selected from such groups for the performance of the aforesaid compulsory public service, must not be held exempt.[41]

This rescript is directed to the prefect of Egypt and shows that Jews were engaged in shipbuilding in Alexandria at the end of the fourth century. The *navicularii* were often ship-owners and the rescript may point to the existence of a colony of wealthy Jews in Alexandria at the time. It assumes that Jews were charged with the responsibility of dispatching ships with grain to Constantinople. At the same time the rescript also implies that there were Jews who were not so wealthy, indeed who were "poverty-stricken" and engaged as petty tradesmen. About the same time Synesios, bishop of Ptolemais, mentions a voyage from Alexandria to Cyrene in which half of the crew were Jews.[42] From these bits of evidence as well as the statements of ecclesiastical writers we have a glimpse of Alexandrian Jewry at the end of the fourth

---

his *Commentary on Zachariah* edited by Louis Doutreleau, *Didyme l'Aveugle. Zur Zacharie,* p. 1058 (401, 16), p. 896 (324, 19–25); see also M. Faulhaber, *Die Prophetenkatenen nach roemischen Handschriften,* p. 107. Faulhaber notes that of four fragments on Jeremiah by Didymus numbers two and four are polemical against Judaism. Gustave Bardy, in *Didyme L'Aveugle,* however, shows that number two really belongs to Asterius of Amaseus (p. 45).

41. *Codex Theodosianus* 13.5.18; trans. Pharr, p. 394.
42. Jean Juster, *Les Juifs dans l'empire romain,* 2:265; *CPJ* 1:105.

century. The Jewish community was beginning to come to life again and to regain something of its former strength.

We have now reached the fifth century and the time of Cyril. Most of the evidence considered thus far has pointed to the continuing presence of Jews in Alexandria, but there has been little to indicate that Christians and Jews had much intellectual contact with one another. What contacts they had were marked by bitter animosity and frequently ended in violence. From the beginning of the fifth century, however, we have reports of a number of discussions which took place between Jews and Christians on exegetical and theological issues. In the ancient border town of Pelusium, located on one of the mouths of the Nile not too far from Alexandria, lived Isidore, the famed ascetic, theologian, and counselor to bishops. Isidore was born in Alexandria in the fourth century and came to Pelusium in the beginning of the fifth century to assume the monastic life. He lived in Pelusium for over a generation and wrote 2000 letters during this period to all parts of the Church. The letters cover the period from 392 to 433, the time when Cyril was growing into manhood as well as most of the years of his episcopate.

Isidore knew Cyril well and felt close enough to him to give him much fatherly advice on how to conduct the affairs of the diocese. On at least two occasions he wrote to Cyril, sternly admonishing him about his activities. In one case, he vigorously contested Cyril's handling of the Chrysostom affair. Cyril's uncle Theophilus, former bishop of Alexandria, had been responsible for the deposition of Chrysostom at the Synod of the Oak in A.D. 403, and Cyril had decided to follow his uncle's practice and refuse to allow Chrysostom's name to be entered in the diptychs. Isidore wrote: "Put a stop to these contentions; do not involve the living Church in private vengeance prosecuted out of duty to the dead." [43] Cyril took Isidore's advice and restored Chrysostom's name to the diptychs. In a second case, the controversy with Nestorius, Isidore also intervened and told Cyril in no uncertain terms that his dispute was not solely on theological grounds. He wrote: "Prejudice does not see clearly; antipathy does not see at

43. *Ep.* 1, 370 (*PG* 78:392c).

all. If you wish to be clear of both these affections of the eye-sight, do not pass violent sentences, but commit causes to just judgment."[44]

Isidore wrote a number of letters to others in the Alexandrian diocese on disputes between Christians and Jews. In these letters there is dramatic evidence of continuing interaction between Jews and Christians on a number of theological points. In a letter written to a certain Adamantius he reveals that one matter of dispute between Jews and Christians was the Virgin Birth. "Tell the Jew who has come to quarrel with you about the divine in-carnation and who says that it is impossible for human nature to give birth without intercourse and impregnation, that there is nothing in Christianity which is foreign to the law and the prophets. Whoever is not able to learn the elementary things of the law which are clear and apparent, how can he penetrate into the hidden things or delve into the depths?"[45] Isidore tells us little more about the dispute, but the argument he presents is a familiar one. The Christians claimed that their teachings con-cerning Jesus, in this case the belief in his birth from a virgin, were foreshadowed in the Jewish scriptures. If the Jew would read these Scriptures correctly and understand them he would see that they actually do speak of Jesus. But the Jew is hard of under-standing and cannot even comprehend the law, much less probe into deeper matters. This argument recurs over and over in works against the Jews and Cyril used it extensively.

In another letter, to Ophelius a grammarian, he also gives advice on what to "tell the Jew who disputes with you." In this case the dispute centered about the interpretation of Deuter-onomy 18:15. "The Lord your God will raise up for you a prophet like me from among you, from your brethren—him you shall heed." This text became controversial because Christians took it to be a reference to Jesus. The Jews claimed that it referred to Joshua the son of Nun, the successor to Moses. Isidore again charges the Jews with faulty understanding and proceeds to list no less than seven arguments in support of his view. The arguments themselves are interesting, since they seem to reflect

44. *Ep.* 1, 310 (*PG* 78:361c).   45. *Ep.* 1, 141 (*PG* 276c–d).

the kind of verbal nitpicking which must have characterized Jewish and Christian encounters on exegetical matters. For example Isidore believes that the passage implies that Joshua would be greater than Moses. But it is clear that in fact he was inferior to Moses, says Isidore; it would be untrue if it refers to Joshua. Therefore it must refer to Jesus. Further, the text reads ἀναστήσει. This can only apply to Jesus. If it applied to Joshua it would have to read ἀνέστησε. He concludes then that it must refer to the "true prophet," and this is Jesus.[46]

This passage from Deuteronomy was a matter of some concern in Christian-Jewish disputes at the time. Not only does Isidore go to great lengths to provide arguments in favor of the Christian interpretation, but Cyril also cites Deuteronomy 18 with great frequency in his commentaries and almost always takes the passage to be a point of difference between Jews and Christians.[47] Another parallel between Isidore and Cyril is the interpretation of Haggai 2:9. In a letter to a bishop who is having difficulty explaining this text to Jews, Isidore again writes and gives advice. The text from Haggai refers to the rebuilding of the temple: "The latter splendor of this house shall be greater than the former, says the Lord." Isidore says that "from all the holy writings one can show that Jewish things [πράγματα] have come to an end." A rebirth will not come as a result of this text as the "Jew who contends with you with all his strength thinks." Isidore enters into a discussion of the wording of the text and manages, to his own satisfaction, to show that the "greater splendor" refers to the Church which took the place of the temple.[48] In the *Commentary on Haggai* Cyril also sees the text in the same light and uses it as an opportunity to contrast the temple of Israel with the coming of the Lord. For when the Lord comes, the "worship according to the law" will be replaced by the "evangelical" worship and the "truth" will take the place of the things in shadows."[49]

In a number of other letters Isidore refers to other aspects of

46. *Ep.* 2, 94 (*PG* 78:797c–800a).

47. See for example Cyril, *In Ionam,* preface (P 1:562–64). I will discuss Cyril's interpretation of Deut. 18 in the next chatper.

48. *Ep.* 4, 17 (*PG* 78:1064d).   49. Cyril, *In Aggaeum* 2.9 (P 2:267–68).

the quarrel between Jews and Christians.[50] For example he tells us that some Jews objected to the Christian Eucharist, making fun of the substitution of bread for actual bloody sacrifices. And in another place we learn of Jewish objections to the exaggerations of the gospel record. Specifically Jews took exception to the final sentence of the Gospel of John which reads: "But there are also many other things which Jesus did; were every one of them to be written, I suppose that the world itself could not contain the books that would be written."

Isidore of Pelusium sheds light on what otherwise would be a very dark and fuzzy picture. As a contemporary of Cyril and a priest in the Alexandrian diocese he gives us a unique perspective on the situation at the time. From other sources we have learned that Jews continued to live and work in Alexandria. From Isidore, however, we learn that in Egypt Jews and Christians had more than superficial contact with one another. Jews and Christians also met to dispute exegetical and theological questions. According to the reports from Isidore these questions covered the following topics: the relationship between the Jewish scriptures and Christian writings; Christology; Israel and the Church; Christian practices, such as the Eucharist.

This examination of the relations between Jews and Christians in Alexandria has confirmed the conclusion reached in the first chapter. During the fourth and fifth centuries Judaism was still a force to be reckoned with in Alexandria. Though the destruction and devastation of the first two centuries had great and far-reaching consequences for Egyptian Jewry, the ravages of these centuries did not put an end to Judaism there. It seems that during the later period Judaism turned in on itself more and rejected the "Hellenizing" of an earlier generation, but in its search for identity it found new resources and strength. During these years Christian-Jewish relations worsened considerably, but Jews and Christians continued to discuss and debate exegetical and theological matters of common interest. At the very time that Cyril became bishop our sources give clear evidence of disputes between Jews and Christians.

50. *Ep.* 1, 401; 2, 99; see also *Ep.* 3, 112. *Ep.* 4, 26.

3 Cyril and the Jews

Cyril's episcopate began in conflict. Theophilus, bishop of Alexandria from A.D. 385, died on October 15, 412. At his death there was a great contest for a successor: some promoted Timothy the archdeacon, and others Cyril, the nephew of the late bishop. A great tumult arose among the populace, but after three days Cyril was chosen and he ascended the throne of the patriarchate of Alexandria. Immediately he turned the great power of his office to rid the city of undesirable religious groups. His first target was the Novatians. He shut their churches, took possession of their sacred vessels and religious ornaments, and even deposed their bishop Theopemptus.[1] Several years later he turned to the Jews and waged a campaign to drive them from the city. Socrates the Christian historian has given us a full—though not impartial—account of the affair.

> It happened that the Jewish inhabitants were driven out of Alexandria by Cyril the bishop on the following account. The Alexandrian public is more delighted with tumult than any other people: and if at any time it should find a pretext, breaks fourth into the most intolerable excesses; for it never ceases from its turbulence without bloodshed. It happened on the present occasion that a disturbance arose among the populace, not from a cause of any serious importance, but out of an evil that has become very popular in almost all cities, viz. a fondness for dancing exhibitions. In consequence of the Jews being disengaged from business on the Sabbath, and spending their time, not in hearing the law, but in theatrical amusements, dancers usually collect great crowds on that day, and disorder is almost invariably produced. And although this was in some degree controlled by the governor of Alexandria, nevertheless the Jews continued opposing these

---

1. *Paschal Homily* 1.2 (PG 77:405); Socrates, *Historia Ecclesiastica* 7.7.

measures. And although they are always hostile toward the Christians they were roused to still greater opposition against them on account of the dancers. When therefore Orestes the prefect was publishing an edict—for so they are accustomed to call public notices—in the theatre for the regulation of the shows, some of the bishop Cyril's party were present to learn the nature of the orders about to be issued. There was among them a certain Hierax, a teacher of the rudimental branches of literature, and one who was a very enthusiastic listener of the bishop Cyril's sermons, and made himself conspicuous by his forwardness in applauding. When the Jews observed this person in the theatre, they immediately cried out that he had come there for no other purpose than to excite sedition among the people. Now Orestes had long regarded with jealousy the growing power of the bishops, because they encroached on the jurisdiction of the authorities appointed by the emperor, especially as Cyril wished to set spies over his proceedings; he therefore ordered Hierax to be seized, and publicly subjected him to the torture in the theatre. Cyril, on being informed of this, sent for the principal Jews, and threatened them with the utmost severities unless they desisted from their molestation of the Christians. The Jewish populace on hearing these menaces, instead of suppressing their violence, only became more furious, and were led to form conspiracies for the destruction of the Christians; one of these was of so desperate a character as to cause their entire expulsion from Alexandria; this I shall now describe. Having agreed that each one of them should wear a ring on his finger made of the bark of a palm branch, for the sake of mutual recognition, they determined to make a nightly attack on the Christians. They therefore sent persons into the streets to raise an outcry that the church named after Alexander was on fire. Thus many Christians on hearing this ran out, some from one direction and some from another, in great anxiety to save their church. The Jews immediately fell upon and slew them; readily distinguishing each other by their rings. At daybreak the authors of this atrocity could not be concealed: and Cyril, accompanied by

an immense crowd of people, going to their synagogues—
for so they call their house of prayer—took them away from
them, and drove the Jews out of the city, permitting the
multitude to plunder their goods. Thus the Jews who had
inhabited the city from the time of Alexander the Macedo-
nian were expelled from it, stripped of all they possessed, and
dispersed some in one direction and some in another. One of
them, a physician named Adamantius, fled to Atticus, bishop
of Constantinople, and professing Christianity, some time
afterwards returned to Alexandria and fixed his residence
there. But Orestes the governor of Alexandria was filled with
great indignation at these transactions, and was excessively
grieved that a city of such magnitude should have been sud-
denly bereft of so large a portion of its population; he therefore at once communicated the whole affair to the emperor.
Cyril also wrote to him, describing the outrageous conduct of
the Jews; and in the meanwhile sent persons to Orestes who
should mediate concerning a reconciliation: for this the people had urged him to do. And when Orestes refused to listen
to friendly advances, Cyril extended toward him the book
of gospels, believing that respect for religion would induce
him to lay aside his resentment . . . , however, even this had
no pacific effect on the prefect, but he persisted in implacable
hostility against the bishop.[2]

The date of this outbreak of violence between Jews and Christians is uncertain, but it probably took place in the first two or
three years of Cyril's reign, perhaps in A.D. 414. Our principal
source for the incident is Socrates, and though he was no great
admirer of Cyril, he nevertheless presented the whole affair in a
light prejudicial to the Jews. He chided and ridiculed the Jews
because they did not keep the Sabbath as they were supposed to.
He put the blame for the disturbance primarily on the Jews, because, in his view, they loved to frequent dancing exhibitions

2. Socrates, *Hist. Eccles.* 7.13 (trans. Zenos, 2:159–60). On Socrates' account see Victor Tcherikover and Alexander Fuks, eds., *Corpus papyrorum
judaicarum,* 1:98–100. For similar occurrences in other cities see Ambrose
Epistle 40, and *Excerpta Valesiana* 2.80 (n. 11 in chap. 1).

(ὀρχηστάς). They should have been in the synagogues hearing the law, said Socrates. On the other hand he did not exempt Cyril and the Christians from blame. For example he singled out a certain Hierax, a sycophant of Cyril, as the chief troublemaker. As a result of the treatment of Hierax by the prefect Orestes Cyril called the Jews together and warned them that they would be punished if they did not stop molesting Christians. This infuriated the Jews even more, for they had really done nothing as yet. At this point, they were said to have planned an attack on the Christians and to have succeeded in killing some of them. After this outbreak, Cyril gathered a large crowd of Christians and proceeded to expel the Jews from the city and to allow Christians to plunder Jewish goods.

This is a fascinating, though troubling, account of relations between Jews and Christians in Alexandria at the time. There seem to be no good reasons for doubting its main outlines, though Socrates' explanation of the causes of the outburst are less than persuasive.[3] However, the actual reason for the disturbance is not important. What is important for our purpose is the information that in Alexandria at this time there lived a large and influential Jewish population, and that Cyril had dealings with them. Whether the Jews were actually expelled from Alexandria is a disputed matter, but it seems likely that Socrates is exaggerating the situation. Socrates mentions that the Jews were a "large part of the population" of Alexandria.[4] If this is so, it is hard to believe that they were simply expelled from the city. As the chief port of the empire and a great crossroads of travel and trade, Alexandria was an important part of the life of the Roman world. Without Alexandrian shipping the grain supply to Rome would have diminished rapidly. The Jews played a role in the shipping industry and presumably were involved in the export of grain to Italy. Could the city really do without its Jewish population? And where were they to go? We have no answers to these questions; from Socrates we can only conclude that the Jews did play a role in the life of the metropolis and

3. Socrates reveals his prejudice against the Jews elsewhere in his history. See, for example, *Hist. Eccles.* 3.20; 5.22.
4. See also A. H. M. Jones, *The Later Roman Empire,* p. 948.

that they were a force to be reckoned with by the Christian majority.[5]

Socrates makes clear that Jews and Christians had had outbreaks of this sort before. Apparently none had been quite so severe, but when disturbances did occur the bishop communicated with Jewish leaders. When Cyril learned of the trouble he sent immediately for the "Jewish leaders" (τοὺς Ἰουδαίων πρωτεύοντας), says Socrates. We also learn that the Jews had a number of synagogues, that they observed the sabbath and presumably the principal Jewish festivals, practiced circumcision, and followed other Jewish observances. Christians were familiar with the Jewish way of life, but relations were very bitter between Jews and Christians and each appeared to the other as the enemy.

Cyril was acquainted with Judaism not only by firsthand experience. He also knew Jewish writings and traditions which were not included in the Old Testament. He knew the works of the Jewish historian Josephus, whom he called "a man famous and wise." [6] He referred to the Maccabees in a number of his commentaries and related at one place that "Josephus narrates their history in a book about them." [7] In one place he quoted a short passage from Josephus' *Jewish War*. And he frequently alluded to information which is contained in Josephus' writings.[8]

Cyril was also familiar with Jewish legends of various sorts and at times relied on traditions which are found only in the Talmud.[9] For example, in his commentary on Genesis 4:4–5 in the *Glaphyra,* Cyril discusses the difference between the offering of Abel and that of Cain. A Jewish haggadah on that passage says that the fire from heaven consumed Abel's offering and therefore showed that it was accepted; but no fire came down in

5. We know also that Jews were living in Alexandria in the sixth century. A Christian sermon even mentions a "Jewish street" in Alexandria. See *CPJ* 1:99.

6. *In Zach.* 11:20 (P 2:455, 18–19).   7. *In Is.* 9:13 (*PG* 70:265a).

8. *In Zach.* 12:11–14 (P 2:496,4 ff). Cyril cites *De bello Judaico* 2.1; see Alexander Kerrigan, *St. Cyril of Alexandria: Interpreter of the Old Testament,* pp. 308–9 for other references.

9. See F. M. Abel, "Parallélisme exégétique entre s. Jérôme et s. Cyrille d'Alexandrie," and Kerrigan, *Old Testament,* 308–22.

the case of Cain and this showed that his was not accepted.[10]
Cyril was apparently aware of this interpretation and used it in
his own exegesis of the text. This haggadah does not appear in
a Jewish source until much later and may have been passed on
orally. Cyril's use of Jewish traditions in his commentaries suggests that he found such legends useful in discovering the sense
of the text. He says, for example, that such knowledge is useful
for "an accurate interpretation" of the biblical text.[11]

In the case of Jewish legends Cyril sometimes borrows from
earlier ecclesiastical writers, but also appears to get some material
firsthand.[12] Thus in commenting on Isaiah 10:28 "At Michmash
he stores his baggage," Cyril refers to a Jewish tradition which
says that the Assyrians left their baggage at Michmash because
they feared an attack, believing that the Israelites were pursuing
them.[13] Another instance is Isaiah 5:2: "My beloved had a vine-
yard on a very fertile hill. He digged it and cleared it of
stones, and planted it with choice vines; he built a watchtower
in the midst of it, and hewed out a wine vat." In discussing this
verse Cyril reproduces material from the commentaries of Eusebius
and Jerome, but then he goes on to add further information pos-
sibly drawn from a Jewish source.[14]

The most significant body of material from Cyril on Judaism
comes not from his use of Jewish sources, but from the extensive
polemic against Judaism throughout his exegetical works. Here
we see the animosity between Jews and Christians in Alexandria
most clearly. Reading Cyril's commentaries, one is not surprised
that Jews and Christians set upon one another early in his reign.
His exegetical works are studded with hundreds of references
to Jews and Judaism; Jews provide the occasion for discussion
of theological, historical, and exegetical questions. Unwavering
and intractable in his attack, Cyril never gets the Jews off his

10. *Glaph. in Gen.* 1 (*PG* 69, 56 ff.); see Louis Ginzberg, *Die Haggada
bei den Kirchenvaetern,* 1:22.
11. *In Habac,* 2:15–16 (P 2:110,6 ff).
12. For a discussion of this question see Kerrigan, *Old Testament,* pp.
311–22, and Abel, "Parallélisme."
13. *In Is.* 10:27 (*PG* 70:301c); see Kerrigan, *Old Testament,* p. 314.
14. *In Is.* 5:2 (*PG* 70:137a–b); see Kerrigan, *Old Testament,* pp. 312–13.

mind.[15] His opposition to the Arians or the Antiochenes seems like a friendly intramural contest in contrast to the invective against the Jews.

Like other writers he frequently sets the Jews apart from the Greeks and devotes a special polemic to them. "Moreover, the Jews, all of whom have reached the height of impiety, have found the cross of our Savior Christ a cause of stumbling even to the point where they have surpassed the ravings of the Greeks . . . so that if anyone should be made a judge of these two groups I believe that he would immediately condemn the former [that is, the Jews] and say that the ideas of the latter [that is, the Greeks] were among the lesser evils. For it is not surprising, he might say, if those who have never read the divine Scriptures go astray from the doctrines of the truth. But those who were educated by the law and the prophets in all that leads to piety exceeded the error of the Greeks, since at least the offenses of the Greeks were pardonable. For the Jews, however, there is no means of defense. They have brought upon themselves the poison of consequent ignorance." [16] Cyril wrote a massive apology to the Greeks in the form of a reply to the Emperor Julian's *Against the Galilaeans*. We do not possess a parallel work directed against the Jews. But Gennadius said that Cyril was so troubled by the danger of Judaism that he wrote an apologetic work similar to that of Theodoret entitled "On the Apostasy of the Synagogue." [17] It is probable that Cyril did write such a work but we have only one possible fragment of it, and it is doubtful whether this one fragment comes from the book on Judaism. However in his second major commentary on the Pentateuch, the *Glaphyra,* he includes a lengthy section with the title: "On the Jewish synagogue, that it fell because of unbelief." [18]

Some of Cyril's bitterness about Judaism can be seen in state-

15. See the listing of passages in Kerrigan, *Old Testament,* pp. 386–87.

16. *PH* 4.4–5 (*PG* 77:469d ff.). Also *PH* 6.4–5 (Greeks); 6.6 ff (Jews). See also *Ador.* 9 (*PG* 68:612b); *PG* 70:229a–d.

17. Gennadius, *De viris illustribus,* p. 57. Frag. in *PG* 76:1421–24. Jouassard doubts that the fragment comes from the work *Apostasy of the Synagogue* ("Cyrill von Alexandrien," *RAC* 3:507).

18. *Glaph. in Levit.* (*PG* 69:563a).

ments such as the following: The Jews are the "most deranged of all men" [19] and their madness is greater than that of the Greeks. They have carried impiety to its extreme limit.[20] They are "senseless," "blind," "uncomprehending," and "demented." [21] They are "foolish God haters" [22] and "killers of the Lord"; [23] they are "unbelievers" and "irreligious." [24] Their synagogue is a leprous house which perpetuates their monstrous impiety.[25]

These outrageous charges against the Jews are repeated throughout Cyril's writings. However the most consistent criticism he offers centers about Jewish interpretation of the Scriptures, and here he singles out the problem of the relationship between the two testaments. The Jews do not understand the types of the Old Testament. "How long, O Jew, will you be taken up with the types of the letter? Will you pass by the power of the truth? When will be seen the end of your folly? When will you withdraw your mind from the shadow of the law? When will you offer worship in spirit to God the king of all things?" The Scriptures were given to the Jews, but they were unable to understand them correctly. "The law, destined to be given to Israel by the ministry of angels . . . was able to enlighten if it were understood spiritually. . . . But it proved to be unprofitable to those to whom it had been given, not through any fault of its own, but because they failed to receive the light into their minds and hearts. They enriched themselves instead with the letter, namely, the external appearance of illumination, which they thought they possessed but did not in reality." As a consequence, "the meaning of the law became dead and lifeless" to the Jew. Cyril frequently cites John 4:24 in connection with the "spiritual blindness" of the Jew: "God is spirit, and those who worship him must worship in spirit and truth." This passage provided the title of his first exegetical work on the Pentateuch. It also provided Cyril with a major theme for his exegesis which we will explore in the next chapter. He sets the "true worship" of God practiced by Christians in strong opposition to the

19. *PG* 77:420a.
20. *PG* 77:460d.
21. *In Lucam, Homily* 101.
22. *PG* 77:853c.
23. *PG* 70:229c.
24. *PG* 77:464b; 853d.
25. *PG* 69:565c.

"false" worship in shadows and types practiced by Jews. "You
refuse to worship God in spirit," writes Cyril, "worshiping him
by the law thinking you worship him; but you are really far
from the true understanding of the law, thinking you rightly
understand the Scriptures." [26]

From these general comments about Jewish interpretation of
the Scriptures Cyril proceeds to specific criticism of Jewish practices. For example he lashes out at the observance of the sabbath
as contrary to the true understanding of the Scriptures. In the
Commentary on Isaiah, discussing "if you turn back your foot
from the sabbath," Cyril argues that Paul rejected the ineffective-
ness of the sabbath and made it over into a spiritual theoria.
Neither the sabbath according to the flesh, nor circumcision, as
Paul says in Romans 2:28, is of value any longer; the law is now
transformed and there is no longer value in being a Jew in outward fashion. The Jewish sabbath is a false sabbath, he says; now
we should observe the sabbath spiritually in Christ.[27] In his
homilies on Luke Cyril berates the Jews because they lay in wait
for Jesus to break the sabbath (Luke 14:1–6): "But, O senseless
Jew, understand that the law was a shadow and type waiting
for the truth, and the truth was Christ and his commandments.
Why then do you arm the type against the truth; why do you
set the shadow in array against the spiritual interpretation? Keep
the sabbath rationally; but if you will not consent to do so,
then you are cut off from that sabbath-keeping which is pleasing
to God." [28] Here, as elsewhere, he relies on John 4:24 to support
his argument.

Just as the sabbath was contrary to the Scriptures, so also

26. *PH* 6.6 (*PG* 77:513d ff).

27. *In Is.* 58:13, 14 (*PG* 70:1300c); see also *In Amos* 6:3 (P. 1:483, 24–
484, 11). Almost the whole of Cyril's commentary on Isaiah 56–58 is devoted
to an attack on the Jews. He bases his comments on a number of passages
such as the following: "Blessed is the man who . . . keeps the sabbath,
not profaning it" (Is. 56:2). "His watchmen are blind, they are all without
knowledge; they are all dumb dogs, they cannot bark; dreaming, lying
down, loving to slumber" (Is. 56:10). He singles out the phrase "children
of transgression" (57:4); also "Because of the iniquity of his covetousness
I was angry, I smote him, I hid my face and was angry" (57:17).

28. *In Lucam. Hom.* 101.

circumcision was a thing of the past. "You think it is a great thing and crucial for true worship," says Cyril. "But why should we continue circumcision? If there is no good reason why continue? If it does nothing worthwhile it must be ridiculous. If it was so valuable why was it not given from the beginning?" [29]

Living at the height of the victory of the Church, at a time when Christian influence was shaping the fabric of Roman society, Cyril, like other fathers of his time, relied heavily on the misfortunes of the Jews as a demonstration of the legitimacy of Christianity. He could not only look back on the destruction of Jerusalem by the Romans and the persecution of Jews in Alexandria and elsewhere, but he could also see that Christianity had now become the official religion of the Roman empire. Christianity was no longer a small struggling sect competing with other religions and dodging the blows of emperors. It had conquered Rome! In many places Cyril makes an analogy between the devastation of the Jews in the Old Testament and the destruction wrought by the Romans shortly after the time of Jesus. They were punished because of their hardheartedness and unbelief. Therefore they no longer possess the symbols of piety— no city, no sacrifice; now they are scattered throughout the world. They rejected Christ because they "did not understand the shadows of the Old Testament; if they had believed in Moses they also would have believed in Christ," because Moses was a tutor for Christ. "The manner of Jewish worship is wholly unacceptable to Christ." [30]

Viewed in the light of Christian exegesis, most of the passages in the Old Testament which even hint at Israelite shortcomings become prime texts for supporting Christian polemic against the Jews. Isaiah 40:27 reads: "Why do you say, O Jacob, and speak,

29. *PH* 6.7 (*PG* 77:516b); for the importance of the question of circumcision in Christian polemics against Jews see Simon, *Verus Israel*, pp. 196 ff. Fasting is given a somewhat similar treatment. See *In Is.* 1:10–14 (*PG* 70:32b–36c).

30. See *In Is.* 1:2 ff (*PG* 70:13c ff); *In Is.* 1:17–18 (*PG* 70:44b ff). The appeal to Jewish history as evidence of the truth of Christian claims occurs frequently. See, for example, *PG* 70:1450b; *In Soph.* 1:12 (P 2:185); *In Zach.* 6:1–8 (P 2:359 ff); *In Zach.* 12:10 (P 2:494); *In Joel* 1:11–12 (P 1:304, 19 ff); *In Nah.* 1:4–5 (P 2:15,6 ff); *In Amos* 8:9–10 (P 1:520, 5 ff).

O Israel, 'My way is hid from the Lord?'" This means, says Cyril, that the Jews rejected the gospel. They knew the creator, but they did not receive the "giver of salvation" and separated themselves from the creator. They received the shadows of the law and did not allow the "worship in spirit and in truth, the *latreia* of the gospel." Instead they murmured "my way is hid from the Lord." "Of old, O Israel, you were taught through the law, you know through the prophets the manner of the economy that was to be after the law. The law has been given in oracles having shadows and types of the coming good things, and as with groans in the letter having the power of the mystery according to Christ. For in many ways through the commandments according to the law Christ was prefigured and the mystery about him was signified enigmatically." [31]

In this passage from the *Commentary on Isaiah* Cyril goes beyond an attack on the Jews to the theological issue raised by the polemical situation: the relationship of the Jewish scriptures to the new revelation in Jesus. Throughout his commentaries we find a similar pattern. When he discusses Jews or Judaism he also discusses the relationship between the two testaments. The interpretation of transfiguration is typical, for Cyril takes the presence of Moses and Elijah with Jesus to symbolize the harmony existing between the old and new covenants. The Jews, however, says Cyril, take the presence of Moses to mean that we should follow and obey him. Cyril replies that if this were the case the father would not have said "This is my beloved son, listen to him," but "listen to Moses and keep the law." But the father does not say this and we should take the passage to mean that "law of Moses and the word of the holy prophets foreshowed the mystery of Christ." Moses and Elijah show the continuity which exists between the old and the new. By their presence we know that Christ has the "law and the prophets for his bodyguard, being the Lord of the law and prophets, foreshown in them by those things which they harmoniously proclaimed beforehand. For the words of the prophets are not at variance with the teaching of the law." Cyril concludes by

31. *In Is.* 40:27 (*PG* 70:820a–821d), also *PH* 20.4; 21.3).

citing John 5:46, "If you believed Moses, you would believe me, for he wrote of me." [32]

In connection with his exegesis of John 5:46 Cyril singles out Deuteronomy 18 as one of the chief passages from the Jewish scriptures pointing to Christ. Deuteronomy 18 was one of the passages mentioned by Isidore of Pelusium in connection with Jewish-Christian debates. It comes up for discussion regularly in Cyril's exegetical works and is always viewed in the light of the relationship between Christianity and Judaism, and more particularly the relationship between the Jewish scriptures and the coming of Jesus. Thus it is not insignificant that Cyril cites Deuteronomy 18:15 in his exposition of John 5:46. The text reads: "The Lord your God will raise up for you a prophet like me from among you, from your brethren—him you shall heed." The debate centered about the identification of the prophet who was to come. The Jews claimed that it referred to Joshua, and the Christians took it to be a reference to Jesus. Cyril, of course, chooses the latter interpretation, for the writings of Moses "foreshadowed the mystery of Christ." This is especially true in the case of Deuteronomy for the text clearly points to the coming of the Savior, says Cyril. Moses was a mediator between God and man, but his mediation extended only to the synagogue. Now we "transfer the type to the truth" and see here Christ who is the "mediator of God and men." Moses can therefore be considered a "type of Christ," ministering to the children of Israel. Then Christ comes as the true son of God and unites mankind with God. The writings of Moses prepared the way for Christ but the true end of the law and the prophets is Christ and in him we come to the more perfect knowledge of God. But the Jews refuse to hear the words of Moses and fall under the judgment of Moses himself. For we read in Deuteronomy 18:19: "And whoever will not give heed to my words which he shall speak in my name, I myself will require it of him." "Let the ignorant Jews," says Cyril, "who harden their minds to complete stubbornness, realize that they pour self-invited destruction upon their own heads. They will be under divine wrath, receiving the total loss

32. *In Lucam* 9:27–36, *Hom.* 51.

of good things as the wages of their rage against Christ. For if
they had believed Moses, they would have believed Christ, for
he wrote of him." [33]

Deuteronomy 18 also comes up for discussion in connection
with John 9:28–29. Here the Jews are inquiring about the healing
of a blind man by Jesus. After telling them what has happened,
the blind man urges them to become disciples of Jesus. The
Jews answer: "You are his disciple, but we are disciples of
Moses. We know that God has spoken to Moses, but as for this
man, we do not know where he comes from." Cyril immediately
launches an attack on the Jews. How could they have been
ignorant of Jesus if they had the writings of Moses? They should
have read the words of Moses where he proclaims the time when
Jesus will come: "I will raise up a prophet for them." Surely
anyone, continues Cyril, might have rebuked the Jews with
good reason and said: "O you who only know how to disbelieve,
if you are so readily persuaded by the words of Moses, because
God has spoken to him, ought you not to believe Christ in the
same way when you hear him declaring openly [in John 14:10],
'The words that I say to you I do not speak on my own authority;
but the Father who dwells in me does his works.'" The Jews
then are accused of misunderstanding the writings of Moses for
they do not find Christ there. They "honor the law and pretend
to hold God's will in high esteem" and yet "they violate it and
greatly dishonor it by refusing to accept its message concerning
their time, namely that announced by it concerning Christ that
by his incarnation he should appear in the character of a
prophet." [34]

Behind the exegetical discussion of Deuteronomy 18 lies the
assumption that Jews and Christians share the same book, the
Jewish scriptures or Old Testament. Cyril realized that Christians
and Jews had these writings in common and that Jews could
appeal to these writings to refute Christian claims. The exegetical
and theological problem of the relationship between the Old and

33. *In Jo.* 5:46 (P 1:391 ff).

34. *In Jo.* 9:29 (P 2:186 ff); see also *In Jo.* 8:24 (P 2:21); *In Jo.* 12:49–50
(P 2:337–38); *In Mal.* 4:6 (P 2:625–6), cited in connection with John
5:46. *In Ionam* pref. (P 1:562); *In Lucam, Homily* 82:96.

New Testaments is, as we have seen in the previous chapters, one of the central questions in the Christian literature on Judaism. How can one explain that both Jew and Christian go to the same writings and come up with differing points of view? Christian attempts to answer this question are unusually perverse, for they seem to think that the only legitimate reason was Jewish blindness and spiritual ignorance. "That in the law and the holy prophets there is much said concerning him who is by nature life . . . will I think be plain to all who are lovers of learning." [35] Since the Scriptures foreshadowed Jesus, the Jews are themselves to blame for not recognizing him. The New Testament account of the young lawyer is an illustration of this, says Cyril. One could answer his question by saying: if you had been skilful in the law you would not have failed to recognize who he was. He was depicted to you by the shadowing of Moses. He was there in the lamb, in the arrangement of the ark, in the mercy seat. He was seen in the candlestick with seven lamps, in the showbread, in the serpent on the pole.[36]

Amidst the bitterness of Cyril's polemic against the Jews we can discern certain recurring themes: worship in spirit and in truth contrasted with worship according to the law; shadow and type in contrast to truth and reality; spiritual worship in contrast to keeping the sabbath and circumcision; the relationship between Moses and Christ; the old dispensation and the new dispensation. All of these themes converge on one central problem: the relationship between the Old and New Testaments or the relationship between Christianity and Judaism. Though Cyril's statements on the Jews drip with venom, he constantly turns the discussion to the larger theological and exegetical issues. The issues raised by his confrontation with Judaism provide him with a setting for his exegesis of the Scriptures and the development of his theology.

The great Jewish historian Salo Baron once wrote of Chrysostom: "The very violence of St. Chrysostom's anti-Jewish sermons of 387 was doubtless owing to the great friendliness of the

35. *In Jo.* 5:39 (P 1:385, 1–3); also *Glaph. in Ex.* (PG 69:536c–537a); *Glaph. in Gen.* (PG 69:241b).
36. *In Lucam* 10:25–37, Homily 68; see also *Homilies* 86, 53, 29.

Christian Antiochians toward their Jewish compatriots whom the Arian emperor Valens himself had given 'gardens' for their worship." [37] We cannot go quite so far for Cyril of Alexandria, simply because we are not so well informed about the situation in Alexandria as we are about Antioch. But Baron's point, that the bitterness of the anti-Jewish polemic among Christians did not arise in a vacuum, is applicable to Cyril and Alexandria in the early fifth century.

Cyril, like Chrysostom, is very much aware of the presence of Judaism. We now turn to Cyril's exegesis to see how the exegetical and theological questions raised by Judaism took shape in his thought.

37. Salo Wittmayer Baron, *A Social and Religious History of the Jews,* 2:189.

4 Worship in Spirit and in Truth: The Transformation of the Old

For a man burdened with the responsibility of a large and un-ruly patriarchate Cyril engaged in extraordinary literary activity. During the first few years of his reign he composed the four major exegetical works on the Old Testament and may have written other commentaries. Of these works the earliest are the two on the Pentateuch, the *Adoration and Worship of God in Spirit and in Truth* and the *Glaphyra* (Elegant Comments).[1] The *Adoration,* Cyril's first exegetical work, is written in the form of a dialogue between Cyril and a certain Palladius. The book is intended as an exposition of the Pentateuch, though it does not follow the text verse by verse as Cyril was to do in his commentaries on Isaiah and the minor prophets.[2] Instead he chooses certain passages of particular significance and expounds them under seventeen different headings. The list of topics shows that it is concerned chiefly with various aspects of the Christian life and related theological problems. For example Book 1 is on the fall of man and captivity in sin; Book 2 on death and how man cannot conquer death except through Christ; Book 5 on courage, Book 7 on love, Book 11 on the priesthood, etc.[3]

Since *Adoration in Spirit and in Truth* was Cyril's first exe-getical work, it provides an opportunity to examine his exegetical and theological concerns as they were taking shape early in his life.[4] The work opens with Palladius approaching Cyril. Palladius

1. For the dating of Cyril's works see G. Joussard, "L'activité littéraire de saint Cyrille d'Alexandrie jusqu'à 428. Essai de chronologie et de synthèse," pp. 159–74. Text of *Adoration and Worship in Spirit and in Truth, PG* 68:133–1125; *Glaphyra, PG* 69:9–678.

2. *Commentary on the Minor Prophets* in *PG* 71–72:9–364; there is a better edition by P. E. Pusey: *Sancti patris nostri Cyrilli archepiscopi Alex-andrini in XII prophetas. Commentary on Isaiah* in *PG* 70:9–1450.

3. Texts in *PG* 77:401–98.

4. *PG* 69:512d; 605b; 625d; *PG* 69:385d–388b. "Le *De Adoratione* est un exposé de moral général, exposé à base dogmatique mais présenté dans

is holding a book in his hand and Cyril asks him what it is. Palladius replies that he is carrying two of the Gospels: Matthew and John. He has come to talk to Cyril because he has been studying these two books and cannot understand certain passages. In Matthew he is particularly troubled by the following text: "Think not that I have come to abolish the law and the prophets; I have come not to abolish them but to fulfil them. For truly, I say to you, till heaven and earth pass away, not an iota, not a dot, will pass from the law until all is accomplished" (Matthew 5:17–18). In the Gospel of John he is puzzled by the words of Jesus: "But the hour is coming, and now is, when the true worshipers will worship the Father in spirit and in truth" (John 4:23–24).[5]

The title of the work is based on the second passage. The phrase "worship in spirit and in truth" comes from the discourse of Jesus with the Samaritan woman he met at the well. "Our fathers," said the woman, "worshipped on this mountain but you Jews say the temple where God should be worshipped is in Jerusalem." Jesus replies: "Believe me, the time is coming when you will worship the Father neither on this mountain nor in Jerusalem. You Samaritans worship without knowing what you worship, while we worship what we know. . . . But the time approaches, indeed it is already here, when those who are real worshippers will worship the Father in spirit and in truth. Such are the worshippers whom the Father wants" (New English Bible). Why should Cyril choose this text from the Gospel of John as title for his commentary on the Pentateuch?

In their original setting in the Gospel of John, spirit and truth are part of the familiar Johannine dualism between earthly and heavenly, flesh and spirit. John says that the true worship is to be linked with Christ for in him the temple (cf. 2:13–22) and its offerings and sacrifices now give way to a worship in the spirit.[6]

---

le cadre d'une explication spirituelle du culte mosaïque," writes Jouassard in "L'activité," p. 161, n. 2.

5. PG 68:133b–136a.

6. For the Gospel of John, see especially the recent commentary by Rudolf Schnackenburg, *Das Johannesevangelium,* 1:473; also Raymond Brown, *The Gospel according to John,* 1:180–81; and Rudolf Bultmann, *Das Evangelium des Johannes,* p. 140.

Those who are born of the spirit now participate in this new worship and what was done through blood offerings in the temple is now done sacramentally. Though John gives the notion of spirit and truth a distinctively Christian ring, there are parallels in Qumram where the spirit of truth is associated with an eschatological motif.[7] Truth cleanses the evil deeds of men and casts out the evil spirit. In John, however, worship in spirit and in truth accents the difference between Judaism and Christianity and stresses the character of the new worship in Christ.

The interpretation of the text has an interesting history. Many fathers were attracted by the phrase "God is spirit" and used this passage to support their belief in the incorporeality of God. As such the text was taken not so much as a statement about the differences between Christian and Jewish worship of God, but as a statement about God. Origen, for example, takes it to mean that God is a spiritual being, though he himself qualified his interpretation by his belief that *pneuma* was corporeal.[8] Tertullian also believed it supported the belief that God is a spiritual being.[9] In his *Commentary on John,* Theodore of Mopsuestia gives much the same interpretation: "The time has come, indeed it has already arrived, when God will be worshiped as he should be as is fitting to his nature. For God is of an incorporeal nature; he is not circumscribed by place, but is everywhere, and he should be worshiped according to this conception." [10] Theodore draws out the implication of the passage for Christian worship, but he does

7. For Qumram, see Rudolf Schnackenburg, "Die 'Anbetung in Geist und Wahrheit' (Joh. 4,23) im Lichte von Qumrâm-Texten," pp. 88–94.

8. Origen, *Comm. in Joh.* 4:23–24 (13:17–23, *GCS* 4:242–47); also *Contra Celsum* 2.71; 6.70; 7.27. Origen was not the first to comment on or use John 4:24. See also Irenaeus, Frag. 36 (H 2:501–2), where he contrasts spirit and truth with oblations according to the law; also Heracleon, *Commentary on John,* 4:24, who takes the passage to refer to pure worship which is in accord with the undefiled and invisible divine nature. Those who have the same nature as the father are spirit and their worship is spiritual. Maurice Wiles, in *The Spiritual Gospel,* pp. 67–70, briefly discusses the interpretation of the passage in patristic commentaries on John.

9. Tertullian, *Adv. Praxeas,* 17.8. See also Dionysius, cited by Athanasius, *De sententia Dionysii,* 15.

10. *Comm. in Joh.,* 4:24 (Vosté, *Theodori Mopsuesteni Comm.,* pp. 64–65).

not say anything about its implications for the relationship of Christianity to Judaism. In his *Commentary on John,* Didymus gives a similar exegesis: "God is a spirit and this means he is without a body and invisible." [11] Similarly Augustine believed that John 4 shows that God is incorporeal; for if he had a body, we would worship him on a mountain or in a temple, for mountains and temples are corporeal.[12]

However, many of the same writers take "spirit" to be the equivalent of "truth" and conclude that John is contrasting the types of the Old Testament with the truth of the New Testament. Origen writes: "By these words he [Jesus] taught that God must not be worshipped in the flesh and carnal sacrifices, but in spirit. . . . The Father must not be worshipped by external signs but in truth, the truth which came by Jesus Christ after the law given by Moses." [13] In this sense the text was frequently used to contrast Christianity and Judaism. Chrysostom believed that Jesus was referring here to the end of the sacrifices of the Old Testament. Sheep and oxen are no longer offered, for the offering is now Christ himself, a sacrifice far superior to those of ancient Israel.[14]

John 4:24 is never referred to in Athanasius' works.[15] In itself this is significant, for it suggests that Cyril's approach to the Pentateuch is not so dependent on Athanasius as his works on the Trinity are. In Alexandria, however, both the strictly theological explanation of the text and its interpretation in the light of Judaism were current. We have already noted this in Origen, but it is also true of Didymus. He writes: "Because God is a spirit he is worshiped spiritually in spirit and in truth; the God of all is no longer worshiped typically. He says that the worship in the spirit is in opposition to that of the letter, the truth to the

11. Frag. 3 on John 4:24 (Reuss, *Johannes-Kommentare,* p. 178); see also Apollinaris (Lietzmann, pp. 173,27–174,1.)

12. *Homily* 15 on John 4:20–24 (24–27).

13. *Contra Celsum* 6.70 (trans. Chadwick, p. 385).

14. *Hom. in Joh.* 4:24 (33.2, PG 59:189d–190b). *Hom. in Heb.* 6:19–20 (11.3, PG 63:92a–d).

15. The only reference to the text in Athanasius occurs in a passage cited from Dionysius (*De sent. Dion.* 15).

type. These things were useful until the time when the truth came and at Christ's coming all these things ceased." [16]

Cyril was familiar with both the "theological" interpretation of the text and its use in connection with the relationship between Judaism and Christianity. However, he seldom cites the passage in connection with the doctrine of God.[17] In most cases John 4:24 appears when Cyril is discussing Christianity and Judaism and it provides him with one of the key exegetical bases for his polemic.[18] In his *Commentary on John* he interprets it as follows: Jesus here intimates the change that has come about through his coming. Now that he has come the "type shall be transferred [μετασκευασθήσεσθαι] to truth and the shadow of the law to spiritual worship [λατρείαν πνευματικήν]." In the old covenant Israel worshiped the Lord with "external offerings" paying the "drachm of corruptible matter; but since we are true worshipers we worship God the father in spirit and in truth." Such worship is acceptable to God. "He accepts the spiritual worshiper who does not practice a form of piety in images or types in Jewish fashion but in the fashion of the gospel." [19]

Cyril's exegesis of the text incorporates traditional elements. He follows earlier commentators in identifying "spirit and truth" with the distinction between the types of the Old Testament and the truth of the New Testament. Worship in spirit and truth takes the place of Jewish law. This law was only a shadow of things to come and now that the truth has come in Christ we should follow it instead of the images of the Old Testament. However there are at least two distinctively Cyrillian ideas in the passage and they indicate the significance of this text for his thought. He says that the "types are transformed into the truth." The term used here, μετασκευάζω, is one of a series of words used frequently by Cyril to describe the transformation of the Old Testament types into the new revelation in Jesus. He writes:

16. See Frag. 3 mentioned in n. 11; also Didymus, *Commentary on Zachariah*, 8:23 (Doutreleau, 2:644–48).

17. See *Contra Julianum* 4 (*PG* 76:693c).

18. Luis M. Armendariz, *El Nuevo Moisés*, pp. 117 ff.

19. *In Jo.* 4:23–25 (P 1:283,19–21; 284,20–285,1); *In Jo.* 4:22 (P 1:282, 5–9).

"Emmanuel is the firstfruits of the creation which was being remade [μεταπλαττομένης] into newness," and those who are united to him "have been transformed [μετασκευασμένους] to the newness of the evangelical way of life." Elsewhere: "When Jesus says he came to fulfil the law he does not mean to put away the oracles of God . . . rather there is a kind remaking [μεταπλασμον], and I might say, a transposition [μεταχάραξιν] of the types into the truth." And again: "Moses was minister of types and shadows . . . Christ a son and Lord became the arbitrator of a new covenant. I say new for it is renewing [αναμορφούσης] man to newness of holy life and through the evangelical way of life he is esteemed a true worshiper. For it says that God is a spirit and it is necssary that he be worshiped in spirit and in truth." Finally: "Our Lord Jesus Christ transformed [μεταχαράττων] the things which were in types into truth." [20]

Passages such as these can be multiplied over and over again in Cyril's writings.[21] They indicate that his interpretation of John 4:24 presupposes a set of theological and exegetical ideas which inform his approach to the problem of the relationship between Judaism and Christianity and the relationship between the two testaments. The central idea here is that Christianity is the result of a *transformation* of Judaism into a more God-pleasing way of life marked by worship in spirit and in truth. In one of his more polemical writings he puts the matter as follows:

How long, O Jew, being taken up by the types in the Scriptures, are you going to bypass the power of the truth? When will the limit of your ignorance be recognized? When will you remove the shadow of the law from your mind? How much time will it require for us to show you, you with so much self-control? When will you join in with service in spirit to God, the king of all things? "God is a spirit and those who worship him must worship him in spirit and in truth." For you have neglected to serve in

20. *Ador.* 17 (*PG* 68:1097c–d); *In Is.* 60:4–7 (*PG* 70:1325a); *Ador.* 1 (*PG* 68:140c); *In Is.* 42:8–9 (*PG* 70:857c); *Ador.* 2 (*PG* 68:213a).
21. See, for example, *PG* 77:580d, 937c; *PG* 68:213a, 1061c.

spirit and, more than that, you have chosen the more inferior sacrifice as the most pleasing to yourselves. In the arrogant obtuseness of the letter of the law, you still think that you can honor God through this, and you shake off the more accurate perception of the law as if you had entire knowledge of what was written when you have only perceived trash. Come, now, about those things which you cherish let us have a little discussion. I think that if you really desire to come to your senses you will very easily perceive that you have spent a long time in your error.[22]

The second Cyrillian trait in his exposition of John 4:24 is the emphasis on worship in spirit and in truth as a new way of life. He frequently uses the term πολιτεία to refer to the differences between the way of life under the law and the new life under the gospel. "Through the evangelical teaching the true worshipper, *i.e.* the spiritual man, shall be led to a *politeia* well pleasing to the Father." [23] Christians no longer follow the Jewish form of piety, for they now live according to the evangelical pattern. The term *politeia* is used frequently by the fathers to refer to Judaism. Justin Martyr speaks about the "legal way of life" [τὴν ἔννομον πολιτείαν] when referring to those who have gone back to Judaism after once following Christ.[24] Other writers refer to Judaism as the "way of life [πολιτεία] according to Moses" and sometimes use the term to refer simply to the "religious system" of the Jews. By the same token, πολιτεία also refers to the Christian way as the "evangelical way" or the "new way" which takes the place of the Jewish way.[25] Especially in his exegetical works Cyril employs the term πολιτεία in close conjunction with the text from John 4:24. When the Psalmist writes: "I will accept no bull from your house" (Psalm 50:9), he means, says Cyril, that the "worship in shadows is cast off and the things in types have been taken away, leading us to righteousness in Christ and teaching us to be remade [μεταποιεῖσθαι] in

22. *PG* 77:513d–516b.　　23. *In Jo.* 4:23–25 (P 1:284, 21–23).
24. *Dial.* 47.4.

25. Eusebius, *Demonst, Evang.* 1.2; *Praep. Evang.* 7.8; Chrysostom, *Adversus Iudaeos* 4.5; Theodore of Mopsuestia *In Gal.* 4:24. For other references see G. W. H. Lampe, *A Patristic Greek Lexicon*, p. 113.

the evangelical way of life [ἐυαγγελικἠ πολιτεια] which only is
pleasing to God . . . 'For God is a spirit and those who worship
him must worship him in spirit and in truth.' " [26] At times Cyril
expresses similar ideas but without using the term πολιτεία. For
example, commenting on Jesus' refusal to go to the feast, Cyril
says that he declined because of the words of the prophet Amos,
"I hate your feast days." The Jewish worship has now passed
away and we worship God in "spirit and in truth." No longer
do we perform the "worship of the law, but rather the worship
in spirit and keep the feast of tabernacles in truth." [27] And elsewhere. "All things are new in Christ: worship, life, and law;
we do not adhere to useless types and shadows but rather perform the worship of God in spirit and in truth." We are not
named after a tribe such as Ephraim or Manasseh but we are
named after the "newness of the evangelical life in Christ." [28]

The phrases "new way of life" or "evangelical way of life"
call attention to differences between Judaism and Christianity.
As we observed in the previous chapter, Cyril's polemic against
Judaism, like those of other fathers, dwelt on Jewish practices
such as circumcision, the sabbath, festivals, fasting. By aligning
πολιτεία with "worship in spirit and in truth," Cyril gives shape
to his conviction that everything associated with Judaism has
been transformed to a new way of life in Christ. Thus "evangelical
way of life" becomes along with "incorruption" and "life" the
mark of the redemption accomplished by Christ. "Human nature
blooms again in him to "incorruptibility, and life, and the newness of the evangelical way of life [πολιτεία]." [29]

The choice of John 4:24 as the title for Cyril's first exegetical
work is therefore significant. Indeed it not only gives us some
idea of what he wished to do in this work but also highlights
some of the major exegetical and theological themes which
dominate his thinking. By calling his commentary on the Pentateuch *Adoration in Spirit and in Truth* Cyril wished to demonstrate that the Jewish way of life had been superseded, the Jewish
scriptures had found their true interpretation, and a new way
of life had been established. The institutions of ancient Israel

26. *In Is.* 43:25–26 (*PG* 70:912a–b).   27. *In Jo.* 7:8 (P 1:588–90).
28. *In Is.* 65:16–18 (*PG* 70:1417b).   29. *n Is.* 11:1 (*PG* 70:312d).

have come to an end because they have found their completion and fulfilment in Christ. The Jewish scriptures will not be rightly understood unless they are seen to point to the spiritual worship, the true worship, which now characterizes the new way in Christ. The question of Christianity and Judaism formed the backdrop for Cyril's interpretation of the Bible.

In the introduction to *Adoration* Cyril also cites Matthew 5:17. This passage is as important as John 4:24. It too was part of the arsenal of texts used by Christians in the polemic against Judaism. In his treatise *Adversus Judaeos,* for example, Augustine cites Matthew 5 to show that the prophecies of the Old Testament are fulfilled in Jesus, for "he came to fulfill, not to destroy the law or the prophets." [30] Chrysostom believes that it was spoken by Christ to forestall criticism, for they thought he was "abrogating the ancient institutions." The text, says Chrysostom, is directed against the "obstinacy of the Jews," though it also silences the heretics who say that the "old covenant is of the devil." [31]

Cyril's own exegesis reflects the interpretation of earlier writers, though he once again gives it his own peculiar twist by relating it to his own theological and exegetical framework. Specifically he takes it to be complementary to John 4, and uses it for an explicit polemic against Judaism. In a fragment from Cyril's lost commentary on Matthew 5:17 we read:

> In place of fleshly worship the Lord introduced worship in spirit and in truth. And perhaps what the Jews were not doing in a fleshly way the disciples of Christ are now doing spiritually. Wherefore it says not one jot or tittle shall pass from the law, until all things happen. Evidently the Jews did not do everything, or if they did they had stopped doing them, no longer agreeing to do these things, whether because of fear of the emperors, or because the temple was

30. Augustine, *Adversus Judaeos* 2; see also Clement of Alexandria, *Strom.* 3.6 (46).2

31. Chrysostom, *Homily* 16 on Matt. 5:17 (*PG* 57:257 ff). See also Origen, Frag. 230 on Matt. 11:13; Tertullian, *Adversus Judaeos* 9; *Adv. Marcionem* 4.7.4,9,10; Athanasius, *Festal Epistle* 36 (Lefort, pp. 26–27); Didymus, *Commentary on Zachariah* (Doutreleau, pp. 284, 1000).

destroyed, in which place alone sacrifices had to be carried out.[32]

The two passages from Matthew and John deal with a similar problem but really accent two different aspects of the relationship between the old and the new. John 4 stresses the newness of the dispensation in Christ, whereas Matthew 5 stresses the continuity between the old and the new. Jesus did not put an end to the things of old but brought them to fulfilment. Commenting on John 7:18: "He who speaks on his own authority seeks his own glory." Cyril says that Jesus did not use "strange words which are foreign to the law . . . but rather he exhorts them to be obedient to the former oracles while he removes only the unprofitable and gross shadow of the letter, transforming [μετασκευάζοντα] it persuasively to the spiritual sense, which already lay hidden in types. When he says in the Gospel according to Matthew, "I came not to destroy the law, but to fulfill," he indicates this indirectly. For the way of life according to the gospel transforms the letter into truth [μεταμόρφωσιν] and having fashioned anew [μετασκευάσας] the Mosaic type to what is more fitting, now has knowledge of the worship in spirit. . . . He does not put away Moses, nor does he teach us to reject the instruction of the law, but over what has been shadowed in type, a kind of brighter color, he places over the truth." [33]

We left Cyril and Palladius just as Palladius cited the two passages which had troubled him. Cyril asks his friend: What is it about these passages that you find so difficult and obscure? Palladius replies that the words of Jesus in Matthew seem to suggest that he did not come to dispense with the law but to carry it out and fulfil it. "But elsewhere the sacred text enjoins us to depart from ancient customs and to cease from righteousness of the law." Paul writes: "You are severed from Christ, you who would be justified by the law; you have fallen away from grace" (Gal. 5:4). And in another place: "But whatever gain, I

32. Frag. on Matt. 5:17 (Reuss, *Matthaeus-Kommentare*, no. 46); See also *Ador.* 2 (PG 68:253b).

33. *In Jo.* 7:18 (P 1:606, 16–607,4); see also Cyril *In Jo.* 14:24 (P 2:504), *In Jo.* 15:8 (P 2:567) and *Glaphyra Num* (PG 69:597b).

had, I counted as loss for the sake of Christ. . . . For his sake I have suffered the loss of all things . . . in order that I may gain Christ and be found in him, not having a righteousness of my own, based on law" (Phil. 3:7–9). To these passages Palladius adds Hebrews 7:18–19, "a former commandment is set aside because of its weakness and uselessness (for the law made nothing perfect)," and Hebrews 8:7–10: "If the first covenant had been faultless, there would have been no occasion for a second." Next Palladius cites the long passage from Jeremiah about the new covenant Jahweh will make with his people, and Hebrews 8:13: "In speaking of a new covenant he treats the first as obsolete. And what is becoming obsolete and growing old is ready to vanish away." [34]

Finally Palladius comes to his point: "If the law brought nothing to perfection and there was a rejection of the ancient commandment and a second was brought in to reconcile us to God, why does the Savior say: 'I did not come to destroy the law but to fulfil it,' and 'it is fitting to worship in spirit and in truth'?" It is clear, says Palladius "that we must cease these practices and discontinue worship according to the law." Palladius' question is clear: what we read in Paul and what we hear from Jesus seems contradictory. One says we should continue with the law, the other that we should discontinue. Cyril has listened patiently to the speech and now responds: "What an immense sea of questions you are embarking on. How can the mind even see clearly into such subtle questions?" [35]

Cyril's introduction to the commentary on the Pentateuch skillfully poses one of the central questions in the Jewish-Christian debate of the patristic Church. Though the Church claimed the books of Moses as its own, it could not simply assume without argument that these books were the property of Christians. For example, Eusebius of Caesarea stated that one of the purposes of his *Demonstratio Evangelica* was "to give a more complete answer to the charges of those of the circumcision who say that we have no share in the promises of their Scriptures. . . . I propose to meet these attacks by evidence derived straight from their

34. *Ador.* 1 (PG 68:136b–137a).   35. Ibid., 137a.

own prophetic books." The writings of Israel are "not alien to us, but our own property." [36] In the *Adoration* Palladius points to precisely those passages in the New Testament which expose the weakness of the Christian position and suggest that Christianity has irrevocably broken with the inheritance of Israel. Palladius suggests that Christians have no right to use the Jewish scriptures as they do.

Cyril's introduction to his first major exegetical work attempts a solution to the kind of question raised by the Jewish-Christian debates. [37] In answer to Palladius' questions Cyril replies: "The New Testament is sister and kin to the things spoken of old through the most wise Moses, and made up of the same elements. And the life in Christ is not greatly different from the way of life [πολιτεία] according to the law, *if* the ancient ordinances

---

36. Eusebius, *Praeparatio Evangelica*, preface (trans. Gifford, pp. 3–5). The questions raised by Jews also found their way into the writings of the Greeks against the Christians as we noted in the first chapter. For example, Celsus in the second century and Julian in the fourth bring "Jewish arguments" against Christianity. Julian wants to know "what can be the reason why they [Christians] do not even adhere to the Jewish beliefs but have abandoned them also and followed a way of their own" (*Against the Galilaeans*, 43a, 253a, 262c). Elsewhere: "Why is it that you do not abide even by the traditions of the Hebrews or accept the law which God has given them?" "Why is it that after deserting us you do not accept the law of the Jews or abide by the sayings of Moses?" Julian claims that he can cite ten thousand passages "as evidence, where he [Moses] said that the law is for all time." For Celsus see Origen, *Contra Celsum* 7.18, 25. Cyril's reply to Julian follows the pattern of his exegetical works. He argues that Christ has fulfilled the law (*PG* 76:993b), that he is the end of the law (865b). The law is a tutor for the mystery of Christ. The Jews think they fulfil the law by eating unleavened bread at feasts (996a), but God now requires a spiritual worship (996d).

37. See Simon, *Verus Israel*, pp. 196 ff. For a discussion of Cyril's relationship to earlier interpreters on this topic see Alexander Kerrigan, *St. Cyril of Alexandria: Interpreter of the Old Testament*, pp. 131 ff. For Clement of Alexandria, see Claude Mondésert, *Clément D'Alexandrie;* for Origen, Jean Daniélou, "L'unité des deux Testaments dans l'oeuvre d'Origène"; for Athanasius, Pius Merendino, *Paschale Sacramentum*, pp. 17–29. For the primitive church and the second century see Hans Freiherr von Campenhausen, "Das Alte Testament als Bibel der Kirche vom Ausgang des Urchristentums bis zur Entstehung des Neuen Testaments," *Aus der Fruehzeit des Christentums*, pp. 152–96.

are given a spiritual interpretation. For the law is a type and shadow and the form of piety is as yet in birth pains, and having the beauty of the truth hidden in it." Palladius, however, is not satisfied with Cyril's reply. He presses him further: "How," he asks, "are we to live in an evangelical way and still follow the ancient commands, thinking that we fulfill the things of Moses?" Cyril again reminds Palladius that these are complex and difficult matters, but he proceeds to make another attempt at answering. Citing Psalm 45:14: "The princess is decked in her chamber with gold-woven robes," Cyril says that this applies to the Church for she possesses a spiritual beauty and is lovely to look at to those who can perceive with understanding. But this beauty is hidden from the mind of the Jew. As Paul said, "For he is not a real Jew who is one outwardly, nor is true circumcision something external and physical. He is a Jew who is one inwardly, and real circumcision is a matter of the heart, spiritual and not literal. His praise is not from men but from God" (Rom. 2:28–29). Once again the argument has become a discussion concerning the differences between Jew and Christian; one is marked by worship according to the precepts of the Old Testament, the other by spiritual worship in accord with the gospel. But Palladius now believes he has caught Cyril and again raises the key question. If circumcision in the spirit is now in vogue, and Jewish ways are given up, why did Christ say: "I do not come to destroy"? And if this is not so, why do we not offer bulls and turtledoves? [38] Thus far Cyril has tried to show the need for a spiritual interpretation of the Old Testament, but in doing so he makes it seem as if there is no real value in the Old Testament itself. Now he must turn to that question.

Cyril chides Palladius for his bad thinking: "You have strayed far from the truth, my friend," he warns. "You think that the law is abolished and this means that it is no longer useful. Recall the words of Paul. 'Do we then overthrow the law by this faith? By no means! On the contrary, we uphold the law' (Rom. 3:31). What does this mean? The law tutors us and leads us to the mystery in Christ. We say that the things of old

38. *Ador.* 1 (*PG* 68:137b–d).

through Moses, the ancient decrees, are the foundations of the beginning of the words of God. If we desert the tutor, who will lead us to the mystery of Christ? And if we refuse to learn the foundations at the beginning of the oracles of God, how or whence are we to arrive at the end? Is not Christ the fulness of the law and the prophets according to the Scriptures?" Cyril tries in this passage to move beyond the either-or alternatives suggested by Palladius. Simply because we claim that what happened in Christ is new does not mean that it has no relation to the old. For it is through the writings of the Old Testament that we come to see and recognize Christ and to understand his significance. The Old Testament is a necessary stage in the divine economy. It is a "teacher who leads beautifully to the mystery of Christ." It contains the "first elements of God's words." If we turn our back on this teacher, who will lead us to Christ? if we refuse to learn the fundamentals, how shall we reach the end? [39]

Cyril again turns to a passage from the Gospels to explain his meaning. According to John, Jesus rebuked the Jews for not finding his teaching in the Old Testament. "It is Moses who accuses you, on whom you set your hope. If you believed Moses, you would believe me, for he wrote of me. But if you do not believe his writings, how will you believe my word?" [40] This too is a favorite passage for Cyril and he cites it frequently in connection with the relationship between the two testaments. Commenting on Malachi 4:6 Cyril urges the Jews to remember the law of Moses, for if they do they will see that the "kerygma of Christ is not new or unfamiliar [ἀσυνήθες], but it was there from the beginning and at first." Through the law of Moses he called Israel to knowledge of God. The holy writings sounded forth Christ, and if one would examine the written law he would find Christ there. For Jesus said, "If you believed Moses, you would believe me, for he wrote of me." [41] Thus Christ is "the fulness of the law and prophets." The law is a tutor which leads us from the "worship in the law" to that which is "holy and spiritual." To illustrate this Cyril cites John 5:46.[42]

Cyril has finally come to his own point of view. Rejecting the

39. Ibid., 140a.　　　　　　40. Ibid., 140b.
41. *In Mal.* 4:6 (P 2:625, 16–626,17).　　42. *Ador.* 2 (PG 68:220d).

alternatives proposed by Palladius he argues that the relationship between Christianity and Judaism, between the Jewish scriptures and the New Testament, should be viewed as a *transformation* or a *remolding* of the old into the new. To illustrate this point he draws on the familiar analogy of the painter who first draws a sketch of his painting or the sculptor who first shapes his sculpture in wax. The earlier sketches are in no sense valueless; they have their own purpose and function. But they cannot be compared with the new, the finished product. In the same way the types and shadows of the old covenant had significance in their time, but their time was limited. When the new came and the work of God was brought to completion they had to give way. The sketches and the wax figure do not lose the significance they had, but they must now give way to the finished work. For the new brings the old to its intended fulfilment.[43]

Palladius is still not satisfied, however. If this is so, why was not the evangelical life made known at the outset? Again Palladius puts his finger on the key question. Cyril's analogy does not persuade him because it fails to explain why such a long preparation was necessary. Cyril now switches metaphors and appeals to the Pauline idea of a tutor. In Cyril's hand the metaphor takes on a very anti-Jewish cast. "Much tutoring was necessary for they [the Jews] were dense and quite easily led astray to any kind of absurdities." It is difficult for someone as dense as the Jews to believe that anything as revolutionary as the new life in Christ could spring up without reference to an earlier dispensation. For this life is "very elegant and brilliant and of such exceptional character that it is like walking on earth while having one's citizenship in heaven." Thus it was necessary to have a tutor who taught with types just as we govern children before they reach maturity.[44]

The discussion continues, but the chief points have now been stated. The introduction to *Adoration,* suggests several things about his exegesis: He is deeply concerned to show that Christians have a right to read and interpret the books of the Old Testament.

43. *Ador.* 1 (*PG* 68:140c). See for example Melito of Sardis, *Paschal Homily* 36; J. Daniélou, *Origen,* pp. 144–45.
44. *Ador.* 1 (*PG* 68:141a ff).

He is just as concerned to show that Christianity cannot be confined to the books of the Old Testament, for in Christ there is a
new dispensation which ushers in a new way of life, a life according to the Gospel, a life of worship in spirit and in truth.
What is revealed in Christ is genuinely new, but it can be traced
back to Moses if one reads these writings spiritually. Thus Christians can claim the Old Testament as their own and can meet
the charge of unfaithfulness for failing to observe the law. Finally,
Cyril's approach to the problem is shaped by a number of key
passages from the Gospels, and these provide both an answer to
his critics and a positive statement of what he thinks it is about
Christ that is new. Of these passages the most important is
John 4:24.

The relationship of Christianity to Judaism is not simply a
concern in *Adoration in Spirit and in Truth,* it is a central theme
of Cyril's exegesis. His second major work on the Pentateuch, the
Glaphyra, opens with a discussion of the same problem. The title
of this section reads: "That through all the Mosaic writings, the
mystery of Christ is enigmatically signified." [45] Cyril cites the
words of Jesus: "Search the Scriptures," and applies them directly
to the Jewish people. Jesus here teaches that they would not be
able to receive eternal life "unless uncovering the letter of the law
as a kind of treasure and they would investigate the pearl hidden
there, which is Christ," for Christ is the end of the law and the
prophets. Large sections of the *Glaphyra* are devoted to a discussion of the same problem. For example, two sections are given
over to the topic "the demise of the Jewish synagogue." Other
sections offer an elaborate typology of the narratives of the
Pentateuch, attempting to show that their true meaning is to be
found in the coming of Christ. In a characteristic passage he
argues that the Jewish synagogue has "aged and become shriveled"
whereas the church is a new creation full of life. In many cases
he relies on the same framework of passages—for example, John
4 and Matthew 5—which inform the opening pages of *Adoration.*[46]

45. *Glaphyra* I (*PG* 69:13a); see the comments by Armendariz in *El
Nuevo Moisés,* pp. 19–20.

46. See the following sections in particular: *PG* 69:533b–537d; 564a–
589b; 589d–605a; 676a–677c.

Besides the *Adoration* and *Glaphyra,* Cyril wrote no other commentaries on the Pentateuch or Genesis. His inclination to read the Pentateuch in the light of Jewish-Christian questions and the relationship between the two testaments is significant. Many of the fathers wrote commentaries on Genesis in the decades before Cyril, but most took quite a different approach. In the fourth century Genesis was widely interpreted in the light of cosmological and "theological" questions raised by pagan criticism of Christianity. In the second and third centuries a number of themes suggested themselves to commentators on Genesis, and one of these is the relationship of Christianity and Judaism. This can be seen in the random comments of Justin, Tertullian, and others, as well as Origen. Justin, for example, discusses passages from Genesis in answer to Trypho's claim that Christians had forsaken the regulations of the Old Testament. He tries to show that the Mosaic law had a purpose in the history of Israel but that now its prescriptions have been superseded by Christ.[47]

By the fourth century, however, most expositors of Genesis had turned their attention to other questions. For example, Basil delivered a series of nine homilies on the opening verses. These homilies, of high literary quality and beauty, are chiefly a theological essay on the nature of the created order. Displaying great breadth of learning in the natural sciences he ranges over a host of topics to discuss specific aspects of the created order: plants, animals, fish, birds, etc. The chief purpose of the book is to defend the Christian doctrine of God and creation against the "Greek" view that the world was not created and is eternal. Other writers of the time take a similar approach in their commentaries.[48]

47. Justin, *Dial.* 11.2,5. For the early history of the interpretation of Genesis see Gregory Armstrong, *Die Genesis in der Alten Kirche.* On Justin, see pp. 22–28. See also F. E. Robbins, *The Hexameral Literature.* Origen discusses both cosmological questions and questions concerning Judaism in his homilies on Genesis. See *Homilies on Genesis* (*GCS* 6:24–29; 115,2–3). See also *Homily* 17.1 on Joshua where he cites John 4:21,23 in connection with the ending of types and shadows (*SC*, pp. 371–72).

48. Basil, *Hexameron* 1.1. Gregory of Nyssa completed Basil's work with his *De opificio hominis.* See Chrysostom's comments (*PG* 53:28d). On Athanasius, see P. Athanasius Recheis, "Sancti Athanasii magni doctrina de primordiis seu quomodo explicaverit Gen. 1–3."

Cyril treated the questions most of his contemporaries discussed on the basis of Genesis in the apology against Julian and
his dogmatic works on the Trinity. Thus in *Against Julian* Cyril
defends himself against Julian's charge that Moses teaches in
Genesis that "God is the creator of nothing that is incorporeal,
but is only the disposer of matter that already existed. For the
words, 'And the earth was invisible and without form' can only
mean that he regards the wet and dry substance as the original
matter and that he introduces God as the disposer of this matter."
Plato on the other hand teaches that the world "came into being"
(γέγονεν), that it had a beginning and this by the providence of
God. In his reply to Julian, Cyril discusses these questions at
length and arrives at conclusions similar to those of Basil, Gregory,
and Athanasius.[49]

Cyril's exegetical works are seldom concerned with cosmological
questions. He is generally interested in dealing with exegetical
questions, questions of "biblical theology," the Christian life, or
the relationship of Christianity to Judaism. His preoccupation
with Jewish questions can be seen in his other two extant works
on the Old Testament. In the *Commentary on Isaiah* as well as
the *Commentary on the Minor Prophets* the themes sounded in
the earlier works appear with almost monotonous regularity.[50]
The *Commentary on Isaiah* opens, as we observed in the previous
chapter, with an attack on Judaism. Taking the exile to be a
punishment for Jewish disobedience to God, he argues that this
is only the first in a series of national catastrophes leading up to
the destruction of the temple, the city, and the land. The cause
of such destruction lies in the inability of the Jews to "under-

49. Cyril, *Contra Julianum* (*PG* 76:560c–564c); also *PG* 76:585d–589a.
50. For the *Commentary on the Minor Prophets,* see, for example, *In Zach.*
8:7–8 (P 2:387). The text reads, "I will save my people from the east
country and from the west." "From east and west" refers to Immanuel
"who called all under heaven" and brought them into the holy city, the
church of the living God; there we no longer follow types and shadows but
"receive in mind and heart the brilliance of the evangelical teachings, we
fulfil the true worship . . . for 'God is a spirit,' as the son said, and 'those
who worship him worship in spirit and in truth.'" Also *In Osean* 3:1 (P
1:82–83); *In Joel* 1:13 (P 1:304–5); *In Nahum* 1:9 (P 2:18–19); *In Amos*
9:11–12 (P 1:540–42).

stand the shadows of the Old Testament. If they had believed in Moses they would have believed in Christ." This does not mean that the law is without value, for did not Paul say the law is holy? Indeed, replies Cyril, "the law is good, if it is understood spiritually." [51]

The book of Isaiah then becomes for Cyril another occasion to elaborate his views on Judaism and the relationship of the Jewish scriptures to the new dispensation in Jesus. Isaiah is one of Cyril's favorite biblical books and he freely uses the text of the prophet to elaborate on his favorite themes. Perhaps the fullest exegetical expression of his theology occurs on the basis of what is today known as Second Isaiah. Here more than anywhere else the biblical text provides him with opportunity after opportunity to develop his ideas. The accent on the "new thing" God is doing in Isaiah became for Cyril the basis for a statement of the new life in Christ, the new worship in spirit and in truth, and the transformation of the old into the new.[52]

A few examples will suffice. Isaiah 45:9–10 reads: "Woe to him who strives with his Maker, an earthen vessel with the potter! Does the clay say to him who fashions it, 'What are you making'? or 'Your work has no handles'?" The text means, says Cyril, that the God of all redeemed Israel from Egypt "by the law of Moses, restoring Israel to the light of the true knowledge of God. He taught it to worship the one God and to adore the one Lord . . . Through types and shadows he wished to ascend to the things that are greater and more perfect, i.e. the things in Christ." The law was a tutor for Christ and when the Savior came the "shadows of the law are put off and he brought in the beauty of worship in spirit and in truth." The Jews, however, opposed him

51. *PG* 70:33b, 44b ff. Commenting on Is. 27:11, Cyril writes: Israel is a people without discernment, not knowing the resurrection which "reforms to newness of life . . . showing new life to those on earth—that is the evangelical life—and abolishing the feebleness of worship according to the law; showing forth the truth and establishing for those who worship him the brilliant way of worship in spirit and in truth" (*PG* 70:605c). Also *PG* 70:856b–857d; 860b–d. 892a; 820a–821d.

52. See for example *In Is.* 51:6 (*PG* 70:1117b); *In Is.* 43:7–8 (*PG* 70:892a–b); *In Is.* 45:17 (*PG* 70:976). *In Is.* 40:28 (*PG* 70:820d–821d). *In Is.* 60:4–7 (*PG* 70:1325a).

and did not receive the prophet of the "evangelical kerygma." "We are transformed in Christ [μετεστοιχειώθημεν], . . . to receive the evangelical teachings and newness of worship." Christ came to "re-form [αναμορφῶσα] you to better things and to make you over to what is better," but the Jews rejected him. Those who receive him however are "remade spiritually to a holy and most beautiful life." [53]

And again from Isaiah: "Instead of bronze I will bring gold, and . . . instead of wood, bronze, instead of stones, iron" (60:17). The prophet here takes very different materials to make his point, says Cyril. He wishes to say that "all things are to be transformed [μεταστήσεται] to something better in order to distinguish the first [dispensation] from the second. The *paideia* of the law will certainly end with the *paideia* of Christ—that is, in the evangelical oracles—and the difference will be as great as that between gold and bronze. For bronze has the look of gold but is not gold, and iron has the look of silver for it has a glitter, but it is not silver and is much less to be preferred. Thus some might liken the *paideia* of the law to brass and that of Christ to gold. And again someone might liken the power of the way of life according to the law to sin, which only has limited radiance but [the way of life] in Christ, the evangelical way, to silver, for this has the most perfect, i.e. spiritual, splendor." [54]

The fathers were not fond of magic but here Cyril reveals himself as an alchemist. The text from Isaiah says that gold will replace inferior materials such as wood and bronze and stone, but Cyril changes the metaphor to say that bronze is "transformed" into gold. The slip is not accidental, for the term "transformation" and its correlates runs through these commentaries like a bright thread in a dull carpet. The thread first appeared in Cyril's commentary on John 4:24 where he said that the new life in worship and in truth was a remodeling or transformation of the old way of life which had been governed by the law. The corollary to this idea is Cyril's conviction that the new life in Christ is superior to the old life under the law. These two terms summarize the whole of Cyril's attitude toward the

53. *In Is.* 45:9–10 (*PG* 70:960c–964b).   54. *In Is.* 60:17 (*PG* 70:1341).

relationship between Christianity and Judaism. Judaism has been *transformed* through the coming of Christ and the result is *superior* to what was before.

Cyril's vocabulary to express this idea is exceedingly rich and varied. He has a tendency to form compound words and he has carried this to extreme lengths here.[55] Most of the terms have as root some form of "make" or "create" and the prefix *ana* or *meta*.[56] For example he uses the following verbs: διαπλάττω, ἐπιχρωματίζω, μεθίστημι, μεταπλάττω, μεταχαράττω, μεταχρωματίζω, ἀναμορφόω, παραφέρω. Most of these compounds are used by other authors, but in Cyril they occur with uncommon frequency and generally have a technical sense. For example, in answer to Palladius, Cyril said that with the coming of Christ the old was not overthrown but there was a "transformation and a remodeling [μεταπλασμόν, μεταχάραξιν] of the things in types to the truth." [57]

What does Cyril mean when he speaks of remodeling or transforming the shadows into truth? In the introduction to *Adoration* he indicates that he does not wish to dispense with the Old Testament as such, nor does he wish to deny it a place in the economy of salvation. At the same time the force of his discussion is to accent the new so much that little place remains for the old. In fact, he regularly cites 2 Corinthians 5:17 "if anyone is

55. For Cyril's language, see F. L. Cross, "The Projected Lexicon of Patristic Greek." Cross writes of Cyril: "The material in our files has disclosed that Cyril coined a highly distinctive vocabulary. There are well over 1,000 words which occur either in Cyril alone or in Cyril for the first time or in Cyril more frequently than in the whole rest of Greek literature taken together. These Cyrilline words are compounds of common words or verbal elements with prepositional prefixes. Characteristic instances are ἀναφοιτάω, γραοπρεπής, κατωθέω, προαναθρέω. Especially frequent are compounds with κατα and συν, in each case numbering between 100 and 150. These words are so characteristic that their occurrence is a sure test of Cyrilline authorship" (p. 392). On Cyril's Greek see also A. Vaccari, "La grecità di S. Cirillo d'Alessandria," pp. 38–39.

56. See *In Is.* 62:6 (*PG* 70:1373b); *In Is.* 60:47 (*PG* 70:1325a); *PG* 69:293b; *PG* 69:1061c; *PG* 68:228c; *In Mal.* 3:2–3 (P 1:599). *In Is.* 10:33–34 (*PG* 70:308a); *PG* 68:213a. Other references in Kerrigan, *Old Testament*, pp. 128–29.

57. *PG* 68:140c. See in this connection, Gerhart B. Ladner, *The Idea of Reform*, pp. 79–81.

in Christ, he is a new creation" in connection with the transformation of types into truth. Therefore in the beginning of the year
and in the first month the mystery of Christ is shown forth.
A new age for us, the time of his coming, in which everything
is re-established to what is better, indeed transforming into newness of creation that which is growing old and infirm and close
to disappearing. For the things in Christ are a new creation, the
old has passed away, behold all things have become new. We
live, not in Mosaic fashion, but rather we have been brought into
the evangelical life. Christ refashions us through the Holy Spirit.[58]

The terminology used here is precisely the same as that used
in the opening section of the *Adoration,* but the citation of 2
Corinthians 5 gives the whole passage a different character. The
"old is transformed" is really equivalent to "new creation." This
conjunction of new creation and transformation occurs over and
over in Cyril. "The time of human life in the beginning was holy
as in the forefather of the race Adam, not yet violating the commandments, not despising the divine ordinances. Much more
holy, however, is the one in the last time, that is the one who is
the second Adam, reforming the race of those things which happened in the meantime to newness of life in the spirit." [59]

The burden of Cyril's comments is to stress the newness of
Christianity in contrast to the oldness of Judaism.[60] In spite of
his attempt to stress the continuity of the new with the old, he
really comes down very hard on discontinuity. When he says that
Christianity is a transformation of Judaism, or that the Christian
scriptures are a result of the transformation of the types of the
Jewish scriptures, he is really saying that something radically new
has taken place. The words of Isaiah, says Cyril, are appropriate.
He says, "Sing a new song." Only such a hymn, a "new hymn is

58. PG 69:1068a; see also *In Is.* 65:16–18 (PG 79:1417b).
59. PG 68:1076c–d.
60. Cyril often describes the renewal of mankind as a return to that which
was in the beginning. See PG 69:16; *In Jo.* 7:39 (P 1:694,24); PG 69:241c;
Chr. Un. 744a. Just as often he speaks of a renewal to that which is "better."
In Is. 45:11 (PG 70:965b); *In Is.* 45:9 (PG 70:961b). It is clear that he
does not mean a *return* to the original state, but a new state brought about
through Christ.

suitable to the newness of things. For if anyone is in Christ, he is a new creation." [61]

Now this accent on newness has much to do with Cyril's view of Christ. For the thing that distinguishes Christianity from Judaism is the new man who ushers in the new age. Cyril uses precisely the same set of terms to refer to the transformation of types into truth and to the reformation or renewing of the old creation through Christ. The parallel is exact, and he moves freely from one idea to the other. "We are reformed [μεταπεπλάσμεθα] spiritually in Christ and transformed [μετεστοιχειώθημεν] to receive the evangelical teachings and the newness of worship, not in types, but in the most excellent spiritual beauty." "Since he became man he had the whole human nature in himself that he might re-establish human nature transforming [μετασκευάσας] it into what it was in ancient times." "Since Christ shone forth he transformed [μετέβαλον] the types into the truth." "The shadow in the letter is transformed [μεταχατάττοντες] into the truth." [62] These parallels suggest that Cyril's view of Christ is related to the exegetical discussions concerned with the relationship between Christianity and Judaism.

This significance can also be seen in his use of the imagery of the first and second Adam. Commenting on the blessing of Jacob by Esau, Cyril observes that the blessing was not brought to fulfilment simply in Jacob. The blessing "is not fulfilled in Jacob but in Christ. . . . The sense of the prophecy belongs to Christ himself who is beginning and leader. For he is considered the *second Adam* and he bloomed as a second root of humanity. For all things are a new creation in Christ and we have been renewed [ανεκαινίσθημεν] in him to sanctification and incorruptibility and life." [63] Here Cyril supports his view of the relationship between the old and new covenants by reference to the Pauline idea of the second Adam. The distinctive innovation of Christianity is the new man, Christ, the second Adam. Christ the second Adam

61. *In Is.* 42:10 (*PG* 70:860b); see also *In Hos.* 1:19 (P 1:73).

62. *In Is.* 45:9–10 (961c); *In Is.* 65:21–24 (*PG* 70:1425b); *In Jo.* 7:39 (P 1:693, 8); *Ador.* 2 (*PG* 68:213a); *Glaph. Gen.* 1 (*PG* 69:37c).

63. *Glaph. Gen.* 3 (*PG* 69:172b).

renews and refashions and transforms the Old Testament types into the new life in spirit and in truth.

We have seen that Cyril's approach to the question of the two testaments, to the relationship between Christianity and Judaism, is shaped by a number of exegetical ideas. These ideas were suggested by a number of biblical texts, notably John 4:24 and Matthew 5:17. Of these, John 4 is the more important for it provided an overarching framework in which to discuss the problem. However, John 4 does not stand alone in Cyril's thought for it is supported by a wider framework of exegetical and theological ideas—in particular, that the new worship in spirit and in truth comes about through a *transformation* of the old form of worship. However, Cyril's notion of transformation contains two further motifs, bearing particularly on his view of Christ: the new creation, and Christ as the second Adam. These too are exegetical themes central to Cyril's thought, though not so obviously related to the polemic against Judaism. Sometimes they occur in this connection, but they are also used in connection with Christological and Trinitarian debates. As such they provide us with a bridge from Cyril's polemic against Judaism to his other theological concerns.

5   The Second Adam: I

The typology of the first and second Adam enters the Christian tradition through the writings of Paul. Where Paul got his notions about Adam is still a topic of debate. In Philo, for example, there is some speculation about the "earthly man and heavenly man," but Philo's ideas are just the reverse of Paul's. For Philo Adam is not the earthly man but the heavenly man. Since they were contemporaries, it is unlikely that Paul is directly dependent on Philo, but they may have had access to common traditions which each reworked in a different way. At the same time it may be that Paul is drawing on Adamic speculation passed on in rabbinic materials or Jewish legends.[1]

Paul discusses the typology of Adam and Christ in two places, Romans 5 and 1 Corinthians 15. The fathers drew on both passages and moved freely from one to the other. However, they frequently sensed the difference between the two without explicitly saying so. Thus Romans 5 was often cited to support the solidarity of Christ with mankind. Just as all men were "in Adam" and shared his destiny, all men are "in Christ" and therefore share his destiny. 1 Corinthians 15 led to more speculative exegesis, chiefly because of phrases such as "heavenly man" and "life-giving spirit" and the Pauline statement that Christ is the first-fruits of those who are to be raised.

Paul himself uses the Adamic typology to deal with two different problems. In Romans 5 the subject is the place of Jesus' death in redemptive history. In Chapter 4 Paul had discussed Abraham

---

1. On the Adam typology, see Egon Brandenburger, *Adam und Christus Exegetisch-Religionsgeschichtliche Untersuchung zu Roem 5:12–21 (I Kor. 15)*; also Robin Scroggs, *The Last Adam*. On "Adamic" motifs elsewhere in the New Testament, see Leonhard Goppelt, *Typos*, pp. 155 ff. 166 ff; and Jean Daniélou, *From Shadows to Reality*, pp. 11–21. Oscar Cullman sees the son of man and second Adam as "two different developments of the same Christological idea." (*The Christology of the New Testament*, p. 145). For Philo, see *Leg. Alleg.* 1.31.89. See also Wolfhart Pannenberg, *Jesus. God and Man*, p. 186, fn. 4; p. 200, fn. 13.

as a symbol of the one who is justified by faith. The Christian is justified by faith just as Abraham was. In Chapter 5 he launches on a discussion of the significance of Christ's sacrificial death. Why should the death of one man be the basis for the redemption of all men? Paul resorts to a rigorous parallelism between Adam and Christ. In the history of mankind there are two "representative" figures. What happened to the first man, Adam, affected all men who followed him, and what happened to the second man, Jesus, likewise affected, in reverse fashion, all of mankind. If by one man came sin and death, so by the other came life. In this view Paul envisions two great eras in the career of mankind: the era of death which held sway from the time of Adam, and the era of life which began with Christ. All men are bound up with these two men. "For as through the disobedience of the one man the many were made sinners, so through the obedience of the one man the many will be made righteous."

In 1 Corinthians 15 Paul approaches the typology somewhat differently, since he is not so much concerned with the death of Christ as an event in redemptive history as he is with Christ as the first to be raised in the general resurrection of mankind. Here too he attempts to link the destiny of all men with the destiny of Christ, but the point of reference is now the resurrection. Christ is the "firstfruits of the harvest of the dead" and he foreshadows what will happen to all men. "As in Adam all die, so also in Christ shall all be made alive. But each in his own order: Christ the firstfruits, then at his coming those who belong to Christ" (15:21–23). In this section of the chapter Paul's thought is much closer to Romans. Later he engages in wider speculation about the nature of the resurrected body. Paul may have in mind the creation account, particularly Genesis 2:7, suggesting that in Christ there is a renewing of the fallen creation. The first man became a "living being" and the last man has become a "lifegiving spirit." "The first man was made 'of the dust of the earth'; the second man is from heaven. The man made of dust is the pattern of all men of dust, and the heavenly man is the pattern of all the heavenly. As we have worn the likeness of the man made of dust, so we shall wear the likeness of the heavenly man." By drawing a parallel between Adam, the representative man, and Christ, Paul concludes that the resurrected body of the Christian will resemble that of the resurrected Christ. It too will be transformed and modeled not after earthly bodies but after the heavenly body of Christ.

The words of Paul in Romans and 1 Corinthians have frequently captured the imagination of Christian thinkers. In the history of patristic theology these two passages will have a profound impact on certain thinkers, and many others will draw on them in various circumstances. The history of the interpretation of the Adam-Christ typology builds on the groundwork laid by Paul, but like Paul later writers are seldom content to rest on the work of their predecessors. Most patristic writers, though claiming to expound the Pauline texts, actually go far beyond Paul in employing the typology in new theological and exegetical settings.[2]

During the first two centuries the only author to make extensive use of the Adam-Christ typology was Irenaeus. The apostolic fathers and the apologists are silent, and even in the famous sermon of Melito of Sardis, where typology is used extensively, indeed excessively, there is no reference to the Adam-Christ typology. Toward the end of the second century and the beginning of the third Tertullian toyed with certain aspects of it. For example, he writes about the relation between Adam and the Church: "If Adam was a type of Christ, Adam's sleep was a type of the death of Christ who had slept in death. Eve coming from Adam's side is a type of the Church, the true mother of all living." [3] Tertullian and other writers sometime cite sections of Romans 5 or 1 Corinthians 15, but they do not make extensive

2. There is no monograph on the Adam-Christ typology in the fathers. Daniélou has collected a few passages in *From Shadows to Reality*, pp. 11–65, but the discussion is very sketchy. See also Karl Herman Schelkle, *Paulus Lehrer der Vaeter*. Schelkle discusses the interpretation of Rom. 5 in Irenaeus, Origen, Augustine, Ephraim, Didymus, Theodore of Mopsuestia, Cyril of Jerusalem, Cyril of Alexandria, *et al.*, but his interest is primarily on the question of sin and little is said here of the history of the Adamic typology. See also S. Staerck, "Anakephalaiosis," pp. 411–14; Gerhart B. Ladner, *The Idea of Reform;* G. W. H. Lampe, *PGL,* pp. 28–29.

3. *De anima* 43; for other references see T. H. Waszink, ed., *De anima,* p. 469; see also Tertullian, *De carne Christi* 17; *De anima* 40.1; *Adversus Marcionem* 3.19.1; *De monog.* 5.

use of the typology for exegetical or theological purposes. This is also true of Clement, who refers in one place to the first and second man, and says in another passage that the first man played in innocence and later the Word became man that he might raise mankind. But these are little more than allusions.[4]

The yield is only slightly better in Origen. In his commentary on John, for example, he cites 1 Corinthians 15 and Romans 5 in a number of places, but his interest is primarily in the contrast of life and death rather than the Adamic typology. In another place he links 1 Corinthians 15 to Colossians 1: "the firstborn of creation," and says that Christ is not only the firstborn but also Adam, i.e. man.[5] In the *Commentary on the Song of Solomon* he used Romans 5 in an interesting way to interpret the Song of Solomon 1:10. Here Solomon speaks about the "neck" of the beloved and this is said to signify obedience, for the neck receives the yoke of Christ. "So the adornment of her neck, that is, of her obedience, is Christ. For he himself was first made obedient unto death; and, as by the disobedience of one man—namely, of Adam —many were made sinners, so also by the obedience of one—that is, of Christ—many shall be made just. So the adornment and necklace of the Church is the obedience of Christ. But the neck of the Church too, that is, her obedience has been made like to the obedience of Christ; because his obedience is the necklace of the neck." [6] This curious though highly original exegesis is, however, somewhat atypical of Origen. The typology of Adam-Christ occurs only infrequently in his works and is not a major exegetical theme.

We are left then with Irenaeus. He has gained great fame and notoriety in recent years because of his theory of recapitulation and the related idea of first and second Adam. He deserves such attention for he is a singular figure in this respect in the pre-Nicene church. His use of the Adam-Christ typology occurs in a polemical, not an exegetical context. We have no exegetical works

---

4. *Protreptikos* 11; *Stromateis* 3.7(64)1–2 (*GCS* 2:225).

5. *In Joannem* 8:51 (*GCS* 10:381); *In Jo.* 1:1 (*GCS* 10:23).

6. *Commentary on Song of Solomon* 2 (*In Cant.* 1:10; *GCS* 33:156); trans. R. P. Lawson, *Origen*, p. 147; see also Origen's exegesis of Rom. 5 in Rufinus' translation (*PL* 14:1019–21).

from Irenaeus, though the *Against Heresies* is almost wholly concerned with exegetical matters in relation to theological problems. But Irenaeus' interest in the typology is theological and he uses it to score points against the Gnostics and to develop his own theological views vis-à-vis his Gnostic opponents.

Most recent studies of Irenaeus have shown that the notion of recapitulation is not his central theological idea, but really part of a wider field of ideas.[7] Specifically, Irenaeus' understanding of recapitulation is part of his general notion of the divine economy or dispensation. Recapitulation is only one of the formulas he uses for the economy, and it receives only limited use in his book. Irenaeus, however, did take an important step by combining the notion of "recapitulation" from Ephesians with the Adam-Christ typology of Romans and 1 Corinthians. In doing this he did go beyond Paul by utilizing the Pauline (more accurately Pauline and deutero-Pauline) materials in a new way. Further, in Paul the typology was used primarily with relation to Adam and Jesus. Irenaeus, however, gives the typology a universal dimension by asserting that not simply Adam but all things are recapitulated in Christ. The whole of creation is summed up: "Omnia semetipsum recapitulans." [8] The Adam-Christ typology becomes a convenient way of speaking of the solidarity of Adam and Christ with all things in the created order.

Irenaeus also goes beyond Paul in a number of details. He notes, for example, that Adam had no father but God and this was also true of the second Adam. The "first was of dust" wrought by God and the "second [was] also formed by God" in the womb of the virgin.[9] He observed that in Adam mankind lost the "image and likeness of God," and this image was recovered in Jesus.[10] He draws a parallel between Mary and Eve. "The knot of Eve's disobedience was loosed by the obedience of

7. For Irenaeus' view of recapitulation see André Benoît, *Saint Iréné,* pp. 219–27; Albert Houssiau, *La Christologie de Saint Iréné,* pp. 215–23; J. T. Nielsen, *Adam and Christ in the Theology of Irenaeus of Lyons.* For the use of the recapitulation motif prior to Irenaeus see Houssiau; also W. Staerk, "Der eschatologische Mythos in der altchristlichen Theologie," pp. 83–95, and "Anakephalaiosis."

8. *Adversus Haereses* 3.17.16 (H 2:87).   9. Ibid., 3.19.1 (H 2:95).
10. Ibid., 3.31.1 (H 2:120).

Mary. For what the virgin Eve had bound fast through unbelief, this did the virgin Mary set free through faith." [11] Irenaeus uses the typology to affirm that Jesus was truly man, for if Jesus was to sum up all things in himself he must be of the same flesh and blood as Adam.[12] This particular accent occurs regularly in the later fathers. Irenaeus also draws a parallel between the spirit which descended on the first creation and the spirit which descended on the second Adam at his baptism.[13]

These instances give some impression of how Irenaeus developed the typology beyond Paul and applied it to other events in the life of Jesus. Paul limits the parallel between Adam and Christ chiefly to death and resurrection. But Irenaeus extends it to include Jesus' whole life, though he does not apply it explicitly to every moment in Jesus' life. Irenaeus' chief contribution, however, was to link the Adam-Christ typology to his argument about the unity of God and the wholeness of the created order. The God who created the world and Adam is the same God who redeems it in Christ, the second Adam. The typology establishes the unity of God's redemptive work and the oneness of God. He is, in Benoît's words, a "theologian of unity" who sought to hold together the full history of salvation in a unity against the fragmentation of the Gnostics.[14]

Irenaeus' emphasis on unity led him to play down the element of discontinuity in the relationship between Adam and Christ. He insists on the similarity between the original creation and the renewed creation. Consequently the idea of new creation, though implicit in Irenaeus, seldom becomes explicit in his works. "Irenaeus fights shy of such passages as 2 Corinthians 5:17 and Galatians 6:15, and hardly ever quotes them." [15] The idea of new creation was too susceptible to misinterpretation by his opponents. However, Irenaeus distinguishes between natural

11. Ibid., p. 124.   12. Ibid., 5.14.1–2 (H 2:361).

13. Ibid., 3.10 (H 2:32–33); Ibid., 3.18–1–3 (H 2:92–94). On this passage see Karl Schluetz, *Isaisas 11,2 in den ersten vier christlichen Jahrhunderten*, pp. 46–58; see chap. 6 and also Robert L. Wilken, "The Interpretation of the Baptism of Jesus in the Later Fathers."

14. Benoît, *S. Irénée*, p. 227.

15. Gustaf Wingren, *Man and the Incarnation*, p. 152. See *AH* 3.31.1 (H 2:121); 3.18.1 (H 2:92).

and created endowments of man and those gifts which come from God in Christ and which were not given fully in the first creation. Incorruption, for example, is only a precarious possession in Adam, but in Christ it is given to mankind fully and permanently. Christ then brings to man what he did not possess in Adam.[16]

In the ante-Nicene period Methodius also gave attention to the Adam-Christ typology, though his interpretation is more idiosyncratic than that of Irenaeus and did not have as much influence on later thinkers. Methodius asks whether there is any basis for Paul's comparison of Adam and Christ. "How can Adam be compared to the son of God, the first-born of every creature and one caught in fire?" Paul is justified in this comparison, says Methodius, for "he not only considers Adam as a type and image of Christ, but also that Christ became the very same as Adam through the descent of the Logos into him." At first this sounds similar to Irenaeus, but Methodius has actually struck out on his own course. He says: "It was only fitting that the first born of God, his first and only begotten offspring, should become man and be joined as his wisdom to mankind's first man, first formed and first born." Methodius seems to be thinking not so much of a "second" Adam but a union between Christ and the first Adam. He continues: "Most fitting was it that the eldest of the aeons, the first among archangels, when about to mingle with men, took up his abode in the first and eldest man of humankind—Adam. For thus, in remodelling what was from the beginning and moulding it all over again of the virgin and of the Spirit, he fashioned the same man; just as in the beginning when the earth was virgin and untilled, God had taken dust from the earth and formed, without seed, the most rational being from it." [17]

16. See M. Aubineau, "Incorruptibilité et divinisation selon saint Irénée, pp. 25–52. Irenaeus considers immortality to be a gift of God, not a natural possession of man, and thinks it is achieved through Christ. See particularly *AH* 2.34.4 (H 1:383,7); 3.5.3 (H 2:20,11); also 3.23.1; 3.19.1; 4.20.2. See also J. Gross, *La divinisation du chrétien d'après les Pères grecs*, pp. 144 ff.

17. *Symposium* 3.3–4. *St. Methodius. The Symposium,* trans. Herbert Musurillo (Westminster, Md., 1958), pp. 60–61.

Now this passage in Methodius has been the subject of much discussion and is interpreted in numerous ways. Some scholars have argued that Methodius teaches a union between Adam and the Logos, a hypostatic union at the beginning of the world. Musurillo, on the other hand, thinks this view is false and the passage means that "in Christ, the Word, in being united to human nature, was somehow united with Adam." [18] The context would support Musurillo, for Methodius explains that Adam, while yet soft on the potter's wheel, hardened into incorruptibility; so God moistened the clay once again and "modeled the same man again with honor, united and mingled it with the Word and finally brought it forth dry and unbreakable into the world that it might never again be drowned by the floods of external corruption and collapse into putrefaction." [19] In Methodius' view the same one was needed to conquer the devil. The Word assumed human nature "that He might through himself defeat the Serpent and destroy the condemnation that existed for man's ruin. It was indeed fitting that the Evil one should be defeated by no one else but by him whom the devil boasted he ruled since he first deceived him. For it was impossible otherwise to destroy the state of sin and condemnation unless the same man . . . should renew the contest and undo the sentence that had been passed against all men because of him. Thus, just as in Adam all men die, so also in Christ, who assumed Adam, all were made to be alive." [20] Methodius has carried the similarity between Adam and Christ to the point where there is no significant distinction between them. Christ becomes Adam, and does correctly what Adam did wrongly. The persistent emphasis on the same one (ὁ αὐτός) only serves to emphasize the conjunction Methodius seems to have in mind. It is the same man who was defeated who is now victorious.

We should also note that Methodius goes beyond Paul and Irenaeus in certain details: In Irenaeus the second Eve was Mary, but Methodius now sees the second woman as the Church. Since what is said of Adam can be said of Christ, "it would be in excellent accord with this that the Church has been formed from his

18. Ibid., p. 197.   19. Ibid., 3.5, p. 62.   20. Ibid., 3.6, p. 63.

flesh and bone. For it was for her sake that the Word left his
heavenly father and came down to earth in order to cling to his
Spouse." [21]

The typology of Adam-Christ is not as central to Methodius'
thought as it is to Irenaeus'. In Irenaeus the typology is organically
related to his overall theological conception of the divine economy
and the idea of recapitulation. Methodius' use of the typology is
limited to only a few passages and does not inform his total
theological outlook. We are dealing here with an important,
though somewhat peripheral matter in Methodius' work.

The Adam-Christ typology lent itself to adaptation to varying
theological situations. It was used to assert the unity of the divine
dispensation and to develop a theology of the relation between
Christ and the Church. The ideas suggested by earlier writers
along these lines are developed further in the fourth century. For
example Hilary of Poitiers devotes a chapter in his *Tractatus
Mysteriorum* to Adam. He cites 1 Corinthians 15:47 to show that
Adam is a type of the one to come; to this he adds Ephesians
5:32, that the church is a mystery and relates these ideas to the
sleep of Adam. "Since the Word was made flesh and the church
a member of Christ—the Church which is born of water and
vivified by the blood pouring from his side—and since the flesh,
in which the word, being the son of God and existing from eternity, dwells among us sacramentally, he teaches us, in a simple
manner, that in Adam and Eve the type of himself and of his
Church were contained, showing that it was hallowed after the
sleep of his death, by the communion of his flesh." [22]

Irenaeus had carried through the parallelism between Christ
and Adam in places where Paul had not. The most notable
instance here is the parallel between Mary and Eve. Such an
extension of the typology naturally suggested other parallels
and in one or two authors new steps are taken beyond Methodius
and Irenaeus. Thus in his *Commentary on Luke* Ambrose uses
the typology of Adam and Christ in connection with the tempta-

21. Ibid., 3.8, p. 65.
22. *Tractatus Mysteriorum* 1.3; see Jean-Paul Brisson, *Traité des Mystères*,
pp. 77 ff.; see also *In Ps.* 68.23; Tertullian, *De anima* 43 and references in
n. 3.

tion of Jesus. Commenting on the phrase "Jesus was led into the desert by the spirit that he might be tempted," Ambrose says that in the beginning "the first Adam was cast out of paradise into the desert," whereas in the case of the second Adam he "returned from the desert to paradise." Then he draws the parallel between the birth of Adam and the birth of Christ. "Adam came from the virgin earth, and Christ from the virgin, the first made in the image of God, the second is the image of God, the one is superior [*antelatus*] to all irrational souls, the other to all living things; through a woman foolishness, through a virgin wisdom, death through a tree, life through a cross." [23] By viewing the temptation of Jesus in the light of the parallel between Adam and Christ, Ambrose singles out the *place* where the temptation is said to have taken place, namely the desert, and links this to the garden where Adam was tempted. Such a use of the typology occurs frequently in Cyril.

In the fourth century, however, the more significant discussions of Adam-Christ occur in connection with Christological matters and questions concerning the redemptive work of Christ. The Adam-Christ typology became one of the chief biblical bases for the solidarity of Christ and mankind. If Christ were not truly one with man his redemptive work would have no consequences for mankind. Therefore if he is truly the second *Adam,* then his redemptive work does indeed bring the redemption of other *men.* Gregory of Nyssa, for example, writes: "Just as death was transmitted to all men by a single act, so too, by the action of one man the principle of resurrection is extended to all humanity." And in another connection: "As in Adam all die, so in Christ all are made alive . . . as according to the example of the veil our nature was rent through sin . . . as a result of Christ our nature takes itself up again." [24] The claim that Christ is one with all humanity is part of the argument that Christ is truly man. Basil writes: "If the Lord possessed a nature different from ours we

23. *In Lucam* 4:1 (*CC* 14:108).

24. *Oratio Catechetica* 16; *Ep.* 101.11; *Oration* 30. 5,21. For the parallels between Gregory of Nyssa and Cyril on the solidarity of Christ and mankind, see L. Malevez, "L'Église dans le Christ. Étude de théologie historique et théorique."

who were dead in Adam should never have been restored in Christ . . . and that which was broken would never have been mended, and that which was estranged from God by the serpent's wiles would never have been brought back to him." [25]

Athanasius also reflects the common use of the typology to show the solidarity of Christ with mankind. Discussing the interpretation of Philippians 2 in the *Orations* he raises the question of the meaning of Christ's exaltation. Does this mean that the Word is exalted? Following his familiar pattern he argues that this does not mean that the Word was exalted *qua* Word. But then he goes on to suggest that exaltation here refers to the resurrection of the Word. In this case the "wherefore" in Philippians 2 refers not to a reward based on accomplishment, but to the cause of the resurrection. What was this cause? "All other men from Adam down to this time [of Christ] have died and remained dead," but Christ has risen from the dead. Now that he has risen from the dead all men rise in him. "For all other men, being merely born of Adam, died and death reigned over them; but he, the second man, is from heaven, for 'the Word was made flesh' and this man is said to be from heaven and heavenly, because the Word descended from heaven; therefore he was not held under death." Now it is mankind who is raised and exalted through the resurrection of Christ. "To man it was not possible to succeed in this; for death belongs to man; wherefore, the Word, being God, became flesh, that, being put to death in the flesh, he might quicken all men by his own power." [26] Athanasius' use of the Adam-Christ typology runs along familiar lines. If Christ is the second Adam there is a solidarity between him and mankind; therefore what happens to Christ affects all mankind.

There is, however, another dimension to this passage which is important for the later history. Notice that the typology occurs here in connection with the resurrection of Christ and that Athanasius draws on both Pauline texts, Romans 5 and 1 Corinthians 15. Christ is said to be the *"heavenly man"* because he has conquered death. In a number of other places he develops his

25. *Ep.* 261 (Deferrari, 4:76–78) where Basil polemicizes against the Apollinarian notion of heavenly man.

26. *Oratio contra Arianos* 1.44; see also *Or.* 1.51.

ideas at greater length. In the lengthy exegesis of Proverbs 8:22 in the *Orations* he gives the following interpretation: In Adam the "first way was lost" and we were turned out of paradise to death. For we hear the words "you are dust and you shall return to dust." However, when God wanted to quicken man he opened for us a new way, through the flesh of his son. And this should be taken to mean that if anyone is in Christ he is a new creation; old things have passed away. "But if a new creation has come to pass, there must be some man who is first in this creation; now a man made of earth only, such as we became from the transgression, he could not be. For in the first creation, men had become unfaithful, and through them that first creation had been lost; and there was need of someone else to renew the first creation and preserve the new which had come to be. Therefore, because of love to man, none other than the Lord, the 'beginning' of the new creation, is created as 'the Way,' and consistently says, 'The Lord created me a beginning of ways for his works'; that man might walk no longer according to that first creation, but there being as it were a beginning of a new creation, and with Christ 'a beginning of its ways' we might follow him henceforth who says to us, 'I am the Way.' " [27]

Athanasius' comments are very suggestive. He links the Adam-Christ typology to the idea of new creation and specifically to 2 Corinthians 5:17. In Christ there is a new creation for he has renewed (αναϝεόω) the first creation. He is the first to renew mankind and is the beginning of a new way. Just as there was a creation at the beginning so there is a second creation; just as there was a first Adam who brought men into sin, there is a second Adam who leads men out of sin by the resurrection from the dead. Man was incapable of renewing the fallen creation, for man was not able to break the bonds of death. Therefore the heavenly man came, the Word from God, and by his victory over death he won victory for all mankind. The Adam typology does not simply support the idea of a solidarity between Christ and mankind; it also points to the *uniqueness* of the person of Christ.

27. *Or.* 2.65. This passage from Athanasius and the tradition in which it stands will come up for discussion again in chap. 8 in connection with Cyril's view of new creation.

He is the first man to conquer death and break the spell which mankind has been under since the time of Adam.

In the early stages of the Christological debates Apollinaris appealed to 1 Corinthians 15 in support of his Christology of the heavenly man. Apollinaris takes the phrase "heavenly man" to mean that Christ is a spiritual man and that he does not have a human *nous*. He is a man "united with God and without a *nous*." The first Adam, says Apollinaris, had a body and a *nous*, for he was an earthly man. "The second Adam from heaven is spiritual." "Christ is not an earthly but a heavenly man." [28] Gregory of Nyssa wrote a treatise against Apollinaris, and in it he cites Apollinaris' use of the Pauline terminology. Gregory thought that Apollinaris was saying that Christ's flesh came down from heaven—thus heavenly man—but it seems very unlikely that this is what Apollinaris meant.[29] From a number of places where he employs the Adam typology it appears that he too is really trying to say something about the uniqueness of the person of Christ. Christ is not like other men, for he is the second Adam or the heavenly man. In one of his longest discussions of 1 Corinthians 15 Apollinaris makes quite clear that if Christ had been an ordinary man like other men he would not have been capable of conquering death. "Every man is under death and no one under death destroys death. But Christ destroys death. Therefore Christ is not a man. Every man is earthly. But Christ is not earthly but heavenly." This suggests that Apollinaris really wishes to show that Christ is unique, for he alone conquered death. "Man cannot rise from the dead, only God can

28. Texts of Apollinaris cited by Gregory of Nyssa, *Antirrheticus adversus Apolinarium* (Jaeger and Langerbeck, 3, 1:143, 145). See also Apollinaris, *De unione* 2 (Lietzman, *Apollinaris von Laodicea*, pp. 185–86); *Anakephalaiosis* 4 (Ibid., pp. 243, 3–5); also Timothy of the school of Apollinaris (Ibid., p. 285); E. Muehlenberg (*Apollinaris*, pp. 143 ff), in discussing these and related texts, shows that Apollinaris was polemicizing against the idea, passed on in the anti-Christian philosophical tradition, that Christ was simply a "God-inspired man" (ἄνθρωπος ἔνθεος), and not the incarnate son of God. His analysis sheds a great deal of light on the background of Apollinaris' ideas, but he fails to recognize the importance of the biblical typology of the second or heavenly Adam in Apollinaris' thought.

29. *Oratio Catechetica* 16; *Ep.* 101.11; *Oration* 30.5,21.

rise. But Christ is both. The same one God and man. If Christ were only a man or if he were only God, he would not be intermediate between God and man. If Christ were only man, he would not have saved the world, and if he were only God he would not have saved through suffering." [30]

The Christology of Apollinaris is a matter of some dispute, and the meaning of these texts is not wholly clear. However, it is clear that the typology of the heavenly Adam from 1 Corinthians plays a role in the shaping of Apollinaris' Christology. The argument of Apollinaris for the unique composition of Christ as God and man is supported by appeal to 1 Corinthians 15. Apollinaris seems to be saying that the really significant thing about Christ is that he is *not like* other men, but is different. He is the second Adam, the heavenly man. If he were like other men, he would not be able to conquer death and give life to men. Gregory's argument against Apollinaris' view of the second Adam really misses the point. The difficulty is understandable, however, for Gregory goes on to argue that the Adam imagery proves that Christ is truly a man. If the second Adam is to make it possible for man to share in God, he must be a genuine and perfect man. Thus Apollinaris takes the Adam typology to show that Christ is *unlike* other men, and Gregory uses it to show that he is *like* other men.

The similarities between Athanasius and Apollinaris are noteworthy. Though the terminology differs and the particular Christological formulations are unique to each man, their reliance on the Adam-Christ typology is quite similar. Both Athanasius and Apollinaris appeal to the typology for much the same reason, namely to demonstrate that Christ was capable of conquering death because he was the heavenly man. In Apollinaris the unique composition of the person of Christ receives stronger emphasis, but the controlling idea is the same. Because Christ was the man from heaven he was able to do what no other man had done before.

The seeds of Cyril's view of Christ lie in this interpretation of the Adam-Christ typology and in Cyril they are developed

<hr/>

30. See Apollinaris, *Anakephalaiosis* 1–24 (Lietzmann, pp. 242–45).

much more fully. The views of other fathers helped to shape Cyril's use of the typology,[31] particularly the idea of solidarity between Christ and mankind, but the most significant aspect of Cyril's interpretation is the link he establishes between the Adamic typology and the new creation. And it is this link between the typology and new creation which binds Cyril's discussion to the problem of Christianity and Judaism, or more specifically, the relationship between the two testaments.

We begin our discussion with Cyril's commentary on the Gospel of John, which stands within a long tradition of commentaries on the book stretching back to the middle of the second century. The work is a verse by verse commentary on the text, and at the same time a polemical work against Arianism. Especially in the earlier chapters Cyril focuses his exposition of the text on the Arian theology and attempts to develop an answer

31. The discussion of the Adam-Christ typology in the fourth century has been limited chiefly to those writers whose views foreshadow those of Cyril. The whole subject demands fuller attention than it has received in the past. For example, Theodore of Mopsuestia uses the typology quite frequently. There are some interesting parallels between Theodore of Mopsuestia and Cyril on the Adam-Christ typology. Theodore views the typology in relation to his doctrine of the two ages. "What pleased God was to divide the creation into two states; the one which is present, in which he made all things mutable; the other which is future, when he will renew all things and bring them to immutability." In Theodore's view the future age, the new age is the beginning of a new creation in which Christ is the head of redeemed humanity. "From him we are brought close to our second existence in which rising together with him and gaining in him the grace of the spirit, we shall be immortal. While we were passible we had Adam as our head, from whom we took our origin; but since we became impassible, we have had Christ as our head who makes us impassible." In the new age men will no more "be thought of as Adam's but as Christ's." "The beginning for us of our condition in the present life was Adam. That of our condition in the future life will be Christ our Lord. For as Adam, the first man, was mortal, and thence everyone [else] on his account, so also Christ was the first to rise after death. We are all one body according to nature, and Adam is the head of all of us, because he was the first to be of one nature." Texts in *PG* 66:633c–634a; *PG* 66:888c (trans. R. Greer, p. 67); *In Joannem* 17:11 (Vosté, p. 224); also 10:31 (Vosté, p. 153); 3:29 (Vosté, p. 57). For Theodore, see R. A. Norris, *Manhood and Christ*, pp. 160 ff; and Rowan A. Greer, *Theodore of Mopsuestia*, pp. 66 ff; also Theodore Wickert, *Studien zu den Pauluskommentaren Theodors von Mopsuestia*, p. 26.

to Arianism on the basis of the text of John. The Adam-Christ typology occurs first in Cyril's exposition of John 1:14: [32] "And the Word became flesh and dwelt among us." Cyril comments: "With these words John enters openly on the discussion of the incarnation." [33] Up to this point Cyril had been preoccupied almost wholly with Trinitarian questions in an attempt to use John's prologue to bolster the Nicene faith. For example at verse 4, "in him was life," Cyril states that he wishes to defend the proposition: "That the son is by nature Life and therefore not γενητός, but of the essence of God the father." In one or two places in the prologue he cites Romans 5 but he does not go into the typology in any detail. [34] As soon as the text reaches the point of the incarnation he begins to speak of Christ as the second Adam. For Cyril the imagery of the second Adam is one way of talking about Christ as man. Cyril shares with other commentators on John the view that this Gospel concentrates primarily on the divinity of Christ. [35] However, John also speaks of his life as a man, as is evident from John 1:14. Here the Evangelist "sets forth plainly that the only son became and is called son of man; for it is this and nothing else that the words 'the Word was made flesh' signify; for it is as if he said more openly that the Word was made man." [36] The first part of the verse speaks

32. There is no study of the Adam-Christ typology in Cyril's works. In works on his Christology and doctrine of redemption it is sometimes discussed. See, for example, Eduard Weigl, *Die Heilslehre des heiligen Cyril von Alexandrien*, pp. 52–83; pp. 344 ff.; L. Janssens, "Notre filiation divine d'après saint Cyrille d'Alexandrie," pp. 233–78; Ladner, *The Idea of Reform*, pp. 79–81; G. M. Durand, *Cyrille d'Alexandrie*, pp. 89–98.

33. *In Joannem* 1:14 (P 1:183,4).

34. *In Jo.* 1:4 (P 1:74 ff); 1:9–10 (P 1:123).

35. *In Jo.*, preface (P 1:12, 13–29); see also Origen, *Commentary on Matthew* (GCS 11:210, 14–27); Chrysostom, *Commentary on Matthew* (PG 57, 13 ff); Theodore of Mopsuestia, *Commentary on John* (Vosté, pp. 3–4).

36. *In Jo.* 1:14 (P 1:138 ff). Cyril notes that the term "flesh" is the normal way the Scriptures speak of man, for they "frequently call the whole creature by the name of flesh alone." He cites Joel 2:28 in this connection. "I will pour out my spirit on all flesh." See also his comment on Is. 40:3–5; "But when he became man, or flesh, according to the Scriptures, he destroyed sin." (PG 70:804a–b). Other fathers give a similar exegesis of *sarx* in John 1:14. See, for example, Theodore of Mopsuestia, *Commentary on John* 1:14 (Vosté, p. 23).

of the incarnation, that "in truth he became man." However, the
Evangelist says: "He dwelt among us." This adds something
new, for it teaches that he remained among us and because
he did, the destiny of all men is bound up with the destiny of
this man. "For in him the commonality of human nature rises
up to his person; for this reason he was named the last Adam
giving richly to the common nature of all things that belong to
joy and glory, even as the first Adam gave what belongs to corruption and dejection." [37] What happens to Adam and Christ
happens to all men for all men are joined with these two men.
Cyril puts it this way in another place. "As in the one formed
first we were shut up to death, so in the firstborn, who became
so for our sakes, we shall all come alive again from the dead." [38]
The one is marked by death; the other, by life through resurrection from the dead.

Cyril's parallelism of Adam and Christ is carried out rigorously.
For example, he writes in one place: "We became diseased
through the disobedience of the first Adam and his curse, but we
have become rich through the obedience of the second and his
blessing." Cyril is of course following the strict parallelism of
Paul here, though the terms he uses are not Pauline. In another
passage Cyril uses the same verb to describe the relationship of
Adam and Christ to all of mankind. "Our forefather Adam . . .
did not preserve [$\delta\iota\acute{\epsilon}\sigma\omega\sigma\epsilon$] the grace of the Spirit . . . it was
necessary that God the Word . . . become man, in order that
. . . he might preserve [$\delta\iota\alpha\sigma\acute{\omega}\sigma\eta$] the good permanently to our
nature." And yet in another place he makes a similar point, this
time changing the verb. The first man "transmits [$\pi\alpha\rho\alpha\pi\acute{\epsilon}\mu\pi\epsilon\iota$]
the penalty to the whole race" and the "heavenly man . . . trans-
mits through himself good gifts to the whole race." [39]

Cyril's interpretation of John 1:14 reveals several aspects of
his use of the Adam-Christ typology. He employs the typology
to show that Christ is a man like other men. Thus its appro-
priateness in connection with John 1:14. But he is a representative
man for he is joined to all mankind as Adam was joined to
all mankind. What happened to Adam determined the course of

37. *In Jo.* 1:14 (P 1:141, 6–11).   38. *In Jo.* 6:52 (P 1:520, 25–27).
39. *In Jo.* 19:4 (P 3:63, 13–17); *In Jo.* 7:39 (P 1:693, 13–19); *In Jo.*
1:32,33 (P 1:184,4); *In Jo.* 17:18–19 (P 2:724,11).

mankind and what happened to Christ likewise affects all men. Finally, the Adam imagery calls attention to the uniqueness of Christ. For the first Adam did not preserve the grace of the spirit to mankind, but in Christ the second Adam the gift of God's spirit is again transmitted to all men. Now it is a permanent possession of men, because the second Adam will not fall into sin as did the first. In the first we became the heirs of death, and in the second we became participants in life through the resurrection. In short, Cyril uses the Adam typology to show that if on the one hand Christ is *truly a man,* yet he is a *unique man.*

In these and other passages Cyril accentuates the relationship between Christ as the second Adam and all other men by his use of the term "nature" (φύσις). The term φύσις refers to mankind taken in its totality, i.e. humanity. In the passage cited above where Cyril comments on John 7:39 he says that "in Adam the whole nature [ολη ἡ φύσις], that is, all of mankind" lost the good given it by God. His point is not that the Word assumed mankind in general as though the incarnate Word were not an individual man; what he wishes to say is that Christ, like Adam, is a representative man. As such both Adam and Christ have a unique relationship to all mankind; what happens to Adam and Christ is determinative for all other men. In the *Commentary on Luke* he has Jesus say: "Since I became a man and became like you human nature has in me first attained a divine kingdom." [40]

Cyril proceeds to draw conclusions from the parallel between Christ and Adam. If Christ's relationship to mankind is like Adam's, then mankind shares in the good which he has accomplished.

> The word then dwelt in all through one [δι ἑνὸς] that the one being declared the Son of God with power according to the spirit of holiness, his worth [τὸ αξίωμα] might come to all humanity and therefore because of one of us [ἕνα τῶν ἐξ ἡμῶν] the following might be spoken of us: "I said, You

40. *In Lucam* 11:19–26, Homily 81 (Smith, *Commentary on St. Luke,* p. 371; PG 72:704c); also *In Jo.* 6:51 (P 1:520, 20–23); *In Jo.* 1:32,3 (P 1:184, 4).

are gods and sons of the highest." Therefore in Christ we have been freed from slavery, mounting up to the mystical union with him who bore the form of the slave, yet in us according to the likeness of one because of the common birth in the flesh.[41]

The next place in the commentary where Cyril speaks of Christ as the second Adam is at the baptism of Jesus.[42] However, since I intend to devote a section of the following chapter to this pericope we shall pass over it here. The Gospel of John does not record a temptation scene in the life of Jesus, but in his *Commentary on Luke* Cyril discusses the temptation. The temptation of Adam by the devil and the temptation of Jesus by the devil in the wilderness suggests the parallel between Adam and Christ. In a rhetorical passage reminiscent of Ambrose, Cyril writes: "By eating we were conquered in Adam, by abstinence we conquered in Christ. We won the victory over temptation in Christ" for it had been lost in Adam and "Christ as conqueror handed on to us the power to conquer." [43] This manner of using the typology occurs in a number of other places in the commentary. For example, in the scene before Pilate, Cyril observes that Pilate could not find a charge to bring against Jesus because he had not sinned. This Cyril takes to be a fulfilment of the saying: "The prince of this world comes and he will find nothing in me." But such a verdict is only applicable to Christ, for this certainly could not have been spoken of the first Adam. The first had sinned and was charged guilty by God.

> Just as in Adam he [Satan] conquered the nature of man, showing it to be subject to sin, so now he was conquered by it [human nature]. For he was truly God and had no sin in him, yet he was man. And just as the sentence of condemnation for transgressions went forth over all mankind through one man, the first Adam, so likewise, also the blessing of justification by Christ is extended to all through one man, the second Adam. Paul is our witness who says:

41. *In Jo.* 1:14 (P 1:141, 13 ff).   42. See *In Jo.* 1:32–33 (P 1:183 ff).
43. *In Lucam* 4:1–2 (*PG* 72:529c).

"As through one the judgment came to all men to condemnation; even so through one the free gift came to all
men to justification of life." [44]

Cyril concludes by drawing the parallel further; through the
one came disease and through the other rich blessings. We see
again the emphasis on the solidarity of Christ and mankind and
the unique role of the two representative men. What is interesting, however, is that the discussion is really an exposition of
John 19:4 and is Cyril's way of explaining the fact that Pilate
could bring no charge against him. He has extended the parallel
to another event in the life of Christ.

Let us look at several further examples. According to the
Gospels, Pilate wrote a title over the cross on which Jesus was
crucified. It read: "Jesus of Nazareth, the King of the Jews."
This title, says Cyril, signifies the curse against all men which
came about through Adam and was broken by Christ. "Through
Adam's transgression we were all condemned, but the Savior
wiped out the handwriting against us by nailing the title to
his cross—very clearly pointing to the death upon the cross
which he underwent for the salvation of men." The cross is the
turning point in the history of mankind for here mankind recovered what had been lost in Adam. "Just as by the wood the
evil of our apostasy was contrived, so also by the cross our return
to that which we were in the beginning took place and the
acceptable recovery of heavenly blessings; Christ, as it were
gathering up into himself the origin of our infirmity." [45] Here
Cyril establishes the parallel between the cross and the tree as
had been done by other writers, and he also joins the imagery
of Adam and Christ with the idea of a return to the original
state of things. For Cyril, however, such a return to the way
things were in the beginning is another way of speaking of the
restoration which comes about through Christ and the transformation through his resurrection. But he does not make that explicit
at this point and it can only be drawn by inference from related
passages.

44. *In Jo.* 19:4 (P 3:63,3–17).
45. *In Jo.* 19:40–41 (P 3:106,11–25); *In Jo.* 19:19 (P. 3:85, 8–14).

This can be seen in Cyril's discussion of the death and burial of Jesus. The purpose of the incarnation was to restore and re-fashion man's nature to what it was in the beginning. This re-fashioning takes place through death on a tree.

> The first man was indeed in the beginning in the paradise of delight, being ennobled by the absence both of suffering and corruption; but he despised the commandment that had been given him, and fell under a curse and condemnation . . . by eating the fruit of the forbidden tree. Christ, as I said, by the very same thing restores him again to his original condition. For he became the fruit of the tree by having endured the precious cross for our sakes, that he might destroy death, which by means of the tree had invaded the bodies of mankind.[46]

Cyril applies the typology to the burial of Jesus and sees in the details surrounding his burial a sign of the true meaning of his death. According to the Evangelist, Jesus was buried "in the garden in a new tomb where a man has never been laid." Cyril is struck by the word "new," and this provides the occasion for his exegesis:

> The writer of the Gospel says that this sepulchre in the garden was new; as if to signify to us by a type and figure of the fact that Christ's death is the harbinger and beginning of our entry into paradise. For he himself entered as a forerunner for us. . . . And by the newness of the sepulchre is meant the untrodden and strange pathway of the restoration from death to life and the intended innovation against corruption signified by Christ.[47]

We can see even more clearly here the significance of the Adam typology for Cyril's thought. Like Athanasius, Cyril sees the death of Christ as the beginning of a new way for mankind. This new way is the victory over death which was first achieved in the second Adam.

46. *In Lucam* 23:32–42 (Smith, *Commentary on St. Luke*, pp. 718–19).
47. *In Jo.* 19:40, 41 (P 3:105, 27–106,7).

> In ancient times the dread presence of death held our human
> nature in awe. For death reigned from Adam until Moses,
> even over those who had not sinned after the likeness of
> Adam's transgression; and we bore the image of the earthly
> in his likeness and underwent the death that was inflicted
> by the divine curse. But when the second Adam appeared
> among us, the divine man from heaven, and contending
> for all life, won by the death of his own flesh for all and
> destroyed the power of corruption, and rose again to life,
> we were transformed into his image . . . the likeness of him
> who has made this new path for us that is Christ.[48]

Cyril mentions Moses in connection with Adam and Christ.
He also uses the term μεταπλάσσω to designate the transformation of mankind from death to life through the second Adam.
The term is the same term used in *Adoration* and elsewhere to
refer to the transformation of the types and shadows of the law
into the new way of life of worship in spirit and in truth. In
this passage, however, it refers to the "new path" which Christ
opened up through the resurrection from the dead. The new path
is contrasted not only with the old path of a fallen creation, but
also with the way of life under Moses. As the heavenly man,
Christ brings deliverance from the power of corruption caused
by Adam, but he also brings a transformation of the way of
life instituted by Moses. The Jews rejected Christ when he
came, but he was "renewing human nature for the *first* time in
himself to incorruption and eternal life." Mankind did not find
renewal through Moses even though he gave mankind the law.
In the economy of salvation there are only two great moments:
"For as it [mankind] died in Adam, the curse on it running
to the whole race, thus we came to life in Christ. A second root
of humanity and a second Adam, he transmits his life to all
men."[49]

The newness of Christ is therefore contrasted with both the
oldness of creation and the oldness of the law of Moses. Christ
transforms the shadows into a new way of life in spirit and in
truth *and* he transforms the dying creation into newness of life.

48. Ibid. (P 3:106, 11–25).   49. *PH* 27.4 (*PG* 77:940d–941a).

Commenting on Christ as bread of life Cyril writes: He was "lifegiving and firstfruits of the dough of those being recreated to newness of life. Adam was the firstfruits of the ancient dough, since being given a commandment by God and neglecting it, he fell into transgression and was immediately accused, and the human race was condemned to death and corruption in him. Christ was the firstfruits of a second dough and went through the curse, . . . He rose striking down death . . . he became a kind of firstfruits of mankind making it anew." Since he is the "bread from heaven," he is a new food and "neither the time of the law nor the chorus of the prophets had the new food, that is the teachings which came through Christ, nor the re-creation of human nature, except perhaps as a prediction." By his resurrection Christ presented himself as the firstfruits to God and we are "transformed [μεταστοιχειούμεθα] to a new life. We now live in evangelical fashion 'not in the oldness of the letter, but in the newness of the spirit.' " [50]

Re-creation, renewal, transformation, restoration are all used to describe the new thing which comes through the second Adam. Newness is the chief characteristic of Cyril's view of Christ as the second Adam. Cyril opens the *Glaphyra* with a discussion of Adam. When Paul wishes to speak of the "mystery of salvation through Christ he says that there is in him [Christ] an ἀνακεφαλαίωσις of the things in heaven and earth." The term recapitulation means, says Cyril, that there is a "restitution [ἐπανόρθωσιν] or a restoration [αναφοίτησιν] of all things to their original state [εἰς ὅπερ ἦν ἐν ἀρχῇ]." But what is the meaning of recapitulation, asks Cyril? Recall the words spoken through the prophet: "Remember not the former things, nor consider the things of old. Behold, I am doing a new thing, now it springs forth, do you not perceive it?" And Paul writes: "If anyone is in Christ, he is a new creation; the old has passed away, behold, the new has come." [51]

Cyril regularly speaks of human nature being "transformed into what it was at the beginning" or "reformed into that which

50. *Glaphyra in Num.* (PG 69:616d–625a).
51. *Glaphyra in Gen.* (PG 69:16c–32a); see *in Lucam* 8:19–21, *Homily* 42 (Tonneau, p. 75).

is better," or "transformed into the ancient human image," and there are numerous other variations on this theme.[52] Such language is Cyril's way of talking about the new thing which has happened in Christ. In many places he says, for example, that Christ is a "new beginning," i.e., a new way, for he is the firstfruits of those who sleep. "In returning on his way to the heavens above, he was especially presenting himself to God the father as the firstfruits of humanity and although what was being done was to secure the advantage for all mankind; for he renewed for us *a way of which the human race knew nothing before.*"[53] Interestingly, Cyril is commenting here on John 13:36: "Where I am going you cannot follow me now; but you shall follow afterward." In other places he speaks of Christ as a "second root of our race" and a "second beginning."[54]

We can observe these characteristics elsewhere in the *Commentary on John.* In Chapter 6:51 we read: "The bread which I shall give for the life of the world is my flesh." This means, says Cyril, that Christ is a ransom for the flesh of men. "For death shall die in my death, and with me shall rise again the fallen nature of man." The idea of Christ as ransom is translated to mean that Christ is one with mankind and a representative figure. "We think that Christ extends the mystery of the resurrection to all humanity, and in him *first* we believe that all mankind [human nature] has been released from corruption. For all shall rise after the likeness of him that was raised for our sakes, and has all in himself in that he is man."[55] Christ is pictured as the first man to rise from the dead and through this innovation in human nature, that a man should conquer death, all men come to share in the new thing which Christ has accomplished. Cyril develops this idea further in another place. "Christ was the first and only man on earth who did not know sin, nor was guile found in his mouth. He was established as the root and firstfruits of those being reformed to newness of life in the spirit and the incorruption of the body . . . transmitting it to the

52. *In Jo.* 7:39 (P 1:692, 24 ff.); *In Is.* 45:9 (*PG* 70:961b); *In Jo.* 1:34 (P 1:183, 21–23); *Glaphyra in Gen.* 1 (*PG* 69:16).

53. *In Jo.* 13:36 (P 2:392,12–17). [My italics.]

54. *In Jo.* 16:33 (P 2:657, 16).   55. *In Jo.* 6:51 (P 2:518–20).

whole human race." By this we understand that in Christ there
is a "return and a re-doing of death and corruption into incorruption and life." [56]

What is it that is new about Christ and the second Adam?
Does he bring mankind something which it did not have before
the fall? Or does he bring newness only in the sense of re-
establishing the state of perfection before the fall? [57] From the
discussion in this chapter we have seen that for Cyril the distinguishing mark of Christ, his uniqueness, is the resurrection
from the dead. He brought to mankind what no one had ever
done before his time. He was victorious over the power of death
and rose again to give mankind a new way which had never
been traveled before. Therefore the coming of Christ brings
to men something which they did not have even before the fall.
The time of Adam was "holy" says Cyril but the time of Christ
was "far greater" for he is the "second Adam renewing the race
. . . to newness of life in the Spirit." [58] Adam was an ordinary
man, but Christ is the heavenly man who has come from God.
Since it is God's son who is the second Adam, mankind gains in

56. *Inc. Unigen.* 691e–692a.

57. This question came up in connection with Irenaeus. Cyril, like Irenaeus, maintains that Christ does not simply return man to his original state,
but offers him gifts from God which were not the possession of Adam.
Cyril, however, develops the idea of "newness" much more fully than Irenaeus. The question has been discussed in detail by Burghardt, Janssens, and
others. They have shown that, according to Cyril, Adam did not possess
"radical kinship" with God for he did not partake of the divine nature.
Only in Christ does mankind receive divine sonship. Our discussion supports
this conclusion, though I have tried to show that Cyril's approach to this
question is bound up with the exegetical motif of new creation and the
second Adam. In Chs. 8 and 9 I will consider Cyril's view of newness and
of Christ as the new man in greater detail. The exegetical materials demonstrate, in contrast to the treament of Burghardt and Janssens, that Christ's
uniqueness does not rest on the Incarnation as such, but on his whole
career, and particularly the Resurrection. Divine sonship is won for mankind through the death and resurrection of the heaveny man, God's son,
who has become man. For a discussion of the problem in Cyril, see Janssens,
"Notre filiation divine," pp. 233–78; Walter Burghardt, *The Image of God
in Man according to Cyril of Alexandria,* pp. 114–15; Gross, *La divinisation,*
pp. 277 ff.

58. *Ador.* 17 (*PG* 68:1076).

Christ far more than it ever possessed in Adam. He became the firstborn among many brethren "in order that in him and through him we might be sons of God by nature and by grace; by nature, in him and in him alone; by participation and by grace, through him in the spirit." [59]

The typology of Adam-Christ is not univocal in Cyril's thought. It is made to function in a number of situations and holds together a series of related ideas. At times it is closely tied to the rigorous parallelism of Paul in Romans 5 and the view that as the second Adam, Christ is one with all mankind. The destiny of all men is tied to the destiny of one man. In this same connection the typology also serves to establish that Christ is truly man, as for example in the commentary on John 1:14. But in other places these aspects of the typology are subordinated to the emphasis on new creation, new beginning, firstfruits of creation, and related ideas. In this setting Cyril employs the typology to show that Christ has set himself apart from all other men and accomplished what other men could not do. He is the heavenly man who does a new thing. When Cyril uses the typology to accent the newness of Christ he either contrasts the newness of Christ with the oldness of *creation* or the oldness of the *law of Moses,* i.e. Judaism. Creation is transformed into a *new creation,* or the shadows of the law are transformed into a *new way of life,* a life of worship in spirit and in truth. Finally, Cyril uses the imagery of the second Adam and heavenly man to call attention to the unique relationship between Christ and God. As the "heavenly man" he comes from God and shares in God. Thus the Adam imagery is a way of speaking of Christ as man, for he is one with other men, but it is also a way of speaking of him as God, for he is sent from heaven and is God's son.

59. *De recta fide, ad Theodosium* 30 (*ACO* 1:1, 1, 61).

6 The Second Adam: II

In this chapter I shall examine Cyril's exegesis of Romans 5, 1 Corinthians 15, 2 Corinthians 5:17, and his interpretation of the baptism of Jesus. The baptism of Jesus posed a number of knotty exegetical and theological problems for patristic thinkers, and Cyril attempts to deal with these by using the Adam-Christ typology.

The introduction to Cyril's *Commentary on Romans* [1] is lost. But the commentary itself, like the one on the Corinthian epistles, is a verse by verse exposition of the text. The commentaries on Paul do not seem to have been delivered as sermons, nor are they directed at a specific theological problem, as was the *Commentary on John*. However, the verse by verse exposition does not prevent Cyril from introducing his favorite theological ideas. Cyril feels particularly at home in these commentaries, for it is on the basis of Paul that his central theological ideas took shape.

The opening chapters of the *Commentary on Romans* contain little of interest for our topic. At 3:31, "do we overthrow the law by means of faith?" Cyril cites Deuteronomy 18:18–19 and engages in a brief polemic against Judaism. "The truth does not take away the types, but it establishes them even more clearly." [2] But it is not until Chapter 5 that he begins to warm up to the text. The first part of the chapter is missing and his exposition begins at verse 11 with the words, "boasting in God through our Lord Jesus through whom we have now received our reconciliation." God's Son became flesh, says Cyril, and dwelt in us that he might put down Satan and free us from corruption. "The ancient curse finally became ineffective, the curse which human

---

1. Fragments collected and edited by P. E. Pusey, *Sancti patris nostri Cyrilli archiepiscopi Alexandrini in d. Joannis evangelium,* vol. 3. For patristic commentaries on Paul see Karl Staab, *Pauluskommentare aus der griechischen Kirche,* and the bibliography listed there; for Romans see the study of K. H. Schelkle, *Paulus, Lehrer der Vaeter.*

2. *In Rom.* 3:31 (P 3:180,5–8).

nature endured in Adam as in a first fruit of the race and as
in a first root." Adam had transgressed the commandment and
set himself against his creator; therefore the "son came from
heaven justifying by faith the impious, as God fashioning anew
[μεταχαλκεύων] human nature to incorruption, returning
[ανακομίζων] it to what it was in the beginning. For in Christ
all things are a *new* creation, for a *new* root has been established.
He became a second Adam." This is what Paul means, says
Cyril, when he writes that "through one man sin entered the
world," for through sin death entered into the "first formed and
into the beginning of the [human] race. Then the whole human
race was successively taken possession of." As a result of Adam's
sin "we have all become imitators of him." [3]

Following Paul Cyril uses the Adam-Christ parallel to assert
the solidarity of Adam and Christ with all mankind. "Human
nature" here, as elsewhere, refers to the whole human race, and
Cyril sees the actions of Adam and Christ as having an effect
on all men. He also speaks of Adam as the "first fruit of the
race" just as he speaks elsewhere of Christ as the "first fruit of
the renewed nature of man"; Adam and Christ are also called
the root of the race, Adam the first root and Christ the second
or "new root." The idea of transformation or renewal is expressed in a word we have seen elsewhere, namely μεταχαλκεύω.
The term signifies a refashioning of metal. He also uses another
favorite term, ανακομίζω, to designate a return to the beginning.
However, in the very next line he makes clear that the restoration or refashioning is not actually a return but a new beginning,
for there is a *new* creation and in Christ, the second Adam,
mankind has a new root. He cites the familiar 2 Corinthians 5:17.

Cyril's exegesis of Romans 5 runs according to form. Except
for the metaphor of root most of the ideas expressed here are
already familiar to us. This particular metaphor occurs frequently
in Cyril. "He was the first born on account of us in order that
as by a kind of immortal root all creation might be made new
and might shoot up again from the eternal being." And in
another place. "He was established as the root and firstfruits of

3. *In Rom.* 5:11 (P 3:182–83).

those being re-formed to newness of life in the Spirit." Cyril uses the metaphor of root quite literally, namely to indicate that just as the root is necessary for the life of the plant, so mankind must be nourished by its own life-giving root if it is to have life. "For as the plant will not shoot up from the earth, if it is not surely sprung from its own root (for so is the beginning of its growth), so it is impossible that we, having for our root in incorruption our Lord Jesus Christ, should be seen springing up before our root." Christ then as the "firstfruits of those being re-formed to newness of life" is the source of a new life which replaces the old which had its source in Adam.[4]

Throughout the exegesis of this chapter Cyril portrays Adam as the man who brought death and Christ as the second Adam who brings resurrection and life. A sub-theme in the chapter, however, is the relationship between Christ as the second Adam and Moses. In spite of the prominence of Moses in the Scriptures as the deliverer of Israel, Cyril is reluctant to give either Moses or the Mosaic law any real place in the economy of salvation. Again and again Cyril says that there are but two roots, two representative men, two moments in mankind's history. Consequently Moses appears to be not so much a forerunner of Christ, or even a minister of an outmoded and imperfect way of life, but a minister of a covenant of death. Moses, because he lived after Adam and before Christ, was nourished by the first

4. See *Thes.* 25 (*PG* 75:405c); *De recta fide ad Theodosium,* 20 (*PG* 76:1161d–1163a). Adolf von Harnack was highly critical of Cyril's use of the Adam-Christ typology and ideas such as that represented here by the analogy of root. In Harnack's view such solidarity between Christ and mankind implied that Cyril rejected "the view that an individual man was present in Christ." Christ can be the second Adam, says Harnack, "only if he was not an individual man like Peter and Paul, but the real beginner of a new humanity." (*History of Dogma,* 4:176–77. This is a gross misrepresentation of Cyril. If it is true that Christ is not an individual man, then it follows that Adam too could not have been an individual man, for the parallel Cyril draws between Adam and Christ is complete in every respect. But in Cyril's view, Adam is surely an individual man who by his action brought sin into the world; simply because his action had universal consequences does not annul the individuality of the actor. Christ is not only said to be the beginner of a new humanity, but he is also said to be the *first* to rise, the first to travel a new way, the first who did not sin.

root of mankind, the first Adam. Even Moses could not break
the curse Adam laid on mankind, because he did not overcome
death. "The law which came through Moses was a reproof, as he
[Paul] said, of the shortcomings of those who stumbled; it did
not destroy sin. Rather it worked wrath." Therefore "just as
Adam was condemned, so also the power of the curse subdued
Moses, subjecting all those on earth to corruption." The curse of
Adam extends through history down to Christ who as the "second
Adam was declared righteous, and righteousness comes to us for
the first time. We say that Christ was made righteous, not that
he was once unrighteous, and that he progressed by advancing
to that which is better, namely righteousness, but that he is the
first and *only* man on earth who did not know sin, and guile
was not found in his mouth." [5]

Cyril's argument is that Christ was the first man to overcome
the power of sin because he was the first to rise from the dead.
For this reason he is called the second Adam or the heavenly
man in whom "we bloom again to life." [6] The net effect of
making Adam and Christ the pivotal points in history is to deny
any significance to Moses. Because Moses was unable to free himself or mankind from Adam's sway, he is considered to have
made little positive contribution to the history of salvation.

By contrasting him not simply to Adam but also to Moses
Cyril is able to lay particular emphasis on the uniqueness of
Christ. His uniqueness lies in his accomplishments, namely that
he was the *first* to do what no one else could do, that he began
something new. The same stress appears in the fragments of his
commentary on 1 Corinthians 15. Commenting on 1 Corinthians
5:12,"if Christ is preached as raised from the dead," Cyril says:
"Christ died not that he might remain dead, but that he might
be found superior [$\kappa\rho\epsilon\acute{\iota}\tau\tau\omega\nu$] to death and corruption, that he
might become a kind of way or door for human nature to be
able to crush corruption and return again to life." [7] Cyril changes
his language somewhat in this passage, but his point is the
same. Christ is better or superior to others, for he was "able" to
crush death. Therefore he is the beginning or the entrance by

5. *In Rom.* 5:13 (P 3:183); 5:16 (P 1:185).
6. *In Rom.* 5:15 (P 3:184,18).   7. *In I Cor.* 15:12 (P 3:299).

which human nature enters upon life. "He rose and became a kind of first fruit of mankind, transforming [μεταφοιτώσης] it into life, re-creating [ανακτιζομένης] it into incorruption, and conquering death. For in Christ there is a new creation."[8]

Throughout the exegesis of 1 Corinthians 15 he reiterates his view of the centrality of the resurrection of Christ. It is the resurrection which initiates the new creation and is its chief mark. Christ is the beginning of the new creation or the first to make it possible. The term "firstfruits" means that he was the "first of those on earth who struck down death,"[9] just as "Adam was the first to fall into death and became the firstfruits of those who fell into corruption." Cyril is very careful to insist that Christ conquered death as man. "Through man came death and through man came the resurrection of the dead," for it was "necessary that it be a man who conquers death." Death must be "crushed through obedience and righteousness for it had come through disobedience and sin. For this the only begotten Word of God, who did not know sin, became man. Since in Adam all were condemned, human nature suffering death, thus being justified in Christ we will be made alive, again being blessed in him in equal fashion because of righteousness." But what takes place in Christ is transmitted to all men: "In time the others will follow and come to life again." Since Christ is the second *Adam* he is a man among men, but because he is the *second* Adam or the *heavenly* man he is superior to other men, he is exceptional and able to bring about a victory over death. There were "saints" in Israel, admits Cyril, but things are now "better" in Christ for "we have been justified by faith, become sharers of the divine nature, and been enriched by the spirit of sonship." Through the resurrection, mankind is now the recipient of gifts from God which were not obtainable under the law.[10]

Cyril's treatment of the resurrection and "new creation" in these pages gives us a glimpse of how he links together various sections of Scripture and uses certain biblical themes to interpret seemingly unrelated texts. For example, he cites Isaiah 26:19, an Old Testament passage mentioning resurrection in connec-

8. *In I Cor.* 15:13 (P 3:301).   9. *In I Cor.* 15:20 (P 3:303,6–8).
10. *In I Cor.* 15:20 (P 3:304–5).

tion with 1 Corinthians 15:35, "how will the dead be raised?"
He also cites Psalm 103:28–30 which includes the phrase "you
renew [ἀνακαινιεῖς] the face of the earth." He then says, "Human
nature suffered a turning away from God because of the transgression of Adam," and it fell into "death and corruption. Since
the only begotten word of God became like us, we have been
enriched by sharing in the Holy Spirit and we are being re-
formed [αναμορφούμεθα] to what we were in the beginning and
created anew [ἀνεκτιόμεθα]. We have been called to newness of
life, escaping the power of death." [11] The term ανακαινίζω occurs
in the psalm and this is a cognate of ανακτίζω and αναμορφόω.
The psalm, because it has a term referring to "renewal," becomes
the pivotal text on which he builds his interpretation. A similar
procedure occurs in connection with 1 Corinthians 15:42: "It is
sown in corruption; it is raised in incorruption." Again he
discovers an Old Testament text with the term "renew." In this
case it is Zephaniah 3:16–17, "Do not fear, O Zion; let not your
hands grow weak. The Lord, your God, is in your midst, a
warrior who gives victory; he will rejoice over you with gladness,
he will renew you in his love." The Septuagint reads καινιεῖ but
Cyril cites the text with ανακαινιεῖ. Taking Zephaniah 3 as his
point of departure he proceeds to 1 Corinthians 15:42. The mark
of God's love is that he renews us in Christ and turns us away
from the things that are old and corrupt. "When God the father
loved us, he renewed [ἀνεκαίνισεν] us in Christ. For it is true that
all things in him are a 'new creation,' and the old things have
passed away and become new." What does he mean by old?
They are the things passing away. What sort are the new? The
things which are being introduced. The old is corruption . . .
the new through Christ is glory, and incorruption, power and
spiritual discernment." [12] Not surprisingly, Cyril gives precisely

11. *In I Cor.* 15:35 (P 3:307).
12. *In I Cor.* 15:42 ff. (P 3:311–12). Cyril passes over I Cor. 15:47, "the
first man was of the earth, the second from heaven," with just a few
sentences, though he does polemicize against the view that Christ's body
came from heaven. "Both are, as Paul says, in earthly bodies, though not
in equal bodies, according to will [γνώμην] or manner of life. For the first
was ἐν φρονήματι σαρκικῷ, the second was from heaven a lifegiving spirit"
(P 3:315, 3–8).

the same interpretation of Zephaniah 3 in his *Commentary on Zephaniah*. He writes, "When he gave up his life and died on account of us, who was life according to his nature, he came to life again, re-forming [ἀναμορφῶν] us to newness of life, and fashioning us anew [αναχαλκεύων] to what we were in the beginning. 'For if anyone is in Christ, he is a new creation.' [2 Cor. 5:17] For it pleased the God and father to 'recapitulate all things in him' [Eph. 1:10] as it is written." [13]

Cyril's procedure here is fairly typical. He employs a number of biblical texts throughout his exegesis and they occur over and over again. The contexts in which these texts appear vary considerably, but there is an underlying unity which allows Cyril to move freely from one section of the Scriptures to another. In some cases he does not rely on the actual citation of a text but on a term or idea which strikes him as a parallel. This is usually a sufficient warrant for him to launch on a statement of his chief theological and exegetical ideas. Obviously such a procedure gives a certain consistency to his exegesis, but it also tends to make it highly repetitious. The same motifs appear over and over again.

Thus his interpretation of 2 Corinthians 5:17 really has little to add to what he has already said. In fact, his comments are surprisingly brief as if admitting that he has cited the text so often in other places that little is required at this point. The term τὰ ἀρχαῖα refers, says Cyril, to two passages: "You are of the earth and you will return to the earth," and "The imagination of man's heart is evil from his youth." The choice of texts is interesting, for they suggest that the contrast between the old and new is a contrast between death and life, evil or corruption and incorruption. "The ancient things refer to these things and the things in the law [τὰ ἐν νόμῳ]." By this he means that all these things have passed away. Again Cyril places the law in the category of things which lead to death. In Christ there is a new beginning, for he has broken the power of the curse and of death. "We are justified through faith in Christ, and the power of the curse has ceased. He came to life again for us striking

13. *In Zeph.* 3:16–17 (P 2:236–37).

down the power of death, and we have known the one who is
God by nature and in truth, and we fulfil the worship in spirit
and in truth, the son mediating the things from above and
giving blessings to the world from the Father." [14] Cyril's exposition is interesting, not so much because he says anything new
—which he doesn't—but because he makes it quite explicit that
he views the new creation in the light of the Mosaic law. The
phrase "old things" refers to the "old covenant" which has now
passed away. Further, he cites John 4:24 in connection with the
new creation and the new way of life which comes about
through the resurrection. The relationship between Cyril's various
ideas can be seen clearly in these few sentences. The old is
equivalent to the dispensation of Moses, the new to the dispensation in Christ. The old led to death, the new leads to life
through the resurrection and takes shape in a life of worship in
spirit and in truth. As Cyril put it elsewhere, "We are transformed
to a new life. We now live in evangelical fashion, not in the
oldness of the letter, but in the newness of the Spirit. Moses was
a minister of shadows and types, but Christ mediates a new
covenant renewing man to 'newness' of life and making him an
approved and genuine worshiper through the evangelical polity.
For God is a spirit and those who worship him will worship
him in spirit and in truth . . . for in Christ there is a new creation." [15]

There is a kind of curious and perverse logic which drives
Cyril to these conclusions. Much of the impetus comes from
Paul's letters and Paul's attitude toward Mosaic law. But just as
much comes from Cyril's adaptation of the Pauline materials and
the Adam-Christ typology to his own situation. The centrality
of the resurrection, the motif of new creation, the Adam-Christ
typology itself all come from Paul. But the particular configura-
tion of ideas which appears in Cyril is the result of Cyril's own
synthesis of the tradition. The problem he faced not only con-

14. *In II Cor.* 5:17 (P 3:353). Didymus gives a similar interpretation in
his commentary on 2 Corinthians. The "old" refers to the things of the
law and prophets and the "new" refers to the gospel (frag. *In 2 Cor.* 5:17,
Staab, *Pauluskommentare*, p. 29).

15. *In Is.* 42:8–9 (*PG* 70:856b–857d).

cerned the relationship of Christianity to Judaism, but also the difficulty of finding some way of expressing the mystery of the union of God and man in Christ. Throughout these fragments we can see him struggling with this problem: in what sense is Christ truly a man, and in what sense is he unique among men? The typology of Adam-Christ, seen against the backdrop of the relationship of Christianity to Judaism, provides him with a context for dealing with this question. No man from Adam to Christ, including Moses, was able to turn back the power of death and initiate a new way for mankind.

The Baptism of Jesus [16]

It is perhaps a truism to say that the fathers bound theological and exegetical problems together in one bundle. But it is something else again to discover which theological problems were wrapped in which exegetical bundles. In Christology the Gospels frequently stirred up controversy because the picture of Christ presented there did not always harmonize with the Church's theological understanding of Christ.[17] The problem arose long before the Christological controversies of the fourth and fifth centuries. In the primitive church there was tension between the memory of the historical Jesus and the growing Christological consciousness of early Christianity. In the earliest accounts of the baptism of Jesus the tradition that Jesus was baptized "for the remission of sins" and the belief that Jesus was sinless and not in need of such a baptism came into conflict. In the Gospel of

16. The baptism of Jesus has frequently been the object of study, but we have no thorough monograph on the history of its interpretation in the fathers. The following are useful for the early period: Herbert Braun, "Entscheidende Motive in den Berichten ueber die Taufe Jesu von Markus bis Justin"; Walter Bauer, *Das Leben Jesu im Zeitalter der neutestamentlichen Apokryphen,* pp. 110–41; Johannes Bornemann, *Die Taufe Christi durch Johannes in der dogmatischen Beurteilung der christlichen Theologen der vier Jahrhunderte;* Robert L. Wilken, "The Interpretation of the Baptism of Jesus in the Later Fathers." Also K. Schluetz, *Isaias 11, 2 in den ersten vier christlichen Jahrhunderten.*

17. See the interesting study of Werner Elert, *Der Ausgang der altkirchlichen Christologie.*

Matthew, for example, John tries to dissuade Jesus from being baptized. "I need to be baptized by you," says John. Jesus replies, "Let it be so for now; for thus it is fitting for us to fulfil all righteousness." In Mark the baptism of Jesus is presented without these qualifying comments, and there is no indication that it was improper for Jesus to be baptized. But Matthew attempts to give a reason "why" Jesus had to be baptized.[18]

The problem of the baptism of Jesus presented itself to the early Church in several different forms. Some writers were concerned primarily with the question: "Why was Jesus baptized?" Ignatius, for example, uses almost the same wording as Matthew when he says that Jesus was baptized "in order that he might fulfil all righteousness." [19] In another place he says that Jesus was baptized "in order that he might cleanse the water by his suffering." [20] However, in the second century another aspect of the problem emerged. According to the accounts in the Gospels the Spirit descended on Jesus at the baptism. The descent of the Spirit frequently became the central point of discussion in connection with Jesus' baptism. At times the baptism itself is almost wholly subordinated to the descent of the Spirit, and the descent is presented in the form of an adoption of Jesus. In a fragment from the Gospel of the Hebrews, the baptism of Jesus is reported as follows: "And it came to pass when the Lord was come out of the water, the whole font of the Holy Spirit descended upon him and rested on him and said to him. 'My son, in all the prophets I was waiting for you that you should come and I might rest in you. For you are my rest and you are my firstborn son who reigns forever.' " [21] Among some Gnostic writers the baptism is frequently the time in Jesus' life when he

18. See the commentaries of E. Lohmeyer and W. C. Allen on Matthew. For more recent discussion see Ferdinand Hahn, *Christologische Hoheitstitel,* pp. 340–46.

19. The dilemma of Jesus' baptism is stated clearly in the *Acta Archelai.* Manes asks Archelaus: "Is baptism given for the remission of sins?" A. answers, "Of course." Manes responds, "Then Christ sinned, because he has been baptized." Hegemonius, *Acta Archelai* 60, pp. 88–9.

20. Ignatius, *Smyrnans* 1.1; *Ephesians* 18.2.

21. Text in Epiphanius, *Haereses* 30.13.7 (trans. Hennecke-Schneemelcher-McL. Wilson, *New Testament Apocrypha* [Philadelphia, 1963], 1:163–4).

receives the "name," or Christ descends, or he receives the "son." [22]

As a result of this preoccupation with the descent of the Spirit, Isaiah 11:2 was frequently associated with the baptism.[23] "And the Spirit of the Lord shall rest upon him, the spirit of wisdom and understanding." In the New Testament this text is not used in connection with the baptism of Jesus, though a similar passage, Isaiah 61:1, "the Spirit of the Lord God is upon me, because the Lord has anointed me to bring good tidings to the afflicted" is cited in Luke in connection with Jesus' appearance in the synagogue in Nazareth. Because of the interest in the Spirit in connection with Jesus' baptism, the theological issue associated with Jesus' baptism was broadened beyond the simple "why was Jesus baptized?" to the problem of "why should Jesus need the Spirit?" Writers such as Irenaeus and Justin only intensify the problem by allowing Isaiah 11 to be cited in connection with Jesus' baptism. Irenaeus attempts to meet the problem by viewing the descent of the Spirit as part of God's dispensation in Christ, for by descending on Christ the Spirit now descends on mankind and on the Church. He descends that he may "grow accustomed through fellowship with him [Christ] to dwell in the human race, . . . to renew them from their old habits into the newness of Christ." [24]

22. Clement of Alexandria, *Excerpta ex Theodoto* 22.6–7, pp. 102–4. See Hippolytus, *Refutatio Omnium Haeresium* 7.35.2, p. 222; 7.35.1,2, p. 220; also Irenaeus, *AH* 3.18.1 (H 2:92). Also *Excerpta ex Theodoto* 16. *Peristera* (when the letters are given their numerical equivalents) numbers 801; similarly, Alpha and Omega equal 801, says Irenaeus.

23. See Schluetz, *Isaias 11:2*, pp. 39–58. Irenaeus, *AH*, 3.18.1–3 (H 2:92–94); Justin, *Dial. Trypho* 87. Even within the New Testament there is a tendency to single out the descent of the Spirit as the chief element in Jesus' baptism. See John 1:29–34; Acts 10:37–38.

24. The parallel between Irenaeus and Cyril is striking. This is precisely the same type of expression Cyril uses for the baptism of Jesus, though he employs the Adam-Christ typology here, while Irenaeus does not, and Cyril's interpretation is much more elaborate. Cyril mentions Irenaeus at one place in his *Commentary on Matthew* with regard to an exegetical point (*In Matt.* 3:10, frag. 24; Reuss, *Matthaeus-Kommentare*, p. 160). There are also parallels on exegetical matters: for example a comparison between Rachel and the church. Irenaeus, *AH* 4.35.3 (H 2:227) and Cyril, *PG* 69:231–33.

The shift in the focus of the baptism of Jesus was to cause innumerable difficulties in the fourth and fifth centuries. In the homiletical and exegetical literature the question "why was Jesus baptized?" is a frequent topic of discussion, but in the polemical literature the question of the Spirit and Christ becomes acute. The problem of Jesus' baptism becomes part of the larger question: Why does the Son, if he is truly God, need the Spirit to descend on him? Does not he as God possess the Spirit by nature? In the Arian controversy certain passages from the Gospels became the center of discussion. The Arians were quick to point to any passage which explicitly stated or implied that Jesus did not bear the characteristics of God. For example, they singled out Luke 2:52, "Jesus increased in wisdom and in stature," and claimed this showed he was not equal with the father, because the text says he grew. God, it was assumed could not "grow" in wisdom or change in any way. Other examples are the following passages: "The son of man did not know the day or the hour" (Mark 13:32), which suggested that Jesus was ignorant; "my soul is very sorrowful, even to death" (Matt. 26:38), and others. The baptism of Jesus fitted into this category, for it suggested that Christ was not fully God, and needed this Spirit as did other men.[25]

In Oration 3 against the Arians Athanasius takes up these disputed passages and attempts a comprehensive interpretation. In this work he develops the classical form of the "twofold" exegesis of the Gospel texts. When the Gospels say that "Jesus advanced in wisdom" or that "he did not know the day or the hour" they are speaking of the Logos according to the flesh [κατὰ σάρκα], or humanly [ανθρωπίνως]. Therefore they cannot be used to defend the subordination of the son to the father. Athanasius' principle reads as follows: [26]

---

33. For the influence of Irenaeus on Cyril see G. M. de Durand, ed., *Cyrille d'Alexandrie. Deux Dialogues Christologiques*, p. 90.

25. On the exegetical arguments between Athanasius and the Arians, see Robert L. Wilken, "Tradition, Exegesis, and the Christological Controversies"; and Maurice Wiles, *The Spiritual Gospel* pp. 112–47.

26. Athanasius, *Or. contra Arianos* 3.29 (*PG* 26:385a).

The scope and the character [χαρακτήρ] of the Holy Scripture, as we have often said, is the following: in the gospel there is a double account of the Savior; that he was always God and is Son, being the Logos and radiance and wisdom of the father; and that afterwards, on account of us, taking flesh from the Virgin Mary, the θεοτόκος, he became man. And this [σκόπος] is to be found signified throughout all the inspired Scriptures.

According to this twofold scope, certain statements of the Gospels are to be taken as referring to the Logos insofar as he is Logos, and others insofar as he is man. At times the Logos does things "divinely" such as heal the sick and raise the dead; at other times he does things "humanly," such as hunger, thirst, suffer, etc. Thus when the Savior says "all things have been delivered to me by my Father," he does not intend to say there was a time when he did not have these prerogatives. He always had them, and what the passage means is that he now receives them as man. Athanasius makes a similar point with respect to Luke 2:52.[27]

> Therefore, as we have said previously, not Wisdom as Wisdom [ἡ σοφία] advanced according to itself, but the humanity in Wisdom advanced, transcending little by little the human nature, becoming like God, becoming and appearing to all as the organ of wisdom for the working and shining forth of the Godhead. Wherefore he did not stay, 'The Logos advanced,' but 'Jesus' by which name the Lord was called when he became man, so that there is an advance of the human nature as was explained above.

Athanasius discusses the baptism of Jesus in *Oration 1 Against the Arians* with reference to the interpretation of Psalm 45:7–8. Here the psalmist speaks of anointing, which is taken to mean sanctification by the Spirit. How can one who *is* holy be made holy by the spirit? Athanasius answers: He "is said to be sanctified because now he has become man, and the body that is sanctified

27. *Or.* 3.53 (*PG* 26:436a).

is his . . . When he is now said to be anointed humanly it is we who are anointed in him; since when he is baptized, it is we who are baptized in him."[28] Now this exegesis included Athanasius' familiar "two scope" exposition of the Gospels: baptism is appropriate to Jesus insofar as he is man. Athanasius also draws on earlier exegetical tradition which viewed the baptism of Jesus in terms of the baptism of Christians. Jesus was baptized so that Christians might be baptized in him.[29]

Athanasius was faced then with the problem of offering an interpretation of the baptism of Jesus and the anointing of the Spirit which could counter the Arian objections. Jesus' anointing with the Spirit has become part of the larger theological question of Jesus' relationship to God. His baptism had to be interpreted in accordance with the developing trinitarian theology of the fourth century. It is in this setting that Cyril works out his interpretation of the baptism of Jesus. He was quite aware of the theological problems raised by the Arian controversy. In his *Commentary on John* he actually claims to quote the Arians. When they read the account of the baptism of Jesus, says Cyril, they jump up with a "big laugh" and say, "What argument will you bring against what is written? The evangelist says that the Spirit descends on the son; he is anointed by the father; he receives that which he does not have."[30] How can the son be God if he receives the Spirit at his baptism?

The most extensive discussion of the baptism of Jesus occurs in Cyril's *Commentary on the Gospel of John,* though he also discusses it in the *Commentary on Luke,* as well as at several points in his commentaries on the Old Testament, notably Joel 2 and Isaiah 11. The text in John 2 reads as follows: "John testified further: I saw the Spirit coming down from heaven like a dove and resting upon him. I did not know him, but he who sent me to baptize in water had told me, 'When you see the Spirit coming down upon someone and resting upon him you will

28. *Or.* 1.47 (*PG* 26:109b).

29. For the interpretation of the baptism of Jesus in the light of the baptism of Christians, see Chrysostom, *Hom. in Matt.* 3:16 (*PG* 57:206); Gregory of Nyssa, *In baptismum Christi* (*PG* 46:580 ff).

30. *In Jo.* 1:32,33 (P 1:174,7 ff).

know that this is he who is to baptize in Holy Spirit' " (NEB).
In the *Commentary on John,* Cyril regularly relates his exegetical
discussion to certain theological problems. In this case he believes
that the account of Jesus' baptism raises questions concerning the
relation of the son to the Spirit, specifically whether the son has
need of the Spirit. The superscription over the section reads:
"That the Holy Spirit is in the son not by participation [κατὰ
μετοχήν], nor from without [ἐπακτὸν] but essentially [οὐσιωδῶς]
and by nature [κατὰ φύσιν]." [31] This of course is precisely the
question raised by the Arian controversy, which formed the background for much of the fourth century exegesis of the Gospels.

Cyril first presents a theological-philosophical argument on
divine and human nature. The Arians pervert the statements of
Scripture which say the son of God (Matt. 14:33) and then they
proceed to distinguish different "natures" in God: one that is
perfect, namely the father, and another that is not, namely the
son. Then he turns directly to the text. John saw the Spirit descending, and this seems to say that the son has "sanctification
from without, for he receives it as not having it." But this makes
a creature of him. For if he has sanctification from without he
"was not always holy, but he became [γέγονε] so at a later time,
when the Spirit descended on him." How then was the son holy
before the incarnation, so that the Seraphim glorified him? Why
does he need someone to make him holy when he becomes man? [32]

Cyril then proposes a traditional solution along the lines of
Athanasius' interpretation of Psalm 45. Citing Philippians 2, he
argues that these words were spoken of the son after the incarnation—that is, when he descended to lowliness and became a
servant insofar as he was man. "Before the incarnation he was in
the form and equality of the father, but in the time of the incarnation he received the Spirit from heaven and was sanctified like
others [κατ' ἐκείνους]." [33] Prior to the incarnation one could not
ascribe human experiences to the son, but when he became man
he did experience suffering, hunger, etc., and therefore he can
be said to receive the Spirit as do other men.

But once Cyril has given this traditional exegesis he strikes out

31. Ibid., p. 174,1–2.   32. P 1:177,13–15; 178,4–6.
33. P 1:179,20–23.

on a course of his own. In the Holy Scriptures we read, says
Cyril, that man was made in the image and likeness of God.
Through the descent of the Holy Spirit man was "sealed in the
divine image." Man did not, however, live in accordance with
this image, but followed Satan and disregarded God's law. Man's
sin did not immediately efface the imprint of God, but it grew
fainter and fainter as a result of transgression. As a coin gradually loses its imprint, so also man's nature lost the divine stamp.
Eventually this image disappeared altogether. "When the human
race reached an innumerable number, and sin ruled all, it was
stripped of the ancient grace; the Spirit departed altogether, and
the rational creature fell into extreme irrationality, even ignorant
of its creator." Here Cyril follows his familiar pattern. He begins
with the creation of man, and moves to his fall into sin and the
eventual loss of the divine image. The whole process is viewed
as taking place gradually; man does not lose the image immediately, but over a period of time. But the loss has its origin
in the first sin and eventually permeates all mankind. The creator
endured this corruption for a long time, but eventually he turned
again to man and decreed "to transform [μεταστοιχειοῦν] humanity again [πάλιν] to the ancient image through the Holy Spirit.
For the divine impression [χαρακτήρ] could in no other way
shine forth in it [human nature], as it once did." [34]

Cyril provides a new context for considering the baptism of
Jesus. He takes the passage out of its dogmatic frame of reference,
and proposes that it be read in the light of the transformation and
renewal of creation. The baptism of Jesus becomes a key event
in the total restoration of mankind. In the baptism God plants
his grace in men again, and sends the Spirit to "take root among
men." Thus we see in this text, says Cyril, how "[human] nature was re-formed [ἀνεμορφώθη] to its ancient condition [τὸ
ἀρχαῖον]." [35]

> The first man, being earthly and of the earth . . . was caught
> by bitter guile, and having inclined to disobedience, falls to

34. P 1:182-3.
35. P 1:183,28-184,18. For Christ as the second original man, see J.-C.
Dhôtel, "La 'sanctification' du Christ d'après Hébreux II,11," p. 529.

the earth, the mother from whence he sprang, and since he was overcome at that time by corruption and death, transmits the penalty to his whole race. When evil increased and multiplied in us, and our understanding gradually descended to the worse, sin reigned, and thus at length the nature of man was shown to be denuded of the Holy Spirit who dwelt in him. . . . Therefore, since the first Adam preserved not the grace given to him by God, God the Father was minded to send us from heaven the second Adam. For he sends in our likeness his own son who is by nature without alteration or change and not knowing sin in any way, that as by the disobedience of the first we became subject to divine wrath, so through the obedience of the second, we might both escape the curse and the evils from it might come to nought.

We are caught up in the familiar language and imagery of the Adam-Christ typology. If the corruption of mankind came about through the initial sin of Adam and from him spread to all men, there must be another man who can have a similar relationship to mankind but who will engender new consequences. But the one who comes must not be an ordinary man; he must be one who will not repeat what the first Adam did and who will "preserve the spirit of our nature, and again inroot in us the grace which had left us." The Spirit had fled from humanity because it could not bear to dwell amidst such corruption; now another man appears among men and makes possible the return of the Spirit, for this man is without sin. "He [the son] became as one from us, one who did not know sin, that the Spirit might become accustomed [$\pi\rho\sigma\sigma\epsilon\theta\iota\sigma\theta\hat{\eta}$] to abide in us, not having an occasion of departure or withdrawal in him." [36] The second original man makes possible a new beginning for the race of men.

Cyril's exposition of the baptism of Jesus centers almost wholly on the descent of the Spirit.[37] Cyril does not even give passing

36. P 1:184,23–29.

37. Theodore of Mopsuestia sees the Spirit descending on Jesus to unite him with the Word (*In Jo.* 1:34, Vosté, J.-M. ed., *Theodori Mopsuesteni Commentarius,* p. 33; *In Jo.* 3:29, Vosté, p. 57). For Chrysostom the Spirit comes "only to proclaim Christ," for he was not in need of the Spirit (*PG* 59:109).

attention to the baptism itself or to the problems it raised for
earlier writers. The baptism of Jesus has been reduced to this
one consideration; how could Jesus receive the Spirit? Elsewhere
in the commentary Cyril discusses the descent of the Spirit and
amplifies his remarks. The text is John 7:39. "He said this about
the Spirit, which those who believed in him were to receive; for
as yet the Spirit had not been given, because Jesus was not yet
glorified." Commenting on the verse Cyril again rehearses the
creation and fall of man, and the eventual loss of the Spirit. God
wished to "recapitulate all things in Christ" and to "restore
[ἀνακομίσαι] human nature again to its ancient state," he promises to give it the Holy Spirit again, for in no way could it return
[ἀναδραμεῖν] to the "unshaken state [ἀκλόνητον στάσιν] of good
things." In Christ God "began to give again the Spirit, and Christ
first received the Spirit as a first fruit of the renewed nature." [38]

Here Cyril repeats himself but he adds a new note, namely
that Christ is the first one among men to be part of the renewed
nature. In the previous passage he was said to be the beginning
and the way, but here he is the first and the firstfruits. As the
first he leads the way for all human nature which was united in
him. And because our nature was in him he "restored it and
transformed it to its ancient condition." Christ receives the Spirit
that the good things of the Spirit might flow through him into us.
For "since our father Adam . . . did not preserve the grace of the
Spirit, and thus in him the whole nature lost at last the God-given
goods, the Word of God . . . became man, in order that by receiving [it] as man he might preserve the good permanently to
our nature." The son became man that the good things of God
might be preserved "securely" to our whole human nature. The
son gave mankind the "stability" which was not forthcoming from
any other man including Adam. "The divine Scriptures call the
Savior the second Adam. For in that first one, the human race
proceeds from not being to being; . . . in the second, Christ, it
rises up again to a second beginning, reformed [ἀνασκευαζόμενον]
to newness of life and to a return [ἐπαναδρομήν] of incorruption,
for if anyone is in Christ, he is a new creature, as Paul says. There

38. *In Jo.* 7:39 (P 1:691–92),

has therefore been given to us the renewing Spirit, that is, the Holy [Spirit], the occasion of eternal life after Christ was glorified—that is, after the resurrection—when having burst the bonds of death and appeared superior to all corruption, he lived again having our whole nature in him, in that he was man and one from us." [39]

Cyril ends his discussion of the Spirit and Christ with two further comments. He first makes clear that it is the resurrection which stands out as the central event in the life of Christ. The Spirit now returns to mankind because Christ has broken the hold of sin and death which began with Adam. This is the new thing which distinguishes Christ from other men. "Why was the Spirit not poured out before the resurrection?" Only then did "Christ become the firstfruits of the renewed nature, when taking no account of the bonds of death he came to life again. . . . How could those who came after it [the first fruit] be quickened before the first fruit? For as the plant will not shoot up from the earth unless it is surely sprung from its own root (for there is the beginning of its growth), so it was impossible that we who have as our root for incorruption the Lord Jesus Christ should be seen springing up before our root. . . . With the descent of the Spirit the time of renewal [ἀνανεώσεως] is at the doors, yea within the doors. . . . The Spirit who fled away from human nature, the one who can gather and form us in the divine image, this one the Savior gives us anew and returns us to our ancient condition and reforms us to his own image." Finally he raises the question of the presence of the Spirit in the Old Testament, specifically among the prophets. He grants that the Spirit did dwell among the prophets, but says that there is no real comparison between the prophets and Christ. For he dwelt in the prophets "that they might prophecy" but now he dwells in Christ that he may dwell in all mankind and that men may participate in the "good things from God." In Christ we now possess the "full and complete indwelling in men of the Holy Spirit." [40]

39. Ibid., pp. 692–94.

40. Ibid., pp. 695–96. See Walter Burghardt, *Image*, pp. 115 ff. Cyril distinguishes between "illumination" (ἔλλαμψις) and "complete and perfect in-

The Adam-Christ typology is also used to interpret the descent of the Spirit in Cyril's commentaries on the Old Testament where he discusses the baptism of Jesus.[41] Isaiah 11:1-3 reads: "There shall come forth a shoot from the stump of Jesse, and a branch shall grow out of his roots. And the Spirit of the Lord shall rest upon him, the spirit of wisdom and understanding, the spirit of counsel and might, the spirit of knowledge and the fear of the Lord. And his delight shall be in the fear of the Lord." Cyril takes the passage to refer to Christ. The prophet here calls Christ the shoot which comes from the root of Jesse, says Cyril. We should take this to refer to the son of God who became flesh. He also calls Christ a branch to indicate that "human nature shot up in him to incorruption and life and to the newness of the evangelical way of life." [42] Since he has taken the passage Christologically Cyril now faces the same problem he faced in his exposition of John 1. The prophet, says Cyril, does not present to us a Jesus who is a "mere man" [ἄνθρωπον ψίλον] who has become a "bearer of the spirit" [πνευματοφόρον] and by this a sharer in divine graces; rather he speaks clearly of the "word of God incarnate," full of good things yet making his own the things of humanity. But how can he be said to receive the Spirit at his baptism? How can he be both the giver and receiver of the

---

dwelling" (κατοίκησις). The latter comes only with the resurrection and full adoption by the Spirit. "The gift of adoption was conferred only after the resurrection of Christ." See also L. Janssens, "Notre filiation divine d'après saint Cyrille d'Alexandrie," pp. 253 ff. See ch. 7, fn. 51.

41. Note Cyril's comments on the baptism of Jesus in the *Homilies on Luke*. "The Spirit also came down again as on the second firstfruits of our race; and upon Christ first, who receives it not so much for his own sake as for ours; for by him and in him we are enriched with all things." "He has been made our firstfruits, and firstborn, and second Adam: for which reason it is said that 'in him all things have become new,' for we have put off the oldness that was in Adam and gained the newness that is in Christ" (*PG* 72:524b-525a). *In Is.* 11:1-3 (*PG* 70:312d). See also *Pulch.* 28 (*ACO* 1:1,5, p. 45).

42. Cyril uses the term ἀναθάλλω. It is used frequently to designate the new beginning through the resurrection. "In Christ human nature blossoms forth again to what it was in the beginning" (*Glaph.*, *PG* 69:421a; see also *In Rom.* 5:15, P 3:184, 18). For the phrase "not a mere man" see Chap. 10.

Spirit? "[The Spirit] was given in the beginning to the first
fruit of our race, Adam, but he [Adam] became careless about
keeping the commandment given to him . . . and he fell into
sin and the spirit found no rest [ἀνάπαυσιν] in men. 'All have
turned aside, together they have gone wrong; no one does good,
not even one' (Rom. 3:12). Then a man was made, the only son
of God . . . who, though like us, was impregnable [ἀνάλωτος]
to sin, and thus the Holy Spirit rested on human nature, in him
at first, as a second firstfruits of the race that he [the Spirit] might
rest on us for good and dwell in the minds of believers. . . . As
we became co-heirs of the evil things which happened to the one
formed at first, thus we will be sharers of the things which are
economically in the second firstfruits of our race—that is,
Christ." [43]

The descent of the Spirit is pictured here, as in the *Commentary
on John,* as the time when the human race again has the opportunity for a new beginning, for a new man has appeared who
promises to turn back what Adam had done and accomplish
what none since the time of Adam was capable of doing. Cyril
is more explicit here than in the *Commentary on John,* for he
makes clear that the distinguishing mark of the second Adam
is that he is God's son. He is not an ordinary man, a man simply
bearing the spirit, but he is the "word of God become man." In
him appeared a man who was "impregnable to sin" and who
would not fall like Adam. Commenting on Joel 2:28, Cyril says
the same thing in somewhat different terms. With the descent
of the Spirit on Christ the work of renewal had its beginning,
for in Adam the "grace given to man came to nothing, but in
Christ it was renewed for he is the second Adam." The Spirit
"did not remain with human nature" when he descended on
Adam, but now that there is a second Adam "the Spirit remained upon him" and now "he dwells in us steadfastly and for
good" (λοιπὸν ἐμμόνως). He departed from the first Adam, but
now there is a "second firstfruits of our race, Christ, and for this
reason he is called the second Adam through whom we are trans-

43. *In Is.* 11:1–3 (*PG* 70:313a–316a).

formed [ἀνεστοιχειώμεθα) to what is incomparably better, and we gain a rebirth through the Spirit, no longer having the first, that according to the flesh, that in corruption and sin . . . but the second from above, that from God through the Spirit." [44]

Cyril's interpretation of the baptism of Jesus and the descent of the Spirit brings together the various ideas and motifs we have been discussing. It is one of the most complete and thorough-going interpretations of the baptism of Jesus in the patristic Church. He is quite sensitive to the theological problem raised by Jesus' baptism, yet he is also attuned to the exegetical issues. Exegesis and theology blend in his treatment of the problem. Cyril's unique contribution rises out of his own theological point of view. In baptism Jesus emerges as the second original man who makes it possible for the Spirit to return again to mankind.[45] He does this through the resurrection from the dead, and by his resurrection he opens up a new way for mankind which had not been known before. In him there is a new creation. Christ becomes a new root which gives life to the new plant. Adam brought men into sin and caused the Spirit to depart, and none of the prophets were capable of recalling the Spirit for mankind. The Spirit dwells in the prophets, but he was not there in his fulness or completely. Only through Christ, the second Adam, does the Spirit find another introduction to mankind.

In a number of places Cyril hints at the rationale underlying his argument. He says for example that when the Spirit returns in the second Adam he will not have "an occasion of departure or withdrawal in him." The Spirit now returns to man "perma-nently" and Christ gives mankind the "stability" which was not achieved through another man. Furthermore, Christ is the first

44. *In Joel.* 2:28–29 (P 1:336–39).

45. Durand, contrasting Cyril and Irenaeus, writes: "Chez Cyrille en effet, il s'agit d'un nouveau départ à zéro, d'un total recommencement; et à ce propos il se permet des élans poétiques, insolites chez lui, sur le second printemps de l'Humanité. Le Christ est notre deuxième chance, et certes cette chance est plus brillante que la première, en ce sens que les biens récupérés appartiennent à notre 'deuxième racine' de manière incomparable-ment plus stable et naturelle qu'ils n'étaient concédés à la première, la suite ne l'a que trop montré. L'Esprit repose sur le Fils sans qu'il puisse jamais avoir à le quitter" (pp. 90–91).

who did not know sin and is "superior to corruption." [46] All of
these expressions are ways by which Cyril expresses the uniqueness of Christ. These are the characteristics of the second Adam
which distinguish him from other men. But these are also ways
Cyril speaks about God and the differences between God and
man. It is God who is without change, who is superior to death,
who does not sin. These are the marks of the Son of God. "God
sends in our likeness his own son who is by nature without alteration or change and not knowing sin in any way" (see n. 35).
The Adam-Christ typology allows Cyril to accent the unique element in Christ, namely that he is *unlike* other men because he is
God's son and has come "from heaven."

The last two chapters have shown that the Pauline conception
of Christ as the second Adam has a central place in Cyril's exegesis, and have illustrated the way Cyril uses the Adam typology
in several different exegetical contexts but with certain typical
characteristics. For example, the Adam-typology is intimately related to Cyril's idea of new creation and his notion of the transformation or renewal of the old creation. In his exegesis of
Romans 5 and 1 Corinthians 15 as well as in his interpretation
of the baptism of Jesus, the motif of new creation is used to
support and complement his view of Christ as the second Adam.
Furthermore, the Adam-typology is also related to the problem of
Christianity and Judaism and Cyril's attempt to present a solution
of the relationship between the old and new testaments. Just as
in Christ there is a renewal or transformation of creation, there is
also a transformation of the types into truth. Finally, he frequently brings in his idea of "worship in spirit and in truth" or
"evangelical way of life" in connection with the Adam typology
and new creation. Here, then, is a body of exegetical and theological ideas which are central to Cyril's thought, and these conceptions inform Cyril's approach to most of the theological issues he
had to face.

The discussion of Christ as the second Adam has opened up

46. For these phrases see notes 36, 39; also G. Jouassard, "Une intuition
fondamentale de saint Cyrille d'Alexandrie en christologie dans les premières
années de son épiscopat," pp. 175–86.

a number of questions which must now be explored: (1) Since
the problem of Christianity and Judaism came first, this question
must be clarified in the light of the exegetical and theological
ideas we have now uncovered. What is the relationship between
Moses and Christ? (2) The more we have probed Cyril's exegesis,
the more Christological questions have come to the surface. We
have seen, for example, that Cyril's view of "new creation" is
related to his view of Christ. Further, we noted that the Adam-
Christ typology, following traditional practice, is used by Cyril to
affirm the solidarity of Christ with mankind and to assert that
Christ is truly a man among men. On the other hand, in the
tradition of Apollinaris and Athanasius, Cyril also uses the typology to assert the uniqueness of Christ. He is like other men but
also unlike them; he is not an ordinary man. These ideas need
to be examined further. Is there a correlation between Cyril's
view of new creation, of the resurrection of Christ, and Christ as
the heavenly man or the new man? What bearing do these
conceptions have on Cyril's view of Christ?

7 Moses and Christ

In the ancient world Moses was the symbol of Jewish beliefs and practices. He was considered the founder of Judaism and its most authoritative teacher. When men wished to refer to the beliefs of the Jews they spoke of the teachings of Moses, and when they wished to contrast Jewish worship or customs with those of other peoples they singled out Moses as the representative figure. In discussions about Christianity and Judaism it is Moses who was thought to represent the Jews as Christ represented the Christians. The philosopher-doctor Galen, for example, considered Christianity and Judaism to be two philosophical schools founded respectively by Christ and Moses.[1]

Of all the figures in the Jewish Scriptures Moses alone captured the imagination of Jew, Christian, and Greek alike. In Jewish tradition Moses was interpreted and reinterpreted in new and diverse ways.[2] To the Jew he was the author of the chief books of Scripture, the Pentateuch; it was Moses who received the Torah from God on Sinai. Moses led his people out of Egypt and kept alive the vision of the promised land during the wanderings in the wilderness. Moses was the one towering figure to whom the Jew returned again and again. Philo, for example, wrote brief tracts on Abraham and Joseph, but these essays were really an occasion to discourse on specific virtues. Thus the tract *On Abraham* bears the subtitle, "Life of the Wise Man made Perfect through Teaching," and the work *On Joseph* is subtitled, "The Life of the Statesman." Enoch represents repentance and progress, Noah righteousness, and Enos hope. But when Philo turns to

---

1. See R. Walzer, *Galen on Jews and Christians,* pp. 38, 48.

2. For Moses in Jewish and Christian tradition, see *Moses in Schrift und Ueberlieferung* (hereafter cited as *Moses*). This work includes a series of studies by Christian and Jewish scholars on Moses in the intertestamental literature, in rabbinic tradition, in Philo, in the New Testament, and in the fathers. See also Joachim Jeremias, "Μωϋσῆς," pp. 852–78 with bibliography; also Luis M. Armendariz, *El Nuevo Moisés.*

Moses he does not confine him to a particular ethical category. Philo is interested in Moses himself, and only in the case of Moses do we get anything resembling a biography.

In Hellenistic Judaism Moses was made the subject of extensive legendary treatment.[3] His life and actions are repeated and amplified and finally idealized. From birth to death his life is marked by a series of wondrous occurrences. Moses was also used in Jewish apologetics. In reply to the charge that Judaism was too particularistic, Jews replied that Moses was the lawgiver of mankind. He is the only lawgiver whose laws are accepted throughout the whole world. Most lawgivers only receive acceptance among their own people. In other circles Moses was seen as the mediator of revelation. He was not as important for what he himself did as for what he revealed to men from God. He is the teacher of the Torah. "Moses received the Torah on Mt. Sinai, handed it on to Joshua, Joshua to the elders, the elders to the prophets." He is the "divine prophet for all the world," for "all the mysteries of times and the end of the hours has God revealed to him." In some circles his death became the object of speculation and tended to take on aspects of a sacrificial offering. "Why is Moses buried in a foreign land? In order that those who died in a foreign land might come to life again through his merit." Some believed that Moses had been taken up into heaven.

In the New Testament Moses is the most frequently mentioned personage of the Old Testament.[4] He is seen as the mediator of the law, as the prophet, as a type of the believer. In its general outline the picture of Moses in the New Testament is closer to that of Palestinian Judaism than it is to the heroic figure of Philo. In Acts, for example, Moses is the leader of the people of Israel who mediates between them and God and who leads them out of Egypt into the wilderness. Luke records the incident of the burning bush where Jahweh reveals himself to Moses and tells him he has heard the cries of his people and will now deliver them. In Hebrews, Moses is seen as a type of the believer, "By

3. See Jeoemias, "Μωϋσῆς," pp. 854–68; Geza Vermes, "Die Gestalt des Moses an der Wende der beiden Testamente," in Moses, pp. 61–94.

4. See Jeremias, "Μωϋσῆς," pp. 868 ff., and the section in Moses on the New Testament by Albert Descamps and Paul Démann, pp. 185–266.

faith Moses refused to be called the son of Pharaoh's daughter
. . . By faith he left Egypt. . . . By faith he kept the Passover."
In Paul on the other hand Moses is seen as the sign of the old
covenant and thus he is contrasted with the new covenant in
Jesus. In 2 Corinthians (3:7–8) Paul writes: "Now if the dispensation of death, carved in letters on stone, came with such
splendor that the Israelites could not look at Moses' face because of its brightness, fading as this was, will not the dispensation of the Spirit be attended with greater splendor?" Paul does
not really use Moses as a type of Christ, for Moses is the sign of
the old covenant which has passed away.

Jeremias has shown that the typology of Moses-Christ is not
really central to New Testament Christology.[5] To be sure there
are places such as the infancy narratives in Matthew which appear
to be modeled on Mosaic legends. And in Hebrews Moses is
taken as a type of Christ. In Hebrews (3:2 ff.) we read that
Jesus "was faithful to him who appointed him, just as Moses also ➤
was faithful in God's house. Yet Jesus has been counted worthy
of as much more glory than Moses as the builder of a house has
more honor than the house. . . . Now Moses was faithful in all
God's house as a servant, to testify to the things that were to be
spoken later, but Christ was faithful over God's house as a son."
But more frequently Moses is contrasted with Jesus, as in Paul.
This reverse typology was just as influential in shaping the
Christology of the early Church as the positive typological link
drawn between Moses and Christ.

If the picture of Moses presented in the New Testament is
many-sided, the picture drawn by the fathers is even more so.
The figure of Moses intrigued many patristic commentators. In a
study of Moses as he appears in the works of the fathers, Jean
Daniélou said: "From the epistle of Barnabas to the *Glaphyra*
of Cyril of Alexandria the texts devoted to Moses are number-
less." [6] Of the patristic commentators, however, only a few devoted special treatises to Moses. Of these the most important are
Gregory of Nyssa's *Life of Moses,* Origen's homilies on Exodus,

---

5. Jeremias, "Μωϋσῆς," p. 78.
6. Jean Daniélou, "Moses bei Gregor von Nyssa. Vorbild und Gestalt," in
Moses, p. 289.

and Cyril's comments in the *Glaphyra*. According to Daniélou the patristic interpretations of the figure of Moses fall roughly into several classes: Moses as model of the devout believing Christian whose exemplary life is set before the faithful as an ideal; Moses, viewed typologically, as a type of Christ and the events of his life as a type of the redemption. There is also another approach, derived more particularly from Philo, and this is an allegorical interpretation of the details of Moses' life. Now these varying interpretations are by no means neatly divided between various writers. In fact in many cases we can see an admixture of various types of interpretations, though most writers tend to prefer one over the other. But the lines cannot be drawn too sharply. A figure such as Origen, though he inclines toward the first, also uses allegory and sees in Moses a type of Christ. If there is a leit-motif in Origen's interpretation of Moses it is the view that Moses is the model of the spiritual journey of the soul to God.[7]

Gregory of Nyssa's *Life of Moses* is the most extensive treatment of Moses in the early Church. From this work we can gain an impression of two traditions of interpretation. In his earlier works Gregory developed some of the ideas which were to appear in the *Life of Moses*. Already in his commentary on the Psalms he praised Moses as lawgiver and lauded him because he had withdrawn from society for forty years to live in peace in order to contemplate [θεωρία] the invisible realities. After this he was illumined by the light which came from the burning bush.[8] As Daniélou has shown, Gregory depends heavily on Philo. For example, from Philo Gregory took over the idea that Moses had rejected the honor of becoming king and that he had lived an eremetic life in the desert. Moses illustrates the difference between participation in the world of the senses and in the unchanging world of the spirit.[9]

In the *Commentary on the Song of Songs* Moses is pictured as the model of the spiritual life. "For a long time Moses lived by himself in the wilderness only on philosophy, set aside from

7. Jean Daniélou, *Grégoire de Nysse. Contemplation sur La Vie de Moïse,* p. xviii.
8. *PG* 44:456c–457c (Jaeger-Langerbeck, 5:43–44).
9. See Daniélou, "Moses bei Gregor von Nyssa," pp. 292–93.

disturbance. He was enlightened by the fire of the burning bush.
. . . He goes up the burning mountain. He reaches its pinnacle.
He goes into the clouds, and he enters into the place where God
dwells. To those who behold him he appears as an unapproach-
able son. How can one describe all his ascents and his various
theophanies? And although he is so great and perfect, that he
shares in such things, the desire fills him yet once more and he
flees to God, to be able to view him face to face." [10] This passage
represents the central theme in Gregory's view of the life of
Moses, the quest of the soul for God. Moses has been transformed
into the Christian embarked on a spiritual journey.

In the *Life of Moses* Gregory elaborates these same themes.
When Moses is driven out of Egypt he takes this as an opportunity to begin the pursuit of a better philosophy. He sets himself
apart from the crowd and passes his time in solitude. The scene
before the well with Reuel is taken to show Moses' zeal for
righteousness. He saw the injustice of the shepherds who drove
away the daughters and therefore drove them away.[11] The birth
of Moses becomes a model for the life of the devout Christian.
Moses' birth, says Gregory, coincides with the order of Pharaoh
to put the male infants to death. That Moses was not put to death
can serve as a lesson for us. How can we imitate that fortuitous
circumstance? We all know, says Gregory, that men undergo
continual change in the course of their lives. Another way of
describing this change is to be born continually. But if we are born
continually throughout our lives we have control over whether
good or evil will result from the change. This birth is the result
of a free choice and we are our own parents; we create ourselves,
making ourselves according to the model we choose. Thus we see
in Moses the possibility, in spite of the opposition of an evil tyrant,
to be born to a superior life. The one who escapes from dangers
and is born to good imitates Moses.[12]

These few instances give some idea of one way of interpreting
the figure of Moses. In the same work Gregory also offers other

10. *PG* 44:1026bc (Jaeger-Langerbeck, 6:355–56)
11. See Daniélou, "Moses bei Gregor von Nyssa," p. 296.
12. *Vita Moysis* (ed. Jaeger-Langerbeck, 7,1:33 ff).

kinds of interpretation, for the life of Moses and related events
could be seen as a type of the mysteries of Christ. Gregory takes
the withered hand to be a symbol of the mystery of divinity, for
God "is revealed to men through the flesh of the Lord." [13] The
staff turned into a snake is a symbol of Christ. [14] The outstretched
arms of Moses are a type of the cross. [15] The passage through the
Red Sea is taken to be a type of baptism. "The crossing of the
Red Sea was, according to St. Paul himself, a prophecy in action
of the sacrament of baptism. And in fact, now once again, when
the people approach the water of rebirth as they flee from Egypt,
which is sin, they themselves are freed and saved, but the devil
and his aides, the spirits of wickedness, are destroyed." [16] The
wood which makes the waters of Mara sweet is a symbol of the
cross, the manna is the Word who has become man. [17]

In the writings of Gregory we can see something of the richness
and variety of the patristic interpretation of Moses. These same
themes appear in other writers as well. Aphrahat for example,
writing in an ascetic Syrian Christian setting, uses Moses as an
example, against the Jews, to support the practice of celibacy and
virginity among Christians. Moses is also the model for a life of
fasting, as well as for the life of prayer. Through prayer he saved
Israel from the hand of Pharaoh, brought plagues down on
Egypt, divided the sea, made bitter water sweet and manna come
down from heaven. He split the rock which let water flow out. [18]
But Aphrahat also draws a parallel between Moses and Jesus:
"Moses was persecuted as Jesus was persecuted. When Moses was
born they concealed him that he might not be slain by his perse-
cutors. When Jesus was born they carried him off in flight into
Egypt that Herod, his persecutor, might not slay him. In the
days when Moses was born, children used to be drowned in the
river; and at the birth of Jesus the children of Bethlehem and in

13. Ibid., p. 41.

14 Ibid., p. 42. Cyril, *PG* 69:474d takes it in the same way; Tertullian
sees a symbol of the resurrection (*De res. car* 28).

15. *Vita Moysis* (ed. Jaeger-Langerbeck, p. 56).

16. Jaeger-Langerbeck, 9:233.   17. Ibid., 7,1:75, 77–78.

18. See Raymond Marie Tonneau, "Moses in der syrischen Tradition," in
Moses, pp. 267–287. See Aphrahat, *Demon.* 3,4; 18.3.

its borders were slain. . . . Moses brought out his people from
the service of Pharaoh; and Jesus delivered all nations from the
service of Satan. . . . When Moses sacrificed the lamb, the firstborn of Egypt were slain; and when they crucified Jesus the true
Lamb, the people who slew him perished through his slaying. . . .
Moses sweetened the bitter waters by the wood; and Jesus sweetened our bitterness by his cross, by the wood of the tree of his
crucifixion. Moses brought down the law to his people; and
Jesus gave his covenant to the nations." [19]

Western writers also gave attention to the figure of Moses,
though none produced a work comparable to Gregory's life of
Moses.[20] As the political and religious leader of the people of
Israel, as the man of God—not the self-made man but the one
sent to carry out and accomplish God's will—he was praised for
his role as lawgiver and mediator. But he was also viewed as the
forerunner of Christ, the lesser who shows forth the greater who
is to come. In his *Commentary on John,* Augustine writes: "The
law was given by Moses; grace and truth came by Jesus Christ.
The law, given by a servant, made men guilty; pardon, given by
an emperor, delivered the guilty. The law was given by Moses.
Let not the servant attribute to himself more than was done
through him. Chosen to a great ministry as one faithful in his
house, but yet a servant, he is able to act according to the law,
but cannot release from the guilt of the law." [21] Moses prepared
the way for Christ through the giving of the law. Moses was the
greatest man of God to announce and prepare for the Lord.

Augustine frequently refers to Moses as a type or prefiguration
of Christ. Jesus characterized himself by reference to the person
of Moses, "Se autem figuraverat in persona Moysi." [22] The most
extensive typological treatment occurs in the *Homilies on Exodus*
of Gregory of Elvira who is dependent on Origen. Moses freed
the Hebrews from the might of Pharaoh, Christ freed his followers from the power of the world.[23] In this connection the fathers

19. Tonneau, "Moses," pp. 272–73; *Demonstration* 31.
20. Auguste Luneau, "Moses und die lateinischen Vaeter," in *Moses,* pp.
307–30.
21. *In Jo.* 1:17 (*CC* 26:27).   22. *Sermon* 137.6 (*PL* 38:758).
23. *Tract. Orig.* 7.

also elaborated on the symbolism of baptism and the Red Sea. "The Red Sea signifies baptism; Moses, their leader through the Red Sea, signifies Christ; the people who passed through signify believers; the death of the Egyptians signifies the abolition of sins. Under different signs there is the same faith." [24] And Ambrose: "Moses led the Jewish people through the wilderness; Christ led them through a fruitful way, in the midst of lilies; then through his suffering the wilderness bloomed like a lily." [25]

But the fathers also developed the "negative" side of the typology. Thus because Moses was wholly identified with the law, and the law with Judaism, Moses provided the occasion to reflect on the meaning of the law and the fate of the people of Israel.[26] Augustine speculated that the incident at Horeb foreshadows the rejection of Christ, for the Jewish people "did not believe that Christ was the power of God." [27] This is why Moses did not live to see the promised land and died before reaching it. For one reaches the promised land only through Jesus. Augustine draws the double conclusion. "There is no doubt that Moses . . . represents two different persons. In the first instance he is an image of the one who takes part in the divine truth (for he went into the cloud on Mt. Sinai); but secondly he represents the Jews who set themselves against the image of the grace of Christ. They did not understand and did not join in the covenant." [28]

Cyril's most extensive treatment of Moses occurs in his works on the Pentateuch, and particularly in the *Glaphyra*.[29] However,

24. Augustine, *In Jo.* 10:8 (*CC* 26:392). For parallels see Luneau, "Moses," p. 325, n. 110.

25. Ambrose, *De Isaac* 6.56 (*CSEL* 32:680).

26. See Luneau, "Moses," pp. 327 ff.

27. Augustine, *Contra Faustum* 16. 17 (*CSEL* 25:458).

28. *In Hept.* 2. 176 (*CSEL* 28:203 ff).

29. On Cyril's interpretation of Moses see the detailed discussion of Moses' life in Armendariz, *El Nuevo Moisés,* pp. 25–108, and the bibliography cited there. Armendariz' work has the great value of discussing Cyril's predecessors as well as Cyril and is a fine resumé of the interpretation of Moses in the fathers. Since Armendariz has treated Cyril's view of Moses so exhaustively, my comments on Moses are limited only to parts which are relevant to this discussion.

Cyril does not limit his discussion to these works. In the *Commentary on the Gospel of John,* for example, he goes into some detail concerning the relationship between Moses and Christ. In his interpretation of Moses, Cyril is frequently dependent on earlier writers. Cyril, like Gregory, takes the hand of Moses which was placed in his bosom as a type of the incarnation. He sees Pharaoh of Egypt as signifying the spiritual Pharaoh, Satan, who tyrannizes over mankind.[30] However, Armendariz has shown that in most instances Cyril's exegesis is notably different from that of his predecessors. It is much more radically Christocentric, and it is preoccupied with shortcomings of the Mosaic law. On the one hand Moses is a type of Christ, and on the other he is the symbol of all that was passing away and was replaced by Christ.[31] Of the two traditions of interpretation described by Daniélou, Cyril certainly inclines towards a typological view. Moses is not the model of the soul questing after God, but he is viewed in the light of the history of redemption which culminates in Christ. Most of the features of Cyril's positive view of Moses can be seen in his interpretation of Moses' birth.

Philo does not have much to say about the birth of Moses, except to point out that Moses was an exceptionally beautiful and gifted child. "Now, the child from his birth had an appearance of more than ordinary godliness, so that his parents, as long as they could, actually set at nought the proclamations of the despot." When Pharaoh's daughter first saw the baby in the river she was struck by his "beauty and fine condition." As the child began to grow he was "noble and goodly to look upon." [32] Origen too has little to say about the birth of Moses, but gives

30. *Glaph. Ex.* 2 (PG 69:473d–475a); see Armendariz, *El Nuevo Moisés,* pp. 46–48.

31. "De ahí también que Moisés no sea, a los ojos de Cirilo, ni el modelo del perfecto buscador de Dios, como para Gregorio, ni tampoco un símbolo de la Ley como para Orígenes, sino primordialmente un tipo de Cristo. . . . No que en Cirilo Moisés represente siempre y exclusivamente a Cristo; también es figura de la Ley y su debilidad, pero aun entonces al resultar la mayor parte de las veces contrastado no con otra Ley, sino con una persona, con Cristto, acaba siempre por reflejarla en un paralelo personal" (Armendariz, *El Nuevo Moisés,* pp. 105–6).

32. Philo, *Vita Moysis* 1. 9–24.

an allegorical interpretation to a number of the details associated with it. Thus the daughter of Pharaoh signifies the church of the Gentiles. Pharaoh signifies the world and the daughter goes out from the house of the father to the river to wash herself of the sins of her father's house. Moses signifies the law. When men come to the waters of baptism in the church they also receive the law which is hidden in the basket made of pitch; the Jews had caused it to be obscured and it was only found again by the church of the Gentiles. The law passed its infancy among its own, nourished by milk, but when it comes to the church, it is full grown and mature, like Moses who is strong and robust.[33] For Gregory of Nyssa, as we have seen, the birth of Moses became a model for the continuous rebirth of the Christian life.[34]

Cyril discusses the birth of Moses in the opening section of the *Glaphyra on Exodus*. The "scopos" of the book, says Cyril, concerns "redemption through Christ," so we must first see "what danger mankind was in" before looking at the account of Moses. There was a great famine in the land and the Israelites journeyed from Canaan to Egypt. They lived there for many years and grew in numbers. When Pharaoh saw that they had grown so numerous he set harsh taskmasters over them and oppressed and humiliated the people. As they became more oppressed they called on God for deliverance. Pharaoh ordered the midwives to kill all the males, but they chose to please God rather than Pharaoh and refused to follow his order. At this point Moses enters the story. These experiences of the people of Israel under Pharaoh are paradigmatic of the subjection of all humanity to Satan, and for this reason we will examine the "things written about the divine Moses as an image and *hypotyposis* of salvation through Christ." [35]

Cyril cites in full the story of the birth of Moses in Exodus 2:1–10. The "mystery [of Christ] is made apparent in the things about Moses." "Since God had mercy on those who served a cruel and wicked tyrant, he did not spare his own son, as it is written, but handed him over for us all." He came to his own,

33. Origen, *Hom. Ex.* 2 (GCS 6:154 ff).
34. *Vita Moysis* (ed. Jaeger-Langerbeck, 7:1, 33 ff).
35. *Glaph. Ex.* 1 (PG 69:388b–392b).

to the lost sheep. "Moses came from the tribe and blood of Levi." Immanuel was a "pious innocent and completely holy priest." His priesthood was not according to the flesh, as it was among the leaders of the Jews, but it was a priesthood to the king of all things. "Therefore, the type was in material things in order that the truth, which is Christ, may be above flesh, for he is considered the newborn child because of the innocence of the divine and because he has become a new creation. When he put off the oldness which was corrupt, he transformed it to newness of life in himself. The infant is a *new creation*. That the newborn child is a symbol of innocence is easy to grasp, if one wishes, from the words of the Savior: "Let the children come to me and do not hinder them; for to such belongs the kingdom of God." From this Cyril concludes that "Christ is signified by a child because of the innocence of divinity." [36]

Moses' birth becomes a type of the person of Christ. To see Moses as a type of Christ is not unusual, but Cyril brings to the text his own theological point of view and discovers a point of reference in the "newness" which characterizes an infant. Just as a child comes into the world as a new and unblemished creation, so Christ was also without blemish, for he was holy and pure. Purity and holiness are the characteristics of God, so the innocence and newness of the infant child becomes symbols of the divine nature of Christ. Cyril also observes that the Scriptures are silent about Moses' father. This too is a sign of Christ who "according to the flesh was without a father." Furthermore, the beauty of the child fits Christ. This too accords with the Scriptures, for in Psalm 45 we read, "You are the fairest of the sons of men." "No one would doubt," says Cyril, "that that which is divine in glory and by nature is more beautiful than all things," though we must remember that when he came among men he appeared "without form or comeliness" (Psalm 53:2). "There is an infinite and incomparable difference between God and man." [37]

Next Cyril turns to the discovery of the child by the daughter

36. *Glaph. Ex.* 1 (*PG* 69:392b–395c); see also *PG* 69:400a where he reiterates the idea of new creation, contrasting Jesus with Moses.
37. *PG* 69:396b–d.

of Pharoah. What mystery do we find here? "Before the coming of the Savior there was not on earth a man who was unassailable. . . . Man was in danger because Satan had driven him on to worldly pleasures and into the slime and mud. . . . 'They have all gone astray, they are all alike corrupt; there is none that does good, no, not one' (Psalm 14:3). Men were clearly incapable of doing good, not allowed to play the man against the author of sin. Since he came among us Immanuel was numbered among those who are plotted against, a male child by nature and in truth, not knowing moral weakness, for he was not inclined toward sin. At first he escaped the notice of the ruler of this world. The child—that is, Moses—was hidden." [38]

Cyril uses the figure of Moses to illustrate certain characteristics of the person of Christ. Building on his earlier statement that Moses was an exceptional child, he concludes that he was the only one among men who was unassailable by Satan. He was pure and did not know sin. Cyril's interpretation of the birth of Moses indicates that, in contrast to other writers, he is not interested in Moses as a paradigm of the soul seeking God. He is more interested in the fate of humanity as a whole and the role Moses, as a type of Christ, plays in the salvation of mankind. These characteristics can be seen in other events in the life of Moses. Cyril, for example, interprets the incident of the rod turned into a serpent in the following way: The serpent is mankind; the fall to earth is Adam's fall. We should, says Cyril, consider humanity as a living animal. Moses seizes the tail, and this means that Christ comes to men at the end of the ages. "Even though Moses only grasped the tail, the whole serpent was transformed [μεταπλασμός] even up to the head, the serpent was fully changed [μετεστοιχειοῦτο] into a rod." In the same way Christ came at the last time late in the history of mankind, but the "re-forming [ἀναμόρφωσις] which he brought extended to the whole race [εἰς πᾶν διήκει τὸ γένος], i.e. to the head which is Adam." [39] Such fanciful exegesis conforms closely to Cyril's basic

38. PG 69:396d–397a.
39. PG 68:245b–d. In the *Glaphyra* the serpent is the Word who becomes man as the rod became the snake (*PG* 69:470c).

theological scheme. The work of Christ is viewed in the light of his relationship to the whole of humanity of which he is a part; the fruits of his work bring about a transformation or re-creation of mankind and this extends to all of humanity because of the unique relationship of Christ to mankind. In this passage we have precisely the same structure of thought which we have already observed in the many passages concerning the first and second Adam.

Similar ideas find expression in other incidents. The account of the hand in the bosom also receives a Christological interpretation. The natural man, says Cyril, bears the image of God, and there is no sin when man remains in the bosom of God. The leprous hand signifies man in sin. When God receives us in Christ we are healed to our original condition, casting off the curse of death. The ancient curse is cast down and "we spring up anew [ἀναθρώσκομεν] to what we were at first." [40] The plague of water turned into blood signifies the water in baptism which purifies the world.[41] The two chief symbols which run throughout the exegesis of these texts, as Armendariz has shown, are mankind and the Word, and together they form the basis for the history of redemption. Moses then becomes a key to the understanding of the mystery of Christ for in his life this mystery was wondrously shown forth.[42]

Most of the fathers were intrigued by the account of Moses' experience at the bush. In his commentary Philo took the bush of thorns to be a symbol of the Logos, and several early fathers, notably Justin and Clement, followed him in this. For Gregory of Nyssa the burning bush was a theophany; Moses and every man who rids himself of his earthly flame and turns to the light which comes from the bush has a vision of God. Such a man will be capable of helping others free themselves from bondage. In the case of Moses the miracles of the stick and then the hand are the first manifestations of this new freedom. The two miracles

40. *PG* 68:248c–d.
41. *PG* 68:250a. For a different interpretation see *Glaph. Ex.* 2 (*PG* 69:478c ff).
42. Armendariz, *El Nuevo Moisés,* p. 42.

represent symbolically the manifestation of divinity to men in the flesh.[43]

Cyril immediately takes up a different problem. The law was given to men as an aid, he says; in order to show them the more perfect thing that was to come God gave them a shadow of it. But later the truth appeared and Christ brought tutoring through shadows to an end. The bush was not unlike a bush of thorns. There was much fire and one would expect such a bush to be consumed, but it was not. This suggests a deeper meaning. The Holy Scriptures often compare divinity to fire: we read that God is a consuming fire. The Scriptures also call man grass. How can grass bear to come in contact with fire, i.e. humanity with divinity? "In Christ this happened and [they] became compatible." Just as the fire spared the bush, when God became man he did not consume humanity. Moses took off his shoes. What was holy about the ground? Cyril answers: "Everywhere is holy where Christ is." Why does God appear in the desert? From the Scriptures we learn that the desert is a type of the churches of the Gentiles.[44]

Exodus records that Moses was commanded to take off his shoes as he approached the burning bush. Why was this necessary? Cyril contrasts the place of the law and the evangelical way of life in the new dispensation:

> Drawing near, Moses stopped short and was commanded to take off his shoes. They were a sign of death and corruption, for every shoe is made from the remains of dead and decaying animals. Christ was inaccessible to those under the law and under the tutorial worship [παιδαγωγικῇ λατρείᾳ]. It was necessary that all defilement be washed away, and that the filth of sin be scoured clean. The blood of bulls was not capable of taking away sin. For no one is justified in the law. It was necessary for him who wishes to know the mystery of Christ to put away beforehand the worship in

43. Philo, *Vita Moysis* 1. 66; Justin *Dial. Trypho* 59.2; Clement of Alexandria, *Prot.* 1.8.3; Gregory of Nyssa, *Vita Moysis* (ed. Jaeger-Langerbeck, 7:1, 39 ff). For other fathers, see Armendariz, *El Nuevo Moisés,* pp. 34–35.

44. *PG* 69: 409b–412a.

types and shadows, which is superior neither to corruption nor to sin. Then he will know and enter into the holy land—that is, the Church. For those who have not rejected worship according to the law are subject to corruption as the Savior himself clearly said. 'Truly, truly I say to you, unless you eat the flesh of the son of man and drink his blood, you have no life in you.' This is the mystery which is not among those who once were under the law, but from those who have received faith and are justified in Christ, and enriched by the teaching which is superior to that of the law, and by that I mean the evangelical [teaching]. Whoever is not yet freed through faith and is far from Christ is under corruption and as if under the law, which is sin, the mother of death. For if they want to take off the shoe, corruption, which cannot bring about justification and lead to the truly life-giving grace, they will draw near to the one who justified the impious, i.e. Christ.[45]

The transition from Cyril's comments about Moses as a beautiful and extraordinary child and a type of Christ to this passage is noteworthy. Within his total perspective on Moses Cyril is quite willing to let Moses stand as a "positive" type of Christ, but he is more inclined to see in Moses not the type but the antithesis of Christ. Here Moses' sandals are the starting point for Cyril's discussion, but he quickly translates the symbol of the sandals to stand for the Mosaic law and the way of life under it. This way of life brings only death and must be replaced by the new way of life which is found in Christ.

Moses is here contrasted with Christ for the purpose of calling attention to the distinctive and new thing that comes through Christ. The difference between the two lies in their ability to cope with death. The legal way of life was incapable of overcoming death; it was not superior to death and corruption. This accent occurs over and over again in connection with Moses. In *Paschal Homily 16* for example Cyril says that as a result of the fall men worshiped the sun and moon and stars and turned away from the true knowledge of God.

45. *PG* 69:415b–417a,

"God called ancient Israel through Moses, choosing him as a sort of firstfruits from his divinity, and through the best laws brought about a good way of life." But they turned again to their evil ways. Then he sent the prophets to them but they did not heed the prophets and refused to be cured. Finally he sent his son "transforming [μετακομοῦντα] the things among us into what is incomparably better than that of old and saving again those on earth." [46] Cyril is thinking of the total history of mankind and the various attempts on the part of God to bring about man's redemption after the fall in Adam. Moses and the prophets are placed together as unsatisfactory attempts to accomplish redemption. What they offered to mankind was of value, but it was not adequate to the task at hand. Moses and the prophets were unable to overcome that power of the devil and of death. Therefore a new dispensation was needed which could in fact carry out this task. In spite of the favorable things said about Moses as a type he really belongs, according to Cyril, with those between Adam and Christ who were unable to undo Adam's work.

Moses is the minister of the law which does not bring life, and Christ is the minister of the gospel which frees men from the ministry of the law to give them justification and life. Cyril has Christ say:

> For I was not sent, he says, like the hierophant Moses condemning the world by the law nor introducing the commandment for conviction of sin, nor do I perform a servile ministry, but I introduce loving-kindness befitting the master. I free the slave, as son and heir of the father, I transform [μετασκευάζω] the law that condemns grace for justification, I release from sin him that is held with the words of his transgressions, I am come to save the world, not to condemn it. For it was right, he says, that Moses, as a servant, should be a minister of the law that condemns, but that I as son and God should free the whole world from the curse of the law and by exceeding loving-kindness should heal the infirmity of the world. [47]

46. PH 16 (PG 77:764d–765d); see also *Glaph. Ex.* 3 (PG 69:497b–c).
47. *In Jo.* 3:17 (P 1:228).

Jesus saw that Nicodemus, who was holding fast to Moses, could not understand the "new and evangelical polity," for he thought it would be more burdensome than the ancient commandments.

At times Cyril paints the contrast less vividly. He recognizes the value and significance of the accomplishment of Moses but also believes that Christ's accomplishment is greater. For example, he says that Moses brought knowledge of God but not perfect knowledge. For "perfect knowledge of God . . . does not consist merely in believing that he is God, but in believing also that he is the father." The bare belief that God is God, says Cyril, "is no better than that held by those under the law; for it does not exceed the limit of the knowledge the Jews attained." The law, for this very reason, was "incapable of sustaining a life of piety in God's service and brought nothing to perfection," for its knowledge of God was imperfect. . . . But our Lord Jesus Christ sets better things before those who are under the law of Moses, and giving them instruction clearer than the commandment of the law, gave them better and clearer knowledge than that of old." [48]

Moses, who was the only major figure in history to attempt a reconciliation of God and man which would undo the damage done by Adam, was unsuccessful because he "was not capable of bringing salvation." [49] As a consequence of this view Cyril is led to the position that the two pivotal figures in the history of mankind are Adam and Christ. "Holy is the time in the beginning when men came to be, for they had not yet departed from paradise because of the sin of the forefather Adam. . . . Holy again is the last time through Christ, justifying in faith those who come to him and restoring again [ἀνακομίζοντος] that which we were in the beginning." [50]

In the previous chapter we noted that Cyril's interpretation of the descent of the Spirit assumed that the Spirit left mankind after the fall of Adam and did not return again in its fulness until the coming of the second Adam. [51] The descent of the Spirit

48. *In Jo.* 17:6–8 (P 2:681–82).   49. *PG* 76:928a.
50. *PG* 69:436a; see also 612a–b.
51. See Chap. 6, fn. 40. "When Christ rose up with the spoils of hell, then it was that he gave the Spirit of adoption to those who believed in him. . . . That the Spirit of adoption was not in men before his return,

on Jesus marks the beginning of the renewal of creation. The
Spirit was present in Moses and the prophets but its presence then
was only to foreshadow what was to come in Christ. The Spirit
does not come to mankind again until the victory over death has
been accomplished. In Christ mankind had a "second beginning
. . . and the renewing spirit has been given to us . . . after Christ
was glorified, i.e. after the resurrection, when having burst the
bonds of death and appeared superior to all corruption he came
alive again having our whole nature in himself. . . . Christ became the firstfruits of the renewed nature." [52]

Christ, however, is superior not only to the prophets and to
John the Baptist, a "great and exalted man," but even to Moses.
Of Moses God said, "I know you before all and you have found
grace in my sight." But the son is "in every way superior to and
of greater renown" even than Moses. Why should Christ be
superior to Moses? He introduced a way of life which was
"better than the way of life of the law." The "law was condemning the world . . . but the Savior sets it free." The law used to
give men grace by turning them away from idols to the knowledge of God, but it did not impart a perfect knowledge. It was a
knowledge conveyed in types and shadows; now we see things in
truth. "The law baptized the unclean with mere water; the
Savior with the Holy Spirit and with fire." Therefore Moses is
a "minister of condemnation" and Christ is a "minister of righteousness." The "holy prophets will yield the palm to Christ and
will never think that they ought to aim at equal glory with him,
for even he who was above all men known of God, namely

---

the very wise evangelist John makes clear when he says, 'For the spirit
had not yet been given, because Jesus was not yet glorified.' By 'glory'
he means the resurrection from the dead." (*In Luc. Hom.* 38 [*PG* 72:617–
20]). Moses did not bring men full adoption as sons of God through the
Spirit; this came only through Christ. The prophets too were "spirit bearers"
but they did not possess the Spirit by nature and were not able to put an
end to the tyranny of Satan over us (*PG* 69:409c). Also *PG* 76:668b. On
the problem of the spirit in the prophets and in Moses, see Armendariz, *El
Nuevo Moisés,* pp. 156 ff.; G. Philips, "La grâce des justes de l'Ancien
Testament," pp. 543–47; Janssens, "Notre filiation divine," p. 266; Burghardt, *Image of God in Man,* 115–16.

52. *In Jo.* 7:39 (P 1:694–95).

Moses, is brought down to second place." Moses is given a place of honor above all the prophets, but he was still a minister of condemnation for he did not bring about the full and perfect knowledge of God.[53] For in Christ things are "incomparably better" than they were of old.[54]

Moses served Cyril as a foil for Christ and Christianity. Indeed it is the deficiencies of Moses and Judaism that establish for Cyril the conditions which Christ must meet. For if Moses could not bring about the required salvation, then Christ must be able to do it. If Moses and the prophets could not bring about a return of the Spirit, then Christ must be able to do so. If there was no one who could triumph over death and corruption, Christ must do it. If there was no one who could bring about a renewal of the old creation and the beginning of the new creation, Christ must do it. "Neither the time of the law, nor the chorus of holy prophets had the *new* food, the teachings which came through Christ, nor did they have the renewal [ἀνακαινισμόν] of human nature, except perhaps as a prediction. Since our Lord Jesus Christ rose up, as a sheaf, the firstfruits of mankind returning himself to the Father, we are transformed [μεταστοιχειούμεθα] into new life. We now live in evangelical fashion, "not in the oldness of the letter, but in the newness of the Spirit, through whom and with whom be Glory to God the Father." [55]

53. *In Jo.* 1:16–17 (P 1:149–53). See Janssens, "Notre filiation divine," p. 266.
54. *PG* 77:765; also *In Joel.* 2:28–29 (P 1:338).
55. *PG* 69:625a. See also *PG* 69:672b.

8 New Creation

"If anyone is in Christ, he is a new creation; the old has passed away, behold the new has come." This is only one text among many where early Christians spoke of the "newness" of Christianity. Terms such as "new law," "new covenant," "new people" are widespread in early Christian literature. In Galatians 6:15 Paul speaks of "new creation"; in other places he speaks of the "new lump" (1 Cor. 5:7), or "newness of life" (Rom. 6:4) or "newness of the spirit" (Rom. 7:6) or of a "renewal of the mind" (Rom. 12:2). The writer of the Apocalypse envisions a "new heaven and a new earth" (Rev. 21:1), and dreams of a "new Jerusalem" (Rev. 3:12) where men will join in singing the "new song" (Rev. 5:9). In Ephesians Christians are exhorted to be "renewed in the spirit of your minds, and put on the new nature created after the likeness of God" (Eph. 4:23–24). The author of the epistle to Diognetus exhorts him to "become like a new man . . . since you are going to listen to a really new message." Justin Martyr says that men are "being made new through Christ." [1]

In early Christian literature the meaning of "newness" varies considerably, though there is an underlying feeling that Christianity must be distinguished from all that has gone before. In some cases newness calls attention to the moral renewal which came about through the coming of Christ. Now men are called to a new life which shuns the immoral ways of the past. In other cases newness refers to the eschatological hope of the early Christians. At the end of the ages all things will be new and men will share in a new heaven and a new earth. In other situations the

1. There is no monograph on the history of the interpretation of 2 Cor. 5:17, nor a study of new creation in the fathers. The closest we have for the earler period is Adolf von Harnack, *Die Terminologie der Wiedergeburt und verwandter Erlebnisse in der aeltesten Kirche;* some useful material is collected in Gerhart B. Ladner, *The Idea of Reform. Its Impact on Christian Thought and Action in the Age of the Fathers;* in G. Kittel, ed., *Theologisches Woerterbuch zum Neuen Testament,* 3:450–56; and Roy Harrisville, *The Concept of Newness in the New Testament.*

newness of Christianity is contrasted with the oldness of Judaism. Paul, for example, contrasts the "newness of the spirit" with "the oldness of the letter" (Rom. 7:6).

The particular passage from 2 Corinthians 5 itself has an interesting history. Though the theme of "newness" crops up regularly in the earliest fathers, the use they make of 2 Corinthians 5:17 often varies considerably. We can see something of this variety in the works of Tertullian. In a number of passages he cites 2 Corinthians 5 in connection with Christianity and Judaism and uses it to prove that Christians have now given up the practices of the old covenant. If we follow Jewish ceremonies, says Tertullian, we behave like Galatians. "These [observances] the apostles unteach [dedocet], repressing the continuance of the Old Testament which was buried in Christ and establishing that of the new. For if there is a new creation [nova conditio] in Christ our observances [sollemnia] should also be new." [2] In a number of other places he makes a similar point and cites several Old Testament passages from Isaiah and Jeremiah (Is. 43:18–19; 55:3; Jer. 4:3–4; 38:31–2) which mention a new creation.[3] To speak of a new creation is to recognize that God sent his son "that the old order might pass away and that the new might be established." [4]

Tertullian also uses the passage in an ethical eschatological sense to refer to the judgment which will take place at the end of time. On the day of judgment men will be either punished or rewarded, for in Christ there is a new creation. The implication here—again following Paul, 2 Corinthians 5:10—is that there will be a reckoning to determine who has really participated actively in the new creation.[5] In very much the same sense Clement of Alexandria, also citing 2 Corinthians 5:10 as well as 5:17, writes that if there is a new creation the old has passed away and "there is chastity instead of fornication, continence instead of incontinence, righteousness instead of unrighteousness." [6] In a somewhat different context, and with a more thorough eschatological perspective, Methodoius in his *Symposium* takes the pas-

2. *De ieiunio* 14.2.　　　3. *Adversus Marcionem* 4.1.6, 11.9, 33.8.
4. *Ad. Marc.* 5.4.3.　　　5. *Ad. Marc.* 5.12.6.
6. *Stromateis* 3.8, 62.1 (ed. Staehlin, *GCS* 2:224).

sage to refer to that "new creation where there will be no pain, when all the fruits of the earth will have been harvested and men will no longer beget or be begotten, and God will rest from the work of his creation." [7] Here new creation does not refer to the re-creation of mankind through the death and resurrection of Jesus, but to the final consummation when everything will be brought to perfection. Origen emphasizes that the new creation took place after the resurrection of Jesus. "Moreover our Savior after the Resurrection, when 'old things had now passed away and all things had become new,' being himself 'the new man' and the 'first-born from the dead,' says to the apostles who were also renewed by faith in his Resurrection, 'Receive the Holy Spirit.' " [8] This link had been made already by Justin in *Dialogue with Trypho* 138.2.

A somewhat unusual interpretation is to be found in Ambrose's treatise *De sacramentis* where he discusses the meaning of consecration in the Eucharist. To illustrate what he means he compares the change that takes place as a result of consecration to a new creation. "It was not the body of Christ before the consecration; but after the consecration, from then on it is the body of Christ." Mankind was at first an old creation but "after consecration it becomes a new creation, for if anyone is in Christ he is a new creation." [9]

Frequently the fathers were inclined to relate new creation specifically to Christian baptism. Basil says that we can legitimately speak of three creations: the first and most important, from non-being into being; the second, from worse to better; and the third, the resurrection of the dead. Paul's words in 2 Corinthians 5 refer to the second, creation from worse to better. "Man is created again [πάλιν κτίζεται] through baptism. If any man is in Christ he is a new creation." [10] Chrysostom, writing in a different context, relates new creation to baptism and specifically to John 3:6, Jesus' conversation with Nicodemus. We are not only delivered

7. *Symposium* 1.9; trans. Herbert Musurillo, p. 132.

8. *De principiis* 1.3.7; trans. G. W. Butterworth. *Origen. On First Principles* (New York: Harper & Row, 1966), p. 36.

9. *De sacramentis* 4.6.

10. *Epistle* 8 (trans. Roy J. Deferrari. *The Letters of St. Basil*, p. 85).

from punishment, says Chrysostom, but we are also made into something new for he "freely gave us a life much more precious than the first, and introduced us into another world, made us another creature. 'If any one is in Christ, he is a new creation.' " [11]

The idea of new creation was employed by a number of writers to deal with the problems raised by the Arian exegesis of Colossians 1:15, specifically the phrase "first-born of all creation." [12] According to Arian exegesis this was only another instance from the Bible which supported the claim that Christ was not God, but that he should be seen as the greatest and noblest of created things. If he was the firstborn of creation he must be one of the created beings. As in the case of a number of other biblical passages, this passage seemed to be certain proof that the exegesis of the defenders of Nicaea was simply inconsistent with the biblical text. In the same connection Proverbs 8:22 also came in for discussion, for it said outright that the son had been created.[13] "The Lord created me the beginning of his ways." The passage from Proverbs speaks about wisdom, and all parties, Arian and Nicene, took Proverbs to be referring to Christ. The question was not whether this passage had anything to do with the son, but whether it meant to say that he was created.

The problem raised by "first-born of all creation" did not originate in the Arian controversy. Even before that time there are intimations that the phrase "first-born of all creation" was not the most congenial or safest way to refer to the son. Justin is himself quite imprecise on the matter and is somewhat inconsistent. At times he takes *prototokos* to mean that the son comes from the father before all creatures; elsewhere he indicates that it means he is the first of created things, and in another

11. *Homily* 26 (*In Jo.* 3:6). See also Severian of Gabala, *In 2 Cor. 5:17*, (Karl Staab, *Pauluskommentare*, p. 293). Theodoret of Cyrus, *In 2 Cor. 5:17* (*PG* 82:409d–411a). Gregory Nazianzus, *Theological Oration* 16.2; also his *Easter Oration* 45.1.

12. For the history of interpretation of Col. 1:15 see Alfred Hockel, *Christus der Erstgeborene.*

13. Thee is no history of the exegesis of Prov. 8:22, but the following works discuss the subject in connection with the Arian controversy: M. Simonetti, *Studi sull'Arianesimo;* and T. E. Pollard, "The Exegesis of Scripture and The Arian Controversy."

place he speaks of Christ as the beginning of a new creation. In the latter passage Justin takes Noah to be a figure of Christ, and the eight members of his family are said to symbolize the eighth day on which Christ appeared when he rose from the dead "always the first in power. For Christ, who is the firstborn of all creation, became again the beginning of another race which was born anew [ἀναγεννηθέντος] by him through water and faith and wood." [14] Justin interprets firstborn to mean that Christ is the beginning of the rebirth or new creation of mankind. Firstborn of creation refers to the new creation, not the creation of all things at the beginning of time.

During the same period, however, other writers take *prototokos* in the other sense, namely to refer to the generation of the son from the father. For example, Tatian, in a passage discussing the creation of the world, says that the Logos is the "first begotten work of the father." [15] Writing somewhat later, Origen is not wholly clear on the matter. He uses the term *prototokos* to refer to the creation of the world and to the Logos as the first of the created order. "Even if the son of God, 'the first born of all creation,' seems to have become man recently, yet he is not in fact new on that account. For the divine Scriptures know that he is the oldest of all created beings [Τῶν δημιουργημάτων], and that it was to him God said of the creation of man: 'Let us make man in our image and likeness.'" [16] But Origen is not wholly consistent and elsewhere he seems to incline to the other sense.[17] He says that Christ is "uncreated and firstborn of all created nature." As yet there had been no systematic discussion of the meaning of *prototokos,* and its sense varies not only from author to author but within the writings of certain authors. It was not until the fourth century that it became a point of dispute and received fuller attention from the fathers.

From fragments of the works of Marcellus of Ancyra we get a glimpse of the problem raised by the term as well as the direction the history of interpretation will take among Nicene authors. In a work published in 335 A.D., Asterius the Sophist had

14. *Dial. Trypho* 84.2; 138.2.   15. *Oration to the Greeks* 5.
16. *Contra Celsum* 5.37; see Hockel, *Christus*, p. 51.
17. *Contra Celsum* 6.17.

argued that the "son is one among others, for he is the first of things begotten, and one among intellectual natures." Christ is one of the "powers created by the father" and among these powers he is the "firstborn and only begotten." [18] The statement of Asterius is of course very similar to that of Origen cited above.[19] But Asterius has refined the point further and emphasized that "firstborn" and "only begotten" really mean the same thing. This point became the focus of debate, for by equating firstborn and only begotten the Arians seemed to have a foolproof argument against the Nicene party.

Marcellus of Ancyra joins the issue precisely at this point. He attempts to distinguish firstborn and only begotten, for in his opinion they refer respectively to two different creations: the creation of all things at the beginning of time and the new creation or second creation which came through Jesus Christ. The term *prototokos* does not refer to the begetting of the son by the father but to the incarnation of the son and the new creation.

"The most holy word is not called *prototokos* of all creation before the incarnation . . . but the first 'new man' in whom God wished to recapitulate all things, and thus he is called the first-born." [20] προτότοκος and μονογενής are quite different in meaning, says Marcellus; the first applies to the economy but not to the begetting, for what is eternal cannot be the firstborn of created things.[21] Thus firstborn should be taken in the sense of "firstborn from the dead" and refer to the new creation. In this sense, "create" can be used when one speaks about that which was pre-existent according to the new creation.[22]

From Marcellus we have only fragments, but in Athanasius' major dogmatic work against the Arians there is much fuller discussion of the problem, and it is here that we can see the tradition which forms the starting point for Cyril. Athanasius

18. Cited in Athanasius *De synodis* 18–19.

19. This raises the interesting question of Origen's connection with Arianism. There has been no thoroughgoing study of the scriptural exegesis of the controversy, and it may be that on examination this material would throw new light on an old problem.

20. Marcellus, *Frag.* 6 (*GCS* 14. *Eusebius Werke,* ed. Klostermann, 4:186).

21. Frag. 4 (Ibid.).   22. Frag. 7 (Ibid.).

discusses the problem in a number of places. In the *Second Discourse* he takes up the meaning of the word "create" and shows that in the Scriptures "create" not only means the creation of things at the beginning of time, but is also used to speak of the re-creation or renovation of man. "Created" does not simply denote the essence and mode of generation. David shows this in the Psalms (102:18): "This shall be written for another generation, and the people that is created shall praise the Lord," and elsewhere: "Create in me a clean heart, O God" (Ps. 51:10). "David," says Athanasius, "neither spoke of any people created in essence, nor prayed to have another heart than that he had, but meant renovation according to God and renewal." He also cites Ephesians 2:15 and 4:22, passages speaking of the creation of a "new man." [23]

Later in the same discourse Athanasius turns specifically to Colossians 1:15 and Proverbs 8:22 and shows how his earlier distinction applies to this particular exegetical problem. We must see these texts as applying to the new creation in Christ, for they speak not of his generation from the father but of his redemptive work when he became the first to rise from the dead and the beginning of the way of renewal. "He is said to be 'firstborn from the dead, not that he died before us, for we had died first; but because having undergone death for us and abolished it, he was the first to rise as man, for our sakes raising his own body. Henceforth, after he rose we also rise from the dead in due course with him and because of him." Therefore the term "firstborn of creation" does not mean that he was the first creature to be made but it refers to the "condescension" (συγκατάβασις) by which he became a brother of many. "The term 'only begotten' is used where there are no brethren," i.e. to his unique place as son of God, but "'firstborn' is used because he has brothers." Consequently we do not read in the Scriptures that he is "the firstborn of God." [24]

After presenting further scriptural evidence, Athanasius turns to Proverbs 8:22. His point is much the same, but now he elaborates what is meant by the term "beginning of his ways." This

23. *Oratio contra Arianos* 2.46.   24. Ibid., 2.61.

means that there is now a new way open to mankind. "For when the first way, which was through Adam, was lost and in places of paradise we deviated unto death, and heard the words, 'dust you are and unto dust you shall return,' therefore the Word of God who loves man puts on him created flesh at the father's will that whereas the first man had made it dead through transgression, he himself might make it alive in the blood of his own body and might open 'for us a way new and living' as the apostle says 'through the veil, that is to say, his flesh'; which he signifies elsewhere thus, 'Therefore, if any man is in Christ, he is a new creation.' But if a new creation has come to pass someone must be the first of this creation. . . . Therefore . . . none other than the Lord, the 'beginning' of the new creation is created as 'the way' and rightly says, 'The Lord created me a beginning of ways for his works,' that man might walk no longer according to that first creation, but there being as it were a beginning of a new creation." [25]

A similar argument can also be found in Eusebius, Didymus, and Gregory of Nyssa, to mention only three instances.[26] I discuss only Gregory of Nyssa. In his *Contra Eunomium* Gregory was faced with the Arian exegesis of "firstborn of all creation." Gregory points out that the term is used four times in the Scriptures and each time it is qualified in a different fashion: "firstborn of all creation" (Col. 1:15), "firstborn of many brothers" (Rom. 8:26), "firstborn from the dead" (Col. 1:8–9), and simply "firstborn" (Heb. 1:6).[27] We must distinguish these various uses, says Gregory, and in particular we should note the difference between the only son and the firstborn, the first creation and the

25. Ibid., 2.65.
26. See Eusebius *De ecclesiastica theologica* 3.2.11–12; Didymus, *In 2 Cor.* 5:17 (Staab, *Pauluskommentare*, p. 29). Both Eusebius and Didymus point out that the term "create" is used in different senses and does not simply mean the process of bringing things into existence; both cite Ps. 51, "Create in me a new heart," in this connection. Apollinaris also speaks of new creation. "Whoever is in Christ is a new creation; what is the new creation if it is not that he has led us to heaven?" *De fide* (Hans Lietzmann, *Apollinaris*, p. 193, 19).
27. *Contra Eunomium* 3.2.45 (Jaeger and Langerbeck, 2:67).

new creation, and John 1:1 and John 1:14. For example "he became the firstborn from the dead since he was the first to destroy
through himself the pains of death that he might prepare the way
for the offspring of the resurrection." He is the "firstborn of
many brothers because of the rebirth in the waters of baptism."
"We know of a double creation of our nature," says Gregory,
"the first in which we were made and the second in which we
were remade. There would have been no need of a second creation of us, if we had not rendered the first useless by disobedience."[28]

In answer to the Arian exegesis Gregory argues that it is true
that the one who created man is the same one who now becomes
the firstborn of those being re-created. "Then taking dust from
the earth he made man and now again taking dust from the
virgin he made not simply man, but himself with him. Then he
created, now he is created with them; then the word was made
flesh, now he becomes flesh with these things. . . . On account of
the new creation in Christ . . . he is called firstborn, becoming
the firstfruits of all things . . . that not according to the existence
before eternity is firstborn fitting for the son; the words 'only
son' testify to this, for the one who is truly the only son has no
brothers."[29] In Gregory as in Athanasius we not only find a
refutation of the Arian argument, but the beginnings of a positive
statement of a theology of new creation.

Cyril is very much part of the tradition of Athanasius, Gregory,
and other fourth century writers who sought to meet the Arian
exegesis of *prototokos* and Proverbs 8. He rephrases and reiterates
the arguments of his predecessors. In the *Thesaurus* for example
he states the Arian argument that the son is a creature because he
is called the "firstborn of all creation." Cyril replies that the two
terms "firstborn" and "only son" must be distinguished, for the
one refers to the son in his relationship to the father, the other
to the son in his relationship to mankind. Firstborn is appropriate
for the son only insofar as he was incarnate and became man.[30]
The scriptural arguments are quite similar to Athanasius', as is

28. Ibid., 3.2.50 (2:68–69).   29. Ibid., 3.2.52–5 (2:69–70).
30. *PG* 75:401–13; 860–929; see Hockel, *Christus*, pp. 65–68; G. M. de
Durand, *Cyrille d'Alexandrie. Deux Dialogues christologiques*, p. 223, n. 1.

the emphasis on Christ as the beginner of a new creation and a new way. "He is called *prototokos* from the dead because he was the first to raise his own flesh to incorruptibility and to bring it into heaven." [31] On the term "create" Cyril repeats the earlier argument that its meaning is univocal in the Scriptures as can be seen from Psalms 102:19 and 15:12, and elsewhere. To say that Christ is "created" does not mean that he is made in the fashion of a creature, but that he is the beginning of a new way.[32] The son became man that he "might open a way for us, new and fresh, re-forming the body to incorruption." [33]

Cyril also appeals to 2 Corinthians 5:17 to support his interpretation of Proverbs 8:22 and *prototokos*. In the *Thesaurus* he argues that the phrase "created" does not refer to the "being of the Logos," but that it applies to the "time of his coming." For he came and "restored human nature to what it was at the beginning and presented to himself the church not having spot or wrinkle or any of these things, but holy and blameless. For we have become in him a new creation, no longer bearing the imperfections which came through the transgression, but permanently receiving perfection because of the obedience of Christ and the resurrection of the dead. Since he became man because of these things one might rightly say, 'The Lord created me the beginning of his ways.' " [34] A similar argument occurs in the *Dialogue* on the Trinity. Cyril distinguishes between *prototokos* and μονογενής, because the latter refers to his "begetting from above," whereas the former refers to the "loosing of the bonds of death and the bringing of a birth to life for the first time." As "firstborn of the dead" he is the "first who has arisen, opening the gates of death; and he is the 'firstborn of all creation,' since he is the first to be born in the new creation, which when he was born he renewed." About this St. Paul wrote, "If anyone is in Christ he is a new creation, the old things have passed away, all things have become new." [35]

Cyril's approach to the Arian exegesis is therefore beholden to the tradition he received from Athanasius and others. He takes a traditional approach and distinguishes two "creations," the one

31. *PG* 75:405b.   32. *PG* 75:264c-d.   33. *PG* 75:280b-c.
34. *PG* 75:284a.   35. *PG* 75:1160c-d.

at the beginning of time and which does not include the son, and a second creation, the new creation, which comes about through the redemptive work of the son. In his argument he relies on the familiar passage from 2 Corinthians 5:17. Cyril, however, has much more to say about new creation than appears in these works on the Trinity. At one point in his argument he injects a uniquely Cyrillian sentence. He says, commenting on Christ as the beginning of the new way, "In Christ the evangelical life shone forth for the first time." [36] He does not develop this idea in the works on the Trinity, but it is clear that the conception of Christ as the new beginning does not have reference solely to the Trinitarian problem raised by the Arians.

Athanasius uses 2 Corinthians 5:17 in only three places. As we have seen he cites it once in connection with his interpretation of Proverbs 8. The other two instances are really citations of the next part of the verse "all things are from God" and have nothing to do with new creation. In Cyril the text is cited frequently, as we have already seen, and it serves to do a much bigger job in Cyril's thought. A good example is his exegesis of John 13:34. The text reads: "A new commandment I give to you, that you love one another; even as I have loved you, that you also love one another." Cyril comments, "Blessed Paul is surely correct and speaks truly when he writes: 'Therefore if any one is in Christ he is a new creation; the old has passed away, behold the new has come.' For Christ renews us [ανακαινίζει] and refashions us [ἀναπλαττει] to a newness of life which was untrodden and unknown to others who were devoted to a way of life according to the law and persist in the precepts of Moses." [37] Here Cyril sets up his familiar contrast between Christianity and Judaism. Christianity brought a new way of life which had never been practiced before by men; a way of life quite different from that initiated by Moses. It is genuinely new for it has never been tried before. The road has not yet been traveled. Thus it is appropriate to call it a new creation.

Why was a new way required? "The law makes nothing

36. *PG* 75:264c–d.
37. Besides the passage cited above, n. 25, see *Ad Afros* 5 (*PG* 26:1037b); *De decret.* 19 (*PG* 25:449a).

perfect" and the law was not able to achieve the "measure of piety" which the Savior urged, for "except your righteousness exceed that of the Scribes and Pharisees you shall not enter the Kingdom of Heaven." This means, says Cyril, that we must go beyond the Jewish way of life. To be sure, the law given by Moses had value, for it brought us an "imperfect knowledge of the good," and served as a tutor for the "evangelical way of life [πολιτεία]." But it only gave us a dim outline, and to it must be added the "beauty of the evangelical teaching." For this reason Christ gave us a *new* commandment which was "better than the ancient one," a commandment which is "superior to the Mosaic law." In the old way men knew God only partially through shadows and types, but now they know him fully and practice a "true piety," a worship in spirit and in truth.[38]

In Cyril, then, the idea of new creation does not have its *Sitz im Leben* solely in the Trinitarian discussions concerning the creation of the son. He has taken the developing theology of new creation, worked out in answer to the Arians, and given it a much wider setting. In his interpretation of John 13:34 he employs it in connection with the problem of Christianity and Judaism. Thus the new creation about which Paul speaks is equivalent to the "new covenant" which the prophet Jeremiah promised. Commenting on Isaiah 42:9, "Behold the former things have come to pass, and new things I now declare," Cyril says that this text should be read in the light of Jeremiah 31:31: "Behold the days are coming, says the Lord, when I will make a *new* covenant with the house of Israel and the house of Judah, not like the covenant which I made with their fathers." "The divine Moses," writes Cyril, "was a minister of types and shadows. . . . Christ as son and Lord became the administrator of a new covenant." The term "new" refers to the distinction between the two covenants. "I say new for it [the covenant] is remaking [ἀναμορ-φούσης] man to newness of holy life and through the evangelical

38. *In Jo.* 13:34 (P 2:384). See also *PG* 69:340c: "The synagogue of the Jews grew old and shriveled; the new people in faith have sprung up instead. Rejoicing about this let David sing 'the people he creates will praise the Lord' for all things in Christ are a new creation."

way of life he is esteemed and appears as a true worshiper. For
it is written that God is a spirit and must be worshiped in
spirit and in truth." [39]

In his exegesis of Isaiah 42:9–10 and John 13:34 Cyril carries
out the parallelism we have noticed elsewhere. On the one hand
there is Moses. Moses = law = imperfection = partial knowledge
= inferiority to Christ = incapability of conquering death =
minister of death = reign of Adam. On the other hand there is
Christ. Christ = new covenant = renewal of the old = evangelical life = true worshiper = life = victory over death = second
Adam. Without exaggeration, we can say that all of these themes
are packed into Cyril's interpretation of 2 Corinthians 5. To say
that in Christ there is a new creation summarizes everything that
Cyril wishes to say about Christianity and Judaism, the old covenant and the new, the relationship of Christ to the old, the unique
place of Christ in the economy of salvation. The prophet Isaiah
exhorts us to "sing a new song." This is surely fitting, for only
such a "new hymn is suitable to the newness of things. For if
anyone is in Christ he is a new creation as it is written and the
old things have passed away and all things have become new."
To be sure we should admire the things which took place of old;
deliverance from the tyranny of Egypt, from hard labor, deliverance through the Red Sea, manna in the desert, water from the
rock, passage through the Jordan, and entrance into the promised
land. "But the things that happened to us are new and far better
than the ancient things. We are freed not from physical, but from
spiritual slavery . . . we do not flee the slave drivers of Egypt
. . . but rather we flee the evil and unclean demons which compel
us to sin and the one who stands behind this mob, Satan. . . .
We eat the spiritual manna, the bread from heaven which gives
life to the world. We drink water from the rock, reveling in the
spiritual streams from Christ. We passed through the Jordan
being made worthy by holy baptism." Thus, says Cyril, "there
must be a new song for the new accomplishments." [40] We no

---

39. *In Is.* 42:9–10 (*PG* 70:857b–860a). See also *In Is.* 43:7–8 (*PG* 70:892a).

40. *In Is.* 42:10 (*PG* 70:860b–861c). At times Cyril emphasizes that it is the same God who did wonders of old who does such wondrous new

longer speak of the land of Jordan but of the ends of the earth
and everything under heaven. The old was confined to Israel but
now his glory fills all the earth.

This passage captures the spirit of Cyril's view of new creation.
A new age has dawned, a new beginning for mankind. The old
was found wanting and now mankind has found a new way.
"Therefore in the beginning of the year and in the first month
the mystery of Christ shone forth. A new age for us, the time of
the coming of our Savior, changing everything for the better, indeed transforming into newness of creation what is growing old
and infirm and disappearing. For 'The things in Christ are a
new creation, the old has passed away, behold all things have become new.' We live not in Mosaic fashion, but rather brought
into the evangelical way of life, Christ refashioning us anew
through the Holy Spirit." [41]

We have had occasion throughout this book to look at a great
number of different passages where Cyril employs the text from
2 Corinthians 5:17 and the idea of new creation. If we leave out
texts which Cyril cites infrequently and single out the more
important ones we can see a decided pattern to his thinking. The
Pauline notion of "new creation" provides the key exegetical and
theological support for Cyril's interpretation of the following
texts: John 4:24, "worship in spirit and in truth"; Matthew 5:17,
"I come not to abolish . . . but to fulfil." The new covenant is
a transformation of the old. Jeremiah 31:31–34, a new covenant
with Israel. John 5:46, "If you believed Moses, you would believe
me." Moses as a minister of shadows pointing to the new covenant in Christ. Colossians 1:15, Proverbs 8:22, Christ is said to
be "created" because he is the beginning of a new way. 1 Corin-

---

things. "He [God] promises that if they [the people of Israel] thirst while
walking through the desert, he will bring them water from a rock. The
rock will be cleft, water will flow, and my people will drink. And we say
that he shows in these things that it was not another God who freed Israel
from the stupidity of the Egyptians and led her through the middle of the
sea, and gave nourishment in the desert, and brought out water from the
rock. But it is this same one who always is able in the same way and in
like fashion to do wonders equal to what he did of old." *In Is.* 48:20–22
(*PG* 70:1033a–b).

41. *Ador.* 17 (*PG* 68:1068a).

thians 15 and Romans 5, Christ is the second Adam who re-creates and renews fallen human nature by the resurrection from the dead.

For Cyril, then, new creation can mean many things, and it serves to interpret numerous exegetical and theological situations. He even uses 2 Corinthians 5:17 in connection with the interpretation of Micah 4:3–4, "They shall beat their swords into plowshares, and their spears into pruning hooks; nation shall not lift up sword against nation, neither shall they learn war any more." The new creation in Christ foreshadows the end of war. "All things have become new in Christ, and Paul speaks truly when he says that 'in Christ there is a new creation and the former things have passed away.' For they will be transformed into what is better and there will be a new order of things when there will no longer be wars and fighting . . . and the things of war will be transformed into the business of tilling the earth." [42]

The central fact which supports and illuminates all these various senses of new creation is the resurrection of Christ. In the last analysis new creation finally means the rebirth to new life and the beginning of a new way through the resurrection. For this very reason new creation appears most regularly in connection with the typology of the second Adam. For the distinctive work of the second Adam is to conquer death and in conquering death he is the beginning of the new creation.[43] Cyril's most lyrical statement of the centrality of the resurrection is to be found in his *Paschal Homilies.* Cyril wrote one each year to announce the date of Easter, and frequently drew a lovely parallel between the new life of spring and the resurrection of Christ: It is springtime. The earth is bursting with new life, the gloom of winter is gone, bright rays of sun break forth, lighting up mountain and forest, wood and glades. Fields are crowned with flowers. The shepherd rejoices, blowing his flute as he leads his flock to freshly sprouting grass. The grapevines shoot forth new sprouts like tiny fingers reaching for the sun. The meadows are resplendent with color which gladdens the husbandman. "However, it would be nothing to praise spring for these things alone, for what makes

42. *In Micah* 4:3–4 (P 1:662).
43. *In Amos* 11:11–12 (P 1:541); *In Abac.* 3:2 (P 2:125–6).

spring more worthwhile than any other season is this: along with nature, the nature of the one who rules over all things, I mean man, is raised up. For springtime brings us the resurrection of our Savior, through whom all are reformed to newness of life, fleeing the alien corruption of death. . . . In this time of his love for us, when he became man on account of us, he reformed the whole nature in himself to newness of life, and transformed it to what it was from the beginning." [44]

This lovely description of spring is one of the most beautiful passages in Cyril's writings. Indeed it is a refreshing change from much of the monotony and repetition. Nevertheless, the same ideas are expressed here that we have observed elsewhere and the vocabulary is quite similar. He uses, for example, a number of his favorite terms: ἀνακαινίζω, ἀναμορφόω, ἀναστοιχειόω. But what is different here is the self-conscious mingling of the description of the earth coming to life in spring and Christ coming to life in the resurrection. In another place where he presents a similar description of spring he even admits that his comments are modeled on "certain of the Greek poets." [45]

44. PH 9 (*PG* 77:581a–d). See Hugo Rahner, "Oesterliche Fruehlingslyrik bei Kyrillos von Alexandreia," pp. 68–75.

45. *In Jo.* 6:68 (P 1:567, 3–4). For spring in classical poetry see Wilhelm James, *The Cruelest Month.* In "The Vigil of Venus," a Latin poem of the second or third century, there is this description of spring: "Spring is new, the spring of bird-song; in the spring our earth was born." "She herself with jeweled flowers paints the purpling year; with the breath of western wind, swell trembling bosoms, into blossoming buds; she sprinkles the sparkling dewdrops, those glistening water left by the winds of night" (pp. 2–3). In another poem, "It was now the beginning of the spring, the snow was gone, the earth uncovered, and all was green, when the other shepherds drove out their flocks to pasture" (p. 49).
James notes that with the coming of Christianity "the history of the spring song becomes the history of the Easter hymn" (p. 60). Spring and Easter merge. See, for example, Prudentius: "The bird, the messenger of dawn, sings out the light is near, and Christ, the rouser of our minds, now calls us back to life." Spring is a sign of renewal in Christ. "Christ's passion and resurrection took place in spring, and this miracle was imposed over the more obvious empirical fact that trees were leafing again and birds were singing." "Spring qua spring is nothing; spring qua Easter is everything and there is only one word to express its miraculous effect upon the soul: gaudium" (p. 75).

In another paschal homily he develops this further: "The gloomy threat of winter has ended, the bad weather and darkness is past, gone for us are the rains and the rage of savage winds. Days of springtime have come upon us. They awaken the vine-dresser from his stupor and unreadiness, and the farmer as well, calling out that it is now time to go to work. The meadows sprout again with all kinds of blooms. On the mountains and in the gardens plants bring to life their sprouts as though in birth pains, and they generate from their loins the power of their own nature. Young shoots come out, a reminder of the philanthropy of God, as it is said; he gives fodder to the beasts." Cyril then explains that he is not speaking this way without reason. There is good reason to celebrate this "month of new things," for it is the time of the coming of the Savior. Winter is the time of the devil's reign and spring is the time of the giving of the Spirit and the blooming of the firstfruits of the Spirit. Finally he brings his praise of spring into relationship with redemption. "We have cast off the oldness of the former life, the leaf of old, and we are renewed again to another, a way of life [πολιτεία] freshly sprouted and new born. As Paul said 'if anyone is in Christ he is a new creation.'"[46]

In connection with this description of spring Cyril cites Song of Solomon 2:10–12: "My beloved speaks and says to me: Arise, my love, my fair one, and come away; for lo, the winter is past, the rain is over and gone. The flowers appear on the earth, the time of singing has come, and the voice of the turtledove is heard in our land." This text was traditionally taken to be a reference to Christ. Origen, for example, thought it referred to the coming of the Word of God. However, Origen took the mention of winter not in terms of the contrast between the old and new covenants, but as a reference to the personal history of the individual soul. "The soul is not made one with the Word of God and joined to Him, until such time as all the winter of her personal disorders and the storm of her vices has passed; so that she no longer vacillates. . . . When . . . all these things have gone out of the soul, and the tempest of desires has fled from here,

46. *PH* 2 (*PG* 77:429c–432c).

then the flowers of the virtues can begin to burgeon in her." [47]

Cyril differs in two respects. He reads the text, not in the light of the individual soul, but in the light of the history of salvation and the place of Jesus' resurrection in the total dispensation. Secondly, he links the mention of "spring" to the newness which comes through the renewal of new life through the resurrection of Jesus. Thus in the *Commentary on Isaiah* 52:7, Cyril interprets the LXX reading "spring upon the mountains" as follows: He first cites Song of Solomon 2:10–12 and goes on to say: "When the only son appeared with flesh he became to us as spring upon the mountains. . . . In him we bloom again [ἀνεθάλλομεν] and are filled with spiritual fruitfulness." [48] In *Paschal Homily* 13 he also cites Isaiah 52:7 and Song of Solomon 2, concluding that "Through the son we all bloom again to incorruption and life." In winter the trees are frozen and lifeless, the leaves and fruit are gone. Then comes spring. Bright rays from the sun warm all things on earth; the stiff branches become pliable, fresh green sprouts shoot from the earth and the trees blossom, "for Jesus Christ has come to us like spring on the mountains." Spring is more fitting for the Pasch than any other season "for in spring the power of the victory of Christ is written as in a picture." Spring comes with warm sunshine, the forest and mountains are beautiful again, the plains are covered with fresh grass, lilies adorn the meadows, bees and birds fly in the sky, lambs leap about and play, the vine-dresser readies his knife. Christ is the new sun, and the Christian is the "new tree who finds life in the resurrection." [49]

The Pauline idea of new creation is a leit-motif running throughout all of Cyril's writings. With the typology of the second Adam it provides a constant point of reference for his exegesis and theology and gives his work an amazing degree of unity and consistence. Type and truth, life according to the law

47. Origen, *In Cant.* 2:10–12 (*GCS*, 33:224); trans. R. P. Lawson. *Origen, The Song of Songs* (London, 1957), p. 240.

48. *In Is.* 52:7 (*PG* 70:1153c).

49. *PH* 13 (*PG* 77:696b); *PH* 16 (*PG* 77:752a–753d). See also *In Jo.* 6:68 (*P* 1:566–69), for spring and resurrection, Song of Sol. 2:10–12.

and life according to the gospel, worship in the law and worship
in spirit and in truth, Moses and Christ, winter and spring, death
and life, old and new—all fall within the overarching framework
provided by the idea of new creation. The resurrection of Christ
holds all this together and provides at once the basis for the
new creation and the first instance of one who has begun to
travel on a new way. Christ, the new man, did not remain in
death as did other men, but rose up, innovating [καινοτομῶν] for
human nature the new way of the resurrection from the dead.
As Paul testifies: "In Adam all die, so also in Christ shall all
be made alive." In Christ "human nature has a second beginning,
reformed to newness of life . . . for 'if anyone is in Christ he
is a new creation.' " [50]

50. *PH* 29 (*PG* 77:968a); *In Jo.* 7:39 (P 1:694). See also *PH* 28 (*PG*
77:956d).

9 The New Man

Hitherto I have concentrated on exegetical motifs from Cyril's works, using them to analyze some of the general characteristics of his biblical theology, especially as it was formed by the polemical situation vis-à-vis Judaism. I now wish to show how these motifs, specifically the typology of the second Adam and new creation, find expression in his thinking about Christ. In the final chapter I shall turn to the controversy with Nestorius to see how the exegetical materials shape Cyril's approach to the polemical situation.

The chief question raised by the discussion thus far can be stated as follows: What is it that makes Christ different from other men so that he is the second Adam and the beginning of a new creation? Christ is the second Adam and unique among men, says Cyril, because he was "superior to and more powerful than every sin and hindrance in the world." [1] From Adam to Moses and from Moses to Christ no man had appeared who was able to withstand the forces that assaulted mankind. All men were subject to the power of death and led mankind further on the way to death. Christ "put to naught the curse on us . . . that he might become the second Adam, not of the earth but from heaven, and might be the beginning of all good to human nature. . . . For one Lamb died for all, saving the whole flock on earth for God the father, one for all that he might subject all to God. . . . For since we were in many sins, and therefore indebted to death and corruption, the father has given the son as redemption for us, one for all, since all are in him, and he is *superior* to all." [2] According to Cyril the superiority of

1. *In Jo.* 16:33 (P 2:657,2–3).
2. *In Jo.* 1:29 (P 1:170). Cyril links the Adam typology to the imagery of a "spotless lamb." Elsewhere he speaks of the "blameless sacrifice" which is superior to other sacrifices, just as the second Adam is superior to other men. See *In Jo.* 17:2 (P 2:663, 15–20); *In Jo.* 17:9 (P 2:688–89); for Adam and "spotless lamb," see *Ador.* 16 (PG 68:1009a); also *Glaph. Ex.* 2 (PG

Christ over other men lies in his victory over death. He was the
first man to rise from the dead. The uniqueness of Christ lies in
his unique accomplishment.[3] This may seem rather obvious, but
the matter is hardly that simple. Most interpreters of the
Christology of the fathers argue that the fathers subordinate the
work of Christ to his *person*. What is thought to be truly
significant about Christ is that he is God and man and that in
his person God and man are united; because the only son became
man he is a mediator between God and man through the
unique makeup of his person. Adolf von Harnack, summarizing
the Alexandrian theology wrote: "Athanasius . . . subordinated
everything to this thought, namely, that Christ promised to
bring men into fellowship with God—and recognized in redemption a communication of the divine nature." "He reduced the
entire historical account given of Christ to the belief that the
Redeemer shared in the nature and unity of the Godhead itself."
This interpretation of the Alexandrian Christology has gained
wide currency. Jacques Liébaert, for example, discussing the
"goal of the Incarnation," argues that in Cyril's view the son
became incarnate in order to be a mediator between God and
man. The son could not be a mediator between God and man if
he was not at once God and man. "If the word Incarnate
reconciles humanity and divinity, it is because he is fully in the
human condition and because he possesses divinity by nature."[4]
In support of this interpretation he cites passages such as the
following:

> For as he is closely related to the father, and through the
> sameness of their nature the Father is closely related to him;
> so also are we to him and he to us, insofar as he was made

69:417–36), where 2 Cor. 5:17 is cited (*PG* 69:421a). The imagery of
sacrifice, priesthood, lamb, etc. would prove to be a profitable study, especially in the light of the prominence of the book of Hebrews in the Christological controversies. For the imagery of the lamb in the fathers, see Franz
Nikolasch, *Das Lamm als Christussymbol in den Schriften der Vaeter.*

3. Adolf von Harnack, *History of Dogma*, 4:45; also 4:171, 179–80, for
Cyril.

4. Jacques Liébaert, *La Doctrine christologique de Saint Cyrille d'Alexandrie avant la querelle nestorienne,* p. 221.

man. And through him as through a mediator [μεσίτου]
we are joined with the Father. For Christ is a sort of link
[μεθόριον] connecting the supreme godhead with manhood,
being both in the same one [ἐν ταύτῳ], and as it were combining in himself these things which are so different; on
the one hand he is, being God by nature, joined to God
and Father, and on the other, he is in truth man joined
with men.[5]

His analysis of the purpose of the incarnation leads him to
the following conclusion: "It is because he [Christ] united in
himself 'humanity' and 'divinity' [human condition and divine
condition] that he reconciles divinity and humanity [God and
men.] According to St. Cyril, *redemption* is thus rigorously
subordinated to the mediation of Christ and that by his incarnation." [6]
Liébaert is surely correct in calling attention to the importance
of the idea of mediation in Cyril's view of Christ. As a follower
of Athanasius, Cyril regularly refers to the role of Christ as
mediator between God and man and develops this idea in his
exegetical and theological works. The point of Liébaert's observations, however, is to show that by using the idea of mediation
Cyril subordinates the various actions in Christ's life to the one
central fact, namely the incarnation. The son became man so
that by joining divinity to humanity he might join humanity
to divinity. Does Cyril really conceive of the incarnation and
the person of Christ in such static terms? Seldom does he speak
of the incarnation of Christ without making reference to the
passion and resurrection as the culmination of the incarnation.
The newness in Christ is a result of the resurrection. "The
resurrection . . . must of necessity follow death . . . In Christ
we have a new age, for whatever is in him is a new creation."
Cyril is commenting here on the building of the tabernacle and
the words of Jahweh to Moses, "On the first day of the first
month at new moon you shall erect the tabernacle." The new
moon signifies the "new age" begun in Christ and the "first

5. *In Jo.* 10:15 (P 1:232, 24–233,3); *Thes.* 14 (*PG* 75:241d).
6. Liébaert, *La Doctrine de Cyrille,* p. 229.

month signifies the renewal of human nature from death and
decay to life and incorruption . . . the time of its passing at
length from barrenness to fruitfulness . . . like the winter now
passed away and come to its close." [7] Resurrection is not an isolated
event in the life of Jesus but part of the whole pattern of events
including suffering and death. Resurrection follows on suffering.
"For the saving passion of Christ is the first means that ever
brought release from death, and the resurrection of Christ has
become to the saints the beginning of their good courage in
meeting it." [8] Here Cyril links suffering and resurrection as the
means by which Christ has won release from death for mankind.
This was the "first means" by which victory over death was
accomplished. Until the time of Christ mankind was incapable
of overcoming death. "Our natural life failed up to this time to
crush the power of death and had not even destroyed the terror
that it casts over our souls." [9] Christ therefore came among man
"to prepare the way through himself and in himself for human
nature to escape from death and return to its original incorruption." [10]

These statements of Cyril give a large place to the passion of
Christ. The passion is closely tied to the resurrection of Christ
and is also seen as part of the purpose of the incarnation. Christ
became man in order to suffer, die, and rise. The Alexandrian
Christology always had trouble with the suffering of Christ and
went to great pains to find a satisfactory solution to the problems
raised by Christ's suffering. Since the fathers were unwilling to
say that God could experience suffering, they were driven to find
a way of recognizing the suffering of Christ while at the same
time preserving the axiom that in himself God could not suffer.
To do so the Alexandrian theologians distinguished between
those things spoken of the son according to his nature and those
spoken according to the flesh. Cyril follows the Alexandrian
solution in the matter of Christ's suffering, just as he did on
other issues. This leads him at times to the extreme utterance:
"He suffered without suffering." [11]

But there is another side to Cyril's thinking which breaks out

7. *In Jo.* 6:68 (P 1:565).   8. *In Jo.* 13:38 (P 2:393).
9. *In Jo.* 13:36 (P 2:392).   10. *In Jo.* 17:18–19 (P 2:726).
11. *Pulch.* 31 (*ACO* 1:1,5,50,9).

of this mold; it arises out of his exegesis of the Gospels. The
Gospel of John refers to the passion of Christ in several places
as his "glory." For example, we read: "Now is the son of man
glorified" (13:31–32). These words were spoken by Jesus at
the beginning of his farewell discourses, just before his passion.
The text raised a number of difficult problems for Alexandrian
Christology. It is *never* cited by Athanasius. Furthermore any
link between *passion* and *glory* is also missing in Athanasius,
though it does appear in Didymus. Cyril could not avoid the
problem once he had determined to expound the text of the
Gospel of John. It would be stretching the point to say that he
handles the text with ease. Actually it causes him great conster-
nation, but he does make an honest try at expounding it.

Cyril points out that the text suggests that the son is crowned
with glory exceeding what he possesses as God. But this solution
is wholly unacceptable to Cyril and he rules it out: "He is not
brought to a new dignity." The text can only mean that Christ
is now glorified as man and this means something different
from being glorified as Lord from eternity. What then does the
Evangelist have in mind? The glory spoken of here is much
greater than the glory associated with the miracles and wonders
performed by Jesus.

"With a word he rebuked the angry rage of the sea and
checked the violence of the fierce winds . . . when he had
bidden Lazarus at Bethany to return once more to life, the
marvelous deed was noised abroad . . . There was a time when
he broke five loaves and two small fishes and satisfied the
hunger of the crowd." We could, says Cyril, enumerate other
deeds which also demonstrated Christ's glory, but this is not
what the Evangelist has in mind. The clear meaning must be
that his suffering itself is his glory. "The perfect fulfilment of
his glory and the fulness of his fame clearly lie in this, in his
suffering for the life of the world and making a new way
[καινοτομῆσαι] by his resurrection for the resurrection of all." [12]

12. *In Jo.* 13:31–32 (P 2:376–79); see also *In Lucam, Homily* 152; Didymus, *De trinitate* 3 (PG 39:961b); *De spir. sancto* (PG 39:1063a). In this
connection see Augustin Dupré la Tour, "La Doxa du Christ dans les oeuvres
exégétiques de saint Cyrille d'Alexandrie," and Liébaert, *La Doctrine de
Cyrille,* p. 113, n. 7.

Now there is an obvious tension in Cyril's handling of this text. He realizes that it is not sufficient, on the basis of the words of Jesus cited in John, to say that the suffering of Christ is a regrettable interlude in the divine economy. The text prohibits any facile dismissal of the passion as peripheral. It explicitly links glory to suffering. Cyril therefore concludes that it is through suffering that Christ opens the new way for mankind. For suffering leads to death and resurrection. Cyril does not try to explain the text away or subordinate it to a theological principle; rather he tries to integrate the new factor—suffering associated with glory—into his view of Christ. To do this he falls back on another biblical idea, namely new creation. Christ opens up a new way [καινοτομέω] through suffering and death.[13]

Cyril has taken a big step here because he was forced to explain the text of the Gospel of John. His exegesis of the Gospel led him to rethink certain aspects of his theology.[14] The only other places where suffering and glory are associated in Cyril also occur in comments on texts from the *Commentary on John*. In a fragment on John 12:23 Cyril faced a similar problem. The text reads: "And Jesus answered them, 'The hour has come for the Son of man to be glorified.'" Jesus says that the hour is come, writes Cyril, for "the time of his passion was near at hand." He had done everything to bring men to faith and proclaimed the coming of the kingdom and now "he desires to pass onward to the very crowning point of his hope, namely the

13. καινοτομέω is almost a technical term to designate the opening up of the new way and the beginning of the new creation. See *PH* 7.2 (*PG* 77:549d ff); Chr. Un. 772d–e; *PH* 29.2 (*PG* 77:968a).

14. In his interesting work on patristic Christology (*Der Ausgang der altkirchlichen Christologie*), Werner Elert discusses the relationship between exegesis and Christology and argues that the *Christusbild* of the Gospels had an influence on the formation of Cyril's Christology. He considers this an important difference between Cyril and Athanasius. "Die Entgegensetzung von Logoslehre und Geschichtsbild durch Harnack mag vielleicht noch auf Athanasius zutreffen, aber nicht mehr auf Kyrill. Dasz Kyrill einen 'geschichtlichen Christus' auszerhalb oder hinter den Evangelien haette suchen sollen, waere doch zuviel verlangt. Wohl aber hat er ihn as rechtschaffener Exeget in den Evangelien gesucht. Sein Christusbild ist genau so geschichtlich oder ungeschichtliche wie das des Johannesevangeliums, das er in zwoelf Buechern kommentierte" (p. 92).

destruction of death; and this could not otherwise be brought to pass, unless life underwent death for the sake of all men, that in him we all may live. For this reason he says that he is glorified in death. . . . His cross was the beginning of his being glorified upon earth." And a few pages later, commenting on John 12:28 he reiterates his point. His suffering for others "is characteristic of excessive compassion and supreme glory." [15]

These considerations suggest that the question of the "goal of the incarnation" cannot be satisfactorily answered without reference to the passion and resurrection of Christ. Christ became man that he might suffer and die and be raised to renew mankind. Suffering is not an unfortunate interlude in the life of Jesus; it is an integral part of the economy. Commenting on the transfiguration Cyril writes: "As therefore the dispensation was still at its commencement and not fulfilled, how would it have been fitting for Christ to have abandoned his love to the world, and have departed from his purpose of suffering in its behalf? For he redeemed all under heaven, by both undergoing death in the flesh, and by abolishing it by the resurrection from the dead." [16]

Cyril censures Peter because he failed to see the full significance of the incarnation; he did not see that it led to passion and death. He also reminds his readers that the Savior had to rebuke Peter when he drew his sword in the garden, for he did not understand that Christ had to suffer. This incident is similar to a previous occasion when Jesus said he was "going up to Jerusalem" and Peter did not understand the good that would come from the passion. He failed to see that "the suffering was the salvation of the world, the passion the undoing of death, and the mighty cross the overthrow of sin and corruption." [17]

15. *In Jo.* 12:23 (P 2:311); *In Jo.* 12:28 (P 2:319).

16. *In Lucam* 9:27–36, *Homily* 51 (*PG* 72:652c ff). Cyril's interpretation of the transfiguration is markedly different from Origen's. For Cyril the transfiguration points to the passion; for Origen it shows that the Logos appeared to men in different forms. (Origen, *In Matt.* 17:1, ed. Klostermann [*GCS* 40:152 ff]). See Robert Grant, *The Earliest Lives of Jesus,* p. 80.

17. *In Jo.* 8:20 (P 2:3:15–17); also *In Jo.* 18:11 (P 3:25 ff). Cf. also the following passage where Cyril discusses Mary's inability to see the true purpose of Christ's coming. Mary thought this to herself, says Cyril: "I gave

Christ then became man not simply to unite man and God in his person but for the purpose of suffering, dying, and rising from the dead. His mission would not have been complete had he not turned back the work of Adam and given mankind a new way which was not known before his coming. This new way was not opened up for mankind simply because the divine son became man, but because he broke the bonds of death by his resurrection. Cyril's interpretation of John 16:33 develops this point. Jesus is comforting the disciples with the promise of victory. "I have said this to you, that in me you may have peace. In the world you have tribulation; but be of good cheer, I have overcome the world." These words mean that Christ was "superior to sin and victorious over death." In Christ we have overcome corruption and death. "Since as man, for us and for our sakes, Christ became alive again making his own resurrection the beginning of the conquest of death, the power of his resurrection will surely extend even unto us, since he that overcame death was one of us, insomuch as he appeared as man." Death dies "first in Christ" and we then overcome death in him. Therefore, he is the *"beginning* and gate and way for the race of men. They who once were fallen and vanquished have now overcome . . . through him who conquered as one of ourselves, and for our sakes. For if he conquered as God, then it is of no profit to us; but if as man, we are conquerors as well. For he is to us the second Adam come from heaven, according to the Scripture. Just as then we have borne the image of the earthly, according to its likeness falling under the yoke of sin,

---

birth to him that is mocked upon the cross. He said that he was the true son of Almighty God, but it may be that he was deceived; he may have erred when he said 'I am the Life.' How did the crucifixion come to pass? . . . Why does he not come down from the cross, though he bade Lazarus return to life and struck all Judaea with amazement by his miracles?" Cyril comments: "The woman, probably not fully understanding the mystery, wandered astray into some such strain of thought . . . And no marvel if a woman fell into such an error when even Peter himself, the elect of the holy disciples, was once offended when Christ in plain words instructed him that he would . . . undergo crucifixion and death" (*In Jo.* 19:25 [P 3:90, 14-30]).

so likewise also shall we bear the image of the heavenly, that is
Christ, overcoming the power of sin and triumphing over all the
tribulation of the world; for Christ has overcome the world." [18]

This is an immensely important statement of the relationship
between the typology of the second Adam and Cyril's view of
Christ. He appeals to the second Adam and heavenly man to
support his argument that the resurrection of Christ is the
beginning of the new way for the race of men. However,
throughout the passage he says over and over again that Christ
is a man like us and that because he conquered as man all men
share in his victory. As man Christ conquers death, for if he
were to conquer death as God then it would be of no profit to
mankind. Both dimensions of the Adam typology appear here
at once. On the one hand he is arguing for the solidarity of
Christ as a man with all other men, but on the other hand he is
claiming that Christ as man is unlike other men and superior,
because he has come from heaven and did what no others could
do: he broke the bonds of death. The typology of the second
Adam is used to say that Christ is man, but that as man he is
not an ordinary man, but the man from heaven.

What does Cyril mean when he says that Christ conquers as
man, not as God? We can dismiss immediately the view that he
somehow divides Christ into two, claiming that the man conquered death whereas the divine son did not. Such an idea is
completely foreign to Cyril's Christology. In the Alexandrian
theology, however, there was a tradition, as we have seen, by
which certain activities of Christ were predicated of him according to the flesh and others were said to be done according to
divinity. Some things were done "humanly" and others "divinely."
Athanasius, for example, wrote that when Peter's mother-in-law
was sick Jesus "stretched out his hand humanly, but he stopped
the illness divinely. And in the case of the man blind from birth,
the spit was human . . . but he opened his eyes through the
clay divinely. In the case of Lazarus he gave forth a human
voice, as man, but divinely as God he raised Lazarus from the
dead." [19] Cyril shared this point of view. "Divinely, the son is

18. *In Jo.* 16:33 (P 2:656–57).
19. Athanasius, *Orationes Contra Arianos* 3.32 (*PG* 26:392a).

said not to suffer, and humanly he is said to suffer." [20] In this
scheme the resurrection falls in the category of things done
divinely. Christ rises from the dead as God.

It would seem, then, that Cyril contradicts what he says elsewhere. Here he says that Christ rises from the dead *as man*.
The presence of the phrase "heavenly man" is the key to understanding the passage. Cyril explicitly rejects the view that
"heavenly man" means that Christ's human nature or flesh came
from heaven.[21] However, this does not forbid him from using
the phrase "heavenly man" or "second Adam" to call attention
to the divine origin of the son. He often appeals to the second
Adam imagery when he wishes to call attention to the unique
relationship of the son to the father. We saw this, for example, in
Cyril's exegesis of the baptism of Jesus, where he used phrases
appropriate to God to designate the new character of the second
Adam as distinguished from the first. The Spirit had now
found a man in whom he could rest permanently, for this man
was pure and would not fall into sin as had the first Adam.
Now a "man was made who is the only son of God" who "became
like us," though impregnable to sin." The Spirit now came to
rest on him as the "firstfruits of the human race" in order to
remain with men for good. The return of the Spirit signifies a
new beginning for the race of men.[22]

In his study of Cyril's Christology Liébaert called attention
to Cyril's doctrine of the "two times." This idea helps us to
understand Cyril's conception of the uniqueness of the second
Adam. By speaking of "two times" Cyril means to refer to the
time of existence of the son prior to the incarnation and the
time of his existence after the incarnation. The son had an
existence before he became man, for he was with the Father, and

20. *In Lucam* 5:12 (*PG* 72:556b); *Ep.* 46 (*ACO* 1:1.6, pp. 161,7); *In Jo.*
12:24 (P 2:313,7): "It was fitting for him to taste death since he became
man; but he went up divinely, for this was his nature."

21. See for example *Ep.* 39 (*PG* 77:180a–b); *PG* 75:940a; *Apol. orient.*
11 (*ACO* 1:1,7,60, 26 ff).

22. See *In Is.* 11:2 (*PG* 70:313a–316a). Christ was not a "mere man"
and the Spirit rested on him that he "might grow accustomed" to dwelling
in mankind. See *In Is.* 11:2 (*PG* 70:313a–316a), and the section on the
baptism of Jesus in chap. 6, pp. 127 ff.

now this same son enters into a new existence as a result of the incarnation. Liébaert writes: "The Incarnation is viewed then at first not so much on a horizontal plan, from a coming together of human nature and divine nature, as on a vertical plan of a passage of the word from the pure divine condition to the divine-human condition." [23]

Such an approach allows Cyril to distinguish two different aspects of Christ, but these two aspects are conceived chronologically or historically as two successive conditions. The condition of the son is not the same after he has become man, but it is still the same son who now exists in the form of man. Thus it is possible for Cyril to explain how it is that the son can enter into the second condition without giving up the first. He continues to be the divine son, i.e. God, but now he is in a different condition. Therefore he exhibits as man the characteristic of God. In any interpretation of the son, says Cyril, we "must examine the time." By this he means that we must ask whether such and such is the "time of the incarnation," or in some cases the "time of his love." [24]

The distinction lying behind Cyril's view of the two times is the Athanasian notion of a "double scope" of the Scriptures. Cyril has however given the distinction a new shape and his reworking of the Athanasian "double scope" allows him a bit more freedom in approaching the Christological problems associated with the incarnation. For Cyril, then, the "incarnation is the passage of the Word from the pure divine condition to the human state. Remaining immutable in his nature, the Word puts himself in the human condition." [25] Therefore the son in the time of his coming cannot be understood solely in terms of his divinity, nor in terms of his humanity. He is the divine son exhibited in the form of a man.

Cyril never calls Christ the second Adam when he is referring to him prior to the incarnation. The term second Adam or heavenly man refers to the son only after the incarnation. This suggests that the Adam typology is a way of expressing the unique character of

---

23. Liébaert, *La Doctrine de Cyrille,* pp. 158 ff.
24. *Thes.* 22 (*PG* 75:396b); also *PG* 75:216b; 337d; *PH* 9 (*PG* 77:581d).
25. Liébaert, *La Doctrine de Cyrille,* p. 167.

Christ, namely that he is a man yet unlike other men. He is the son of God in the form of man. He is, in short, an exceptional man, or a new man. He is the heavenly man. The statement, then, that Christ conquers as man does not mean that "human nature" conquers death or that the man Jesus conquers death. Cyril means that the son in the condition of man conquers. Because Christ is the heavenly man and not an "ordinary man" he is able to win the victory over death. The typology of the second Adam says precisely what Cyril wishes to say: Christ is neither an ordinary man nor the divine son outside of the human condition; he is a new man.

In the chapter on Moses we saw that Cyril develops this view of Christ by contrasting him to Moses. No one from the time of Adam, Moses included, was capable of undoing the work of Adam. All the great men of Israel failed to crush the power of death. In his apologetic work against Julian he attempted to demonstrate the superiority of Christ over the great men of Greece, just as he showed his superiority over the great men of Israel. In his work against the Christians Julian had praised the great figures of ancient Greece and had compared them to Moses. Moses was far inferior to these men, said Julian. Rome, too, was blessed by great heroes, and the greatness of its kings is evident in its victory over all nations. But Christians do not honor the gods of Rome. They "adore the wood of the cross and draw its likeness on [their] housefronts. Would not any man be justified in detesting the more intelligent among you, or pitying the more foolish, who, by following you, have sunk to such depths of ruin that they have abandoned the everliving gods and have gone over to the corpse of the Jew?" [26]

Cyril's answer to this is at once a criticism of the supposed greatness of the gods and heroes of ancient Greece and Rome and an argument for the superiority of Christ over all other men. Christ came among men that he might, through enduring the cross, destroy the power of corruption which tyrannized over mankind. One man died for all so that "mankind would be delivered from the snares of death, destroy the tyranny of sin, scare off Satan, and establish spiritual worshipers." One man

26. Julian, *Against the Galilaeans,* 194d–197c (trans. W. C. Wright, 3:369).

died for all so that we should all live in holy fashion for God.[27]
You Greeks honor and revere the Gods: Zeus, Poseidon, Apollo,
Daphne, Aphrodite. But do you really intend us to keep such
gods in mind as models of virtue? You say that we follow a dead
Jew, but do your gods have immortality? How can you say that
they do when they obviously live no longer? [28] You make Christ
a reproach among the gods because he died, but if you would
only look, you would see that he died "for the purpose of
destroying death." "How could he be subject to corruption
who has given to many others the power to come to life again?
He tasted death according to the divine plan. He rose again
and struck down corruption in order to be the first among mankind to have the possibility of being able to overcome death and
corruption. For this reason he is named the firstborn of the dead
and the firstfruits of those who have fallen asleep. As blessed
Paul says 'All die in Adam, so also all come alive in Christ.' " [29]

This passage is interesting and important. The language is
similar to what we have already seen in Cyril, but the context
differs radically. Cyril is no longer polemicizing against the
Jews, but against the Greeks. He uses the reference to the second
Adam to demonstrate that Christ was superior to the heroes of
Greece and Rome. The whole structure of the Adam typology
underlies the passage. Christ is the first man to overcome death,
and for this reason he is called the firstborn, the firstfruits, and
the second Adam. Cyril uses a number of unusual terms in the
passage and they serve to show precisely how he conceives of the
uniqueness of Christ.

Cyril says that Christ was the first man "capable of" ($\beta\acute{\alpha}\sigma\iota\mu\sigma$,
$\grave{\epsilon}\nu\acute{\eta}\lambda\alpha\tau\sigma\varsigma$) conquering death, the first "to be more powerful"
($\kappa\alpha\tau\epsilon\upsilon\mu\epsilon\gamma\epsilon\theta\acute{\epsilon}\omega$) than death or corruption. In general usage
$\beta\acute{\alpha}\sigma\iota\mu\sigma\varsigma$ has the sense of fixed or stable, or the related sense of
"accessible." [30] The former sense interests us here. In Cyril
$\beta\acute{\alpha}\sigma\iota\mu\sigma\varsigma$ sometimes is used to mean "possible" or "capable of
doing something." In *In Zachariah* 8:6 Cyril discusses Sarah and

27. Cyril, *Contra Julianum* (PG 76:797a).   28. Ibid., p. 797a–c.
29. Ibid., pp. 800d–801a.
30. The terms are somewhat rare in Greek literature. Cf. Liddell-Scott-
Jones *ad loc.*

Abraham. Sarah is said to have laughed at the birth of Isaac because of her unbelief; she was old and a birth at her age seemed to be against the laws of nature. "But," writes Cyril, "she brought forth by hope, since God had made the thing possible for her." Here Cyril uses the term to refer to something which under normal circumstances would not happen, but through the power of God does happen.[31] In a similar context Cyril uses the other word from this passage εὐήλατος. Commenting on Isaiah 51:2, "Look to Abraham your father and to Sarah who bore you," Cyril notes that Sarah was old and incapable of bearing children. But with God nothing is impossible, in fact "all things are easy [λεία] and manageable [εὐήλατος]."[32] In conjunction with the term λεία, εὐήλατος signifies that something can be done without difficulty. In another place Cyril uses this same combination of words in connection with the coming of Christ who makes the way easy and straight. He is commenting on a passage from Isaiah, "I will make all my mountains a way, and my highways shall be raised up." "The Savior makes every way easy and without difficulty, so that what was difficult and overwhelming may be smooth and manageable to those who wish to undertake it."[33]

With these terms Cyril says that Christ was the first one among men who had the *capability* to overcome death. No one before him was up to the task required of mankind. This conception is complemented by another rare word used in the passage, namely κατευμεγεθέω. Its basic meaning is "I am stronger or more powerful," able to do what someone else cannot. It is not surprising then, that this is precisely the term used by Cyril in

31. *In Zach.* 8:6 (P 2:384). Cf. *Glaph.* Exod. (PG 69:388a) where βασιμός is used in connection with the difficulty of interpreting the Scriptures. Without Christ it is impossible to interpret the Scriptures.

32. *In Is.* 51:1-2 (PG 70:1105c); see also his comment on John 18:7-9. Cyril is arguing that the death of the apostles could not bring victory over death. "It was necessary . . . that the son of the living father should give over his own body to death as a ransom for the life of all . . . For the Lord is the 'firstfruits of them that are asleep, and the firstborn from the dead' and so, by his own resurrection he makes smooth [λειοτατην] the way to incorruption for those who come after him" (P 3:21).

33. *In Is.* 49:11 (PG 70:1060-61); also *In Is.* 40:3-5 (PG 77:804a-b).

the commentary on John 16:33, "I have overcome the world." Here Cyril emphasized that Christ conquered death and thereby became the first man to overcome the power of death. Christ "overcame the power of sin and became superior [κατευμεγεθοῦντες] to all the tribulations of the world, for Christ has overcome the world." [34]

Cyril's argument against Julian rests on the superiority of Christ to the heroes of Greek antiquity. Julian had accused the Christians of worshiping a dead Jew and Cyril accepts the challenge to show that Jesus is more than a dead Jew. If one compares Christ with the Greek gods one discovers that he actually showed himself superior to the most powerful force of all, namely death. He took part in the corruption which all men shared and gave himself to death so that he could strike death down. In doing this he became the *first* man who was able to conquer death and corruption. In this accomplishment lies his uniqueness, and for this reason he is called the second Adam. Christ's resurrection from the dead shows that he was capable of "striking down death, and was raised from the dead that he might be the firstfruits of those who sleep, and we might fittingly believe that he will destroy corruption and might scare off the way of death of our bodies, since he is life by nature and life-giving as God, that he might show forth to us an easy and accessible way [βάσιμον καὶ ἐνήλατον] to the things above." [35]

Christ is the first man who was able to conquer death, because he shared fully in God. A mere man such as Adam or Moses could not have overcome death, because man's natural life was incapable of breaking the hold of death. When Christ returned to the heavens above "he presented himself to God the father as the firstfruits of humanity. . . . He renewed for us a *way* of which the human race *knew nothing before* . . . since our natural life had failed as yet to crush the power of death." [36] The history of the human race since the fall of Adam is proof of

34. *In Jo.* 16:33 (P 2:657). The term is used of strength in war, e.g. one nation stronger than another; see *In Nahum* 3:4 (P 2:52); of firstborn in Egypt overcoming death, *Nest.* 4.5 (*ACO* 1:1,6,86,33); also with reference to resurrection of Christ, *Arcad.* 6(*ACO* 1:1,5,64,7).

35. *PH* 25.3 (*PG* 77:912b).   36. *In Jo.* 13:36 (P 2:392).

man's inability to meet the challenge set before it. If man was to overcome the sin and death which came from the first man, he could only do it through the power of God.

The typology of the second Adam is Cyril's way of expressing the mystery that the one who conquers death is both God and man. On the one hand Christ is like Adam in that he is *like other men* in every respect save sin; but he is *unlike* other men because he showed himself superior to death and set mankind on a wholly new course. "Christ was the first and only man on earth who did not know sin, nor was guile found in his mouth. He was established as the root and firstfruits of those being re-formed to newness of life in the Spirit and the incorruption of the body and receiving the stability of divinity . . . and transmitting it to the whole human race. For knowing this, the divine Paul said: 'As we bore the image of the earthly, we will also bear the image of the heavenly.' The image of the heavenly, i.e. Christ, is firmly set on sanctification and on the return and renewal of death and corruption to incorruption and life." [37] Christ's unique relationship to God enabled him to accomplish what no other man had done, namely win the victory over death by his resurrection.

Cyril's expression of the uniqueness of Christ takes many different forms in his writings. But he always returns to this central theme. Christ, who was "one of us," made possible what was formerly impossible. "Human nature was *incapable* of destroying death," until the coming of the son.[38] In the last paschal homily of his life he summarized the convictions which had marked his whole theological effort. "Blow the trumpet at the new on this exalted festival day." It is the festival of the new moon because of the "newness and fresh budding which is the time of the coming of our Savior, for in him the old things have passed away and all things have become new . . . and it is the beginning of a new age." [39] The homily contrasts the old worship of Israel according to the law and the new worship according to Christ, the old priesthood with the new high priest

37. *Thds.* 20 (*ACO* 1:1,1,55, 3 ff); parallel in *Inc. Unig.* 691e.
38. *Arcad.* 25 (*ACO* 1:1,5,42). Cyril uses the term ἀνέφικτον.
39. *PH* 30 (*PG* 77:969 ff).

who offers himself. The old worship was a type which gave birth
to the beauty of the truth in Christ. Now men are baptized not
with water but with the Holy Spirit. Through the law came
knowledge of sin, but through Christ comes righteousness. The
new covenant in Christ is not simply a covenant which takes
the place of the old one. It alone is the eternal covenant which
was preordained before the founding of the world. The "mystery
of Christ existed even before the law." "Since worship according
to the law—and there was none other except that through types
and shadows—was not capable of freeing men from the defile-
ments of sin . . . he became man on account of us and on our
behalf . . . and gave his own body to death that he might re-
deem those under death and corruption by his own blood." [40]
But the Jews did not recognize that Christ was different from
other men and that his death could not be compared with the
death of others.

> How can you, O Jew, be ignorant of the great and ineffable
> economy? . . . Perhaps you say that he appeared to be a
> man like us? But how can you forget the Mosaic oracles?
> It was said of him to you: 'The Lord your God will raise
> up for you a prophet like me from among you—him you
> shall heed' (Deut. 18). The birth of Immanuel was miracu-
> lous; he came from a virgin who had not experienced
> marriage. However, he was born of a woman following the
> laws of human nature, and you say you saw him as a man,
> with the form of a body. But also you see him in glory
> which is fitting to God, being crowned with supreme glory,
> fulfilling the deeds of the father. Only a nature superior to
> all things is able to bring to life those who smell of the
> corruption of death, to give light to those deprived of sight,
> and swiftness of foot to the lame. . . . But do you wish the

40. *PG* 77:977b. The phrase for "incapable" is οὐκ ἐφικτόν. Cf. the
following contrast between the old and new. Commenting on Hosea 1,
Cyril writes: "Another manner of betrothal has come to light, one that is
permanent and unshakable and much more brilliant than the first. . . . The
first was not blameless . . . for this reason there was an occasion for the
second, i.e. the new, the gift and grace in Christ not bound by time" *In Hos.*
1:8–9 (P 1:36).

maker of all things to appear to those on earth in naked
divinity? . . . Who could bear this terrible and fearful sight?
. . . Therefore, he appeared as man, putting himself at the
disposal of all, that as one from among us, going to the
same place and living among us, he might show us the path
to a God-pleasing way of life [πολιτεία] in order to free us
from the snares of Greek foolishness, and to show the way
to true spiritual worship. But the abominable malignancy
did not keep still, and the unholy beast, Satan, who subjected everything on earth to himself . . . saw himself losing
his domination over us. . . . He thought that he [Christ]
was a man like the prophets of old and nothing else [ἕτερον
οὐδέν]. He had caused the prophets to be killed by arousing
the Jews against them because of their stupidity. Therefore, he instilled in them again their perversity.

The Jews proceeded to kill Christ, says Cyril, even though they
should have known about him from their prophecies. He then
cites Psalms 68:21 and 22:19, and Isaiah 50:6, and concludes:
Christ "willingly gave his own body to death for a while, that
being raised from the dead he might destroy the power of death,
that he might set us free from the jealousy of the devil, through
whom death came to human nature, that he might forge us
anew to incorruption and everlasting life. 'For as in Adam all
died, so in Christ all will be made alive.' " [41]

Christ is like no other man, yet he is man. When men looked
at him they saw a man like other men, but they did not realize
that he was God's son. He had the form of a man, yet he was
crowned with glory fitting to God. Only such a man could undo
the power of death and free men from corruption. Even Satan
was deceived, for he believed that he was simply another man
like the prophets of old. He had caused the prophets to be killed
and he was confident that he could do the same with Christ.
But Christ willingly gave himself to death and broke through the
bonds of death to rise again to life. Through rising again he
forged men anew to an unending life. For he was the second
Adam who came from heaven.

41. *PH* 30.4 (*PG* 77:977–81).

This concludes the analysis of the exegetical basis of Cyril's theology. The typology of the second Adam and the motif of new creation are not only prominent in the polemic against Judaism and in other sections of the exegetical works, but also serve to support and inform Cyril's view of Christ. I have not entered into a discussion of the technical problems of Cyril's Christology, but have concentrated on its exegetical dimension. However, the exegetical materials have shown that there is a remarkable congruity between the classical questions of Christology and Cyril's use of the Adam typology. Cyril was seeking a way to express the conviction that Christ was at once God and man. The typology of Adam provided Cyril with a biblical category for expressing this mystery. Even more important, however, were the inferences Cyril drew from the Adam typology. If Christ was the second Adam or heavenly man, he must be different from other men, and this difference lies chiefly in the resurrection. Christ was the first and only man to "innovate" a new way for mankind, for he alone conquered death through the resurrection.

Cyril's preoccupation with the resurrection as the central fact about Christ led him, not surprisingly, to take more seriously the place of the passion in Christ's life. The Gospel of John associated "glory" with Christ's suffering, and Cyril sought to give place to this idea in his view of Christ. He had some trouble with it, but he made an attempt to integrate it into his thinking. He recognized that in the Gospels the passion, death, and resurrection of Christ are closely intertwined. Resurrection made no sense without suffering and death, and death alone was no sign of victory or life. All men from Adam to Christ had died —even great men. The passion of Christ became for Cyril the first means by which Christ opened the new way of the resurrection. Christ willingly submitted to suffering and through suffering was led to triumph. The suffering of Christ is not, however, "glorious" only because of the resurrection. The cross itself is a glorious moment, not a regrettable interlude.[42]

Harnack claimed that the Greek theologians, among whom he includes Cyril, were not able to "reconcile the Christ of faith

42. See Dupré la Tour, "La Doxa du Christ," p. 85.

with the picture of Christ given in the Gospels; for the idea of the physical unity of the two natures and of the interchange of properties, which Cyril had worked out in a strict fashion, swallowed up that of the human which remained in him." [43] By no standard does Cyril have a full picture of the humanity of Jesus. This cannot be claimed. But Cyril did not dissolve the picture of Christ in the Gospels. With the help of the second Adam he took an important step in giving a larger place to this picture of Christ in his thinking. The typology of the second Adam enabled Cyril to take seriously what Christ had *done as man*. It pointed to the unique accomplishments of Christ and gave a rationale for the universal significance of his actions. The typology of the second Adam showed that Christ could not simply be compared with other men, yet it affirmed that he was truly man. "The first was from the earth, the second from heaven, though born of a woman. . . . And though he became man, he is no less from heaven." [44] Christ was not an "ordinary man." [45] He had done an extraordinarily new thing—something only God could do. He *had* to be different if he was to win the victory over death. This Cyril expressed in the imagery of the second Adam.

43. Harnack, *History of Dogma*, 4:179.
44. *Arcad.* 124 (*ACO* 1:1,5,95, 25–28).
45. For the phrase "not an ordinary man," see chap. 10.

10 Cyril and Nestorius

Cyril was the chief representative of the Alexandrian tradition in the fifth century and the standard-bearer of the opposition to Nestorius, bishop of Constantinople and voice of the Antiochene tradition. After the years of exegetical labor Cyril sailed to the council at Ephesus to do battle for the theological tradition of his diocese. The outbreak of the controversy between Cyril and Nestorius brought Cyril's exegetical work to an end. What exegesis he did after the beginning of the conflict was devoted primarily to the polemical and theological questions raised by the dispute. Now he put the interpretation of the Bible at the service of ecclesiastical controversy. Cyril's exegesis had never been practiced solely in the study, but the temper of his earlier works differs markedly from that of the treatises against Nestorius. Now the years of study and writing were to be tested in the heat of battle. Now Cyril forgot his earlier opponents—the Jews and Arians—and zeroed in on one antagonist, Nestorius, and one issue, the unity of Christ. How does Cyril's response to Nestorius look when viewed from the perspective of his exegesis?

Nestorius was consecrated bishop of Constantinople in April, 428.[1] Cyril had already been bishop of Alexandria for sixteen years and had had relatively little contact with Constantinople. Shortly after his consecration, in a letter to Celestine, bishop of Rome, Nestorius mentioned the term *theotokos* and indicated that he preferred *christotokos* as a title for the Savior. Apparently this letter did not itself spark a controversy, but shortly afterward a certain presbyter, Anastasius by name, preached a sermon anathematizing those who called the Virgin Mary *theotokos*.[2]

1. For the events surrounding the Council of Ephesus and the controversy with Nestorius see P. Th. Camelot, *Éphèse et Chalcédoine*, pp. 13–78; Robert Sellers, *The Council of Chalcedon;* also the important article by Robert Devreesse, "Les Actes du Concile d'Éphèse." For the theological developments see Aloys Grillmeier, *Christ in Christian Tradition*, pp. 363–418.

2. See Devreesse, "Éphèse," p. 232, n.1.

Nestorius agreed with Anastasius and did not censure him. He received him at the Eucharist. Within a few months a collection of Nestorius' sermons had been made and forwarded to Cyril in Alexandria.

Cyril and Nestorius exchanged a number of letters on these matters but no settlement could be reached. As a result Cyril, encouraged by Pope Celestine, called a synod in Alexandria and there the Egyptian bishops condemned the teaching of Nestorius. Out of this synod came Cyril's third letter to Nestorius including the notorious twelve anathemas condemning Nestorius' teaching. During this period Cyril also composed a major refutation of Nestorius in five books, the *Adversus Nestorium,* and in this work he discussed the position represented in the collection of Nestorius' sermons.

Most of Nestorius' writings have been lost and the remaining fragments do not present a totally satisfying picture of his views. Recently a later work, the *Bazaar of Heraclides,* was discovered, but it comes from a much later period in Nestorius' life.[3] For a full assessment of Nestorius' thought this work is of great importance. However, our purpose here is not to study Nestorius' views but to analyze Cyril's reaction to him on the basis of his own interpretation of the sermons. Fortunately we not only possess Cyril's excerpts of Nestorius, but in one case we still have the original Greek text of one of Nestorius' sermons and this sermon is the chief subject of book three of the *Adversus Nestorium.*[4] Thus we are able to see not only what Nestorius actually

---

3. For Nestorius' works, see Friedrich Loofs, ed., *Nestoriana: Die Fragmente des Nestorius,* pp. 165–68; for the *Bazaar* see G. R. Driver and Leonard Hodgson, ed., *Nestorius: The Bazaar of Heraclides.* Also the recent study of Luise Ambramowski, *Untersuchungen zum Liber Heraclides des Nestorius.*

4. Text in Loofs, *Nestoriana,* pp. 230–42. Latin text: *Homilia in illud, Heb. 3, intueamini, etc.* trans. and ed. W. T. M. Becher, *Joannis Chrysostomi Homiliae* (Leipzig, 1839); reprinted in *PG* 59, cols. 479–492. Of the homily Loofs says: "Der Text der Predigt bei Becher zeigt nicht die geringsten dogmatischen Korrekturen, erweist sich, an den Fragmenten gemessen, ueberall als intakt. Es liegt also in dieser Predigt der einzige in der Originalsprache vollstaendig erhaltene Sermon des Nestorius vor" (p. 107). See also Sebastian Haidacher, "Rede des Nestorius ueber Hebr. 3.1, ueberliefert unter dem Namen des heiligen Chrysostomus."

said in its context, but also what Cyril thought he meant. Two
different things!

The text of the sermon is Hebrews 3:1–2: "Therefore, brothers
in the family of God, who share a heavenly calling, think of the
Apostle and High Priest of the religion we profess, who was
faithful to God who appointed him" (NEB).[5] Nestorius begins
with some pious comments on theology. We are dealing here,
he says, with holy and precious things beyond our understanding. But the heretics do not recognize this and throw prudence
to the winds. For example they twist the words of Paul [sic!] to
their own ends, "imagining themselves to have something of
greater value in theology." [6] They take this text to mean that the
"son is created" because St. Paul says that God "made him."
They wrongly attribute the words of the text to the divine Logos
and conclude that the son is subordinate to the father. "When
they hear the word 'apostle' they think that God the Word is the
apostle; when they read 'office of priest' they imagine that the
Godhead is priest." [7]

From these opening sentences it is apparent that the heresy
Nestorius has in mind is Arianism. Throughout the sermon he
develops his interpretation of Hebrews 3 against an Arian interpretation. The Arians believe, says Nestorius, that the divine
Logos is not one with the Father because he is said to have been
created and because he became a priest. But if it is true that the
high priest is God, why does he make an offering?

> If divinity is a high priest, who is honored by the service
> of the high priest? If God is the one who makes the offering,
> there is no one to whom the offering is made. What is greater

5. This passage from Hebrews 3 is one of the key passages in the Christological debates just as certain texts from the Gospels, Prov. 8:22, and
others were central in the Trinitarian debates. Cyril discusses it in a number of places besides the *Adversus Nestorium*. See for example, *Pulch.* 23
(*ACO* 1:1,5,39, 26 ff; it occurs in the twelve anathemas (no. 10); see *ACO*
1:1,7,53,11–16; also *Chr. Un.* 750d–3.

6. Loofs, *Nestoriana*, p. 231 (23–25). Theodoret's exegesis of Heb. 3:1
also shows the preoccupation with the Arian view in connection with this
text. We cannot, says Theodoret, apply this passage to the Word believing that
he is "made," i.e. if we wish to remain orthodox (*ACO* 1:1,6,137, 11 ff).

7. Loofs, *Nestoriana*, p. 232, 8–11.

than divinity, in order that as something less it [i.e., divinity] may offer to something greater? What is it that makes necessary such an offering? A priest must bring an offering because he himself is in need of perfection from the offerings according to the word of St. Paul. 'For every high priest chosen from among men is appointed to act on behalf of men in relation to God; he can deal gently with the ignorant and wayward, since he himself is beset with weakness. Because of this he is bound to offer sacrifice for his own sins as well as for those of the people.' But the nature of divinity does not need perfection by grace. Why then is the Word of God thought to be called priest by them even though he did not need sacrifices for his own improvement like other priests.[8]

Nestorius answers by saying that the priest who makes offerings cannot be God, because God does not need to make an offering. The priest who makes an offering must be a man if the offering is to have any significance. To bolster this interpretation he appeals to the context of the passage. In the previous chapter St. Paul had said that Christ is "made like his brethren in every respect." This means, says Nestorius, that he is man. Indeed St. Paul said that it is "not with angels that he is concerned but with the descendents of Abraham." "Is the Godhead the seed of Abraham?" asks Nestorius. "It is not the merciful one who suffers, but the temple which suffers; the life-giving God does

8. Ibid., pp. 232, 233. Theodoret of Cyrus' interpretation is similar. God the Word did not assume the rank of the priesthood of Melchizedek, he says; rather it was the one from the "seed of David who existed free from sin, our priest, and became a victim by offering himself to God for us, having in himself clearly the Word of God united to him and inseparably joined to him" (ACO 1:1,6,137,14–19). See also Andrew of Samosata, ACO 1:1,7,53 18 ff. Theodore of Mopsuestia's comments on Heb. 3:1 are not extant in his Commentary on Hebrews. The extant fragments, however, suggest that he would have given a similar interpretation. Cf. Staab, Pauluskommentare, pp. 204 ff. It is interesting that Theodoret of Cyrus in his more mature and less polemically oriented Commentary on Hebrews assigns this verse to Christos, which title he calls the μήνυμα τῶν δύο φύσεων (PG 82:697b).

not suffer, but the seed of Abraham [suffers]." [9] In the Gospels
we can read of such a distinction. Some texts refer to the Logos
as, for example, "Before Abraham was I am." Others refer to
Jesus and are parallel to the text from Hebrews. Luke 4:18 is an
example: "The Spirit of the Lord is upon me, because he has
anointed me." Nestorius comments: "Humanity was anointed,
heretic, not divinity. This is he who was made a faithful priest
to God for he became a priest, and did not exist as such from
eternity." [10] The passage from Hebrews therefore does not establish the Arian position, says Nestorius, for the texts they cite to
prove that the Logos is subordinate do not refer to the Logos
but to Jesus. The subject of Hebrews 3, or Luke 4, or Luke 2
and similar passages from the Gospels is "the one called the
seed of Abraham, the one who in all things is similar to his
brothers and who became a high priest in time and who was
perfected through suffering." The heretics misinterpret the Scriptures when they say that the "divine impassible Logos" became
a "passible high priest." [11]

Nestorius' reply to the Arians follows the lines of exegesis
developed by "Antiochene" thinkers in the fourth century. Supported by key texts from the Gospels, Arian exegetes presented
a powerful front to Nicene theologians. Eudoxosius of Constantinople wrote, "Let them [the Nicenes] answer how one
who is passible and mortal can be *homo-ousios* with the God who
is above these things and who is beyond suffering and death." [12]
In answer to this argument two different exegetical schemes were
developed, one in Alexandria and the other in Antioch. Athanasius set the pattern for Alexandria by claiming that the Logos
remains the subject of all predications while at the same time
claiming that not everything is predicated of him "according
to his own nature." The Logos suffers, but not according to his
own nature. He suffers "according to the flesh." By distinguishing
two types of predications Athanasius sought to safeguard the

9. Loofs, *Nestoriana*, p. 234.   10. Ibid., p. 235.
11. Ibid., p. 236.
12. Text in August Hahn, *Bibliothek der Symbole und Glaubensregeln
der alten Kirche,* p. 262.

divinity of the son and at the same time to recognize the reality of the incarnation.[13]

Athanasius, however, represents only one tradition responding to Arius. Among another group of thinkers the argument took a different form and it is in this tradition that Nestorius belongs. Take the case of Eustathius of Antioch. He also granted the initial assumption concerning the nature of the deity, but he did not think it was possible to distinguish two types of predication. What is predicated of the Logos is predicated *kata physin*. If this were so, then predicates such as passibility, hunger, thirst, etc. would limit the deity and make him something less than God. The Arians would be correct: the son is not God. Eustathius answered that the "Word" is not the subject of the human actions or suffering of Christ. Passages in the Scriptures which speak of Jesus' suffering must not be attributed to the Logos, either by nature or according to the flesh; they must be ascribed to the man Jesus. It is Jesus who advances in wisdom, who hungers and thirsts, and who suffers.[14]

These two responses to the Arian position gave rise to two contrasting exegetical traditions. Each provided a defense of Nicene theology, a refutation of the Arian arguments and a schema for expounding the Gospels. The one seldom had difficulty recognizing that the Jesus of the Gospels was the son of God, but it tended to diminish the importance of the human portrait of him in the Gospels. The other seldom had trouble taking this portrait seriously, but it always found it difficult, as Theo-

13. For Athanasius see the discussion in chap. 6, pp. 130 ff. On the varying responses to the Arian position, see Francis Sullivan, *The Christology of Theodore of Mopseustia,* pp. 158 ff.

14. See the statement of Eustathius, "Is enim in Christo, inquit, plenitudo divinitatis inhabit, primum quidem aliud est quod inhabit, aliud autem quod inhabitatur, si autem natura differunt ab alterutris, neque mortis passionem neque cibi appetitum neque poculorum desiderium, non somnum, non tristiam, non fatigationem, non lacrimarum fluxus, non aliam quamlibet mutationem plenitudini divinitatis coexistere fas est, cum sit inconvertibilis per naturam. Homini haec adplicanda seorsim sunt, qui ex anima constat et corpore" (Frag. 47); see also Frags. 18, 27, 28, 41, 48, in M. Spannuet, *Recherches sur les écrits d'Eustathe d'Antioche avec une édition nouvelle des fragments dogmatiques et exégétiques.*

dore's exegesis of John amply demonstrates,[15] to show how this Jesus could be one with God. The former, initiated and worked out by Athanasius, was to find expression in his successor in the see of Alexandria, Cyril; the latter was to dominate the tradition centered about Antioch and find expression in Nestorius, Theodore of Mopsuestia, and Theodoret of Cyrus.

In the sermon on Hebrews 3 Nestorius is dealing with precisely this same problem and the answer he gives is characteristically Antiochene. The designation of Christ as priest does not call into question the divinity of the son, says Nestorius, for this passage refers to the man Jesus, the one from the seed of Abraham, and not to the Logos.

Once Nestorius is satisfied that he has answered the Arian objections he turns to a discussion of the priestly work of Christ. He compares Christ to the teachers and prophets of the Old Testament. At the coming of Christ, says Nestorius, the ancient promise was fulfilled. The people of Israel had followed false gods and contaminated the land with sin. How was God's promise to be kept? Who among the people of Israel would carry out this promise? Who among men could fulfil God's purpose? He writes:

> How then were the promises to be kept? Was the divine voice to run the risk of lying? Who is to act as mediator to God for this promise? The lawmaker Moses? He is great as a prophet and indeed as chief of all the prophets, but when he had to act as God's mediator to achieve earthly freedom, he cried out with fear: "O Lord, I pray send another who is able." But is Aaron sufficient for the ministry of blessing? The priest is brilliant, so is the establishment of the priesthood of the law, but he is easily frightened by the impious masses as the making of the calf showed. Even blessed Elias burned with fiery zeal, but he was offensive

15. Cf. for example, the use of pronouns in the following passage. "Deus Verbum, qui *me* assumpsit *sibique* conjunxit, dat *mihi* dum fiducia victoriam iudicii. *Mi* enim semel pro semper fecit suum, quando assumpsit *me;* atque evidens est *eum me* [!] non derilinquere ne temere agam." (Vosté, ed., Theodore of Mopsuestia, *Commentarius in Evangelium Johannis Apostoli,* p. 174; see in this connection T. Camelot, "De Nestorius à Eutyches," pp. 127 ff.

to sinners. There was no mediator from anywhere for the promise of blessing, since the Gentiles were practising idolatry, the Jews were equally ungodly, the prophets cried, "Oh Lord, I pray send another who is able," and the priests either yielded without measure to the sinners or chastised them mercilessly and without reason. A high priest, then, on the one hand from the race of Abraham by nature and, on the other hand, honored above the prophets, was needed to mediate the blessing. He must be a meek and blameless man, capable of suffering as a descendant of Abraham, but one who also knew when, in danger, to call out to God, "Not my will but yours." Christ was born for this, not clothed with the nature of angels, for God did not promise a blessing to men from the race of angels, but from the seed of Abraham, the same as those who received the Gospel.[16]

Mankind needed a man who could do what all the prophets had failed to do. This one is the Christ—not an angel but a man. But why, asks Nestorius, did he who was without sin have to die? St. Paul answers, "Because he himself has suffered and been tempted, he is able to help those who are tempted." Temptation came to one who was without sin that all his brothers might have the power to overcome sin.

"Having undergone this test of suffering in sinless flesh, he received a certain power—an invincible plea for justice—in regard to his kinsmen who were unjustly attacked by an excess of power of the devil, by the sinless man among them not escaping the experience of his assault." [17] Christ was sent to us, concludes Nestorius, from the seed of Abraham, "offering the sacrifice of his body for himself and his race" that man might be reconciled to God.

So far Nestorius on Hebrews 3. Nestorius views this text within the context of the Trinitarian problem and his interpretation attempts to meet objections to the divinity of the son based on this passage. Secondly, he is working within a much different theological and exegetical framework from Cyril's, even though there are some superficial similarities. Nestorius follows the

16. Loofs, *Nestoriana*, p. 238.   17. Ibid., p. 239.

Antiochene exegesis and assigns the texts from the Gospels such as "he advanced," "hungered," etc. to the one from the seed of Abraham, thereby attempting to eliminate the Arian objections. Thus Nestorius has no difficulty in saying that "he [Christ] learned obedience and was made perfect" (Heb. 5:9), or that he "became a faithful high priest." Finally, Nestorius says that Christ makes offering for himself as well as for the race of men. This suggested to Cyril that Christ was in need of an offering. It is here that Cyril begins his attack and the shape of the conflict first emerges.

Cyril's response to Nestorius came in the form of an extended examination of the collection of sermons forwarded to Alexandria. The *Adversus Nestorium* [18] was written in the spring of 430 and represents Cyril's most thorough reply to Nestorius and the most militant statement—except for the twelve anathemas—of his point of view. Cyril has great difficulty understanding Nestorius because he did not recognize that Nestorius is dealing with a Trinitarian, and not a Christological, problem. The Antiochene response to the Arians was unfamiliar to Cyril and it appeared that Nestorius was simply dividing Christ into the divine son and the one from the seed of Abraham. This is not to say that the argument between Nestorius and Cyril was not a real one. It most certainly was, but the form Cyril's attack took tended to cloud the issue. Nestorius was discussing one problem, and Cyril blasts him on quite another matter.

The sermon on Hebrews 3 first comes up for discussion in Book 3 of the *Adversus Nestorium*. Cyril's chief complaint is that Nestorius' explanation of the priesthood of Christ implies that the one who offered himself to God is not the divine son.[19]

18. Text of *Nest.* in *ACO* 1:1, 6, 13–106.

19. Cyril devoted one of the twelve anathemas to Nestorius' view of priesthood. "The divine Scripture asserts that Christ was made the 'High Priest and Apostle of our confession'; moreover He offered himself as 'an odor of sweet savor' to God even the Father. If anyone therefore says that it was not the Word himself who is from God who was made High Priest and our Apostle when he was made flesh and man like us, but as it were another one born of a woman, considered separately from Him; or if anyone says that He offered the sacrifice for Himself also and not rather solely for our sakes—for he 'who knew no sin' would have no need of a sacrifice—

As evidence for this interpretation Cyril cites Nestorius' statement that the priest not only made offering for others, but that he also offered the sacrifice "for himself." If Christ offered the sacrifice for himself as well as for others, he must have been in need of an offering. But this is to say that he had sinned. "If he offers the sacrifice for us and it is fitting for him, he is most certainly and of necessity in need of it, as we who were under the yoke of sin." [20] This is an intolerable position for Cyril, for it suggests that Christ is like other men. He too sinned.

To support his view Cyril cites a number of biblical texts asserting that Christ did not sin (John 14:30; 8:46, etc.). But then he goes on to say that Christ could hardly have been guilty of sin because he is the second Adam.

"Therefore, he was named the last Adam, not enduring the sickness of the first one, but rather in himself first ridding the nature of man of the blame for that ancient transgression. For it was condemned in Adam, but in Christ was seen most approved and worthy of wonder. He was of the earth, but Christ was heavenly. Human nature was put to shame in the first . . . but in Christ it has been preserved inviolable, and as in a second first-fruits of the race it was seen both unafflicted by sins and superior to the curse and doom, death and decay." [21] The second Adam did not need to make offering for himself, because he was "superior to sin as God." The divine son—not an ordinary man —makes offering for mankind. Cyril resorts to the typology of Adam and Christ developed in the commentaries, but now he gives the exegetical materials a somewhat different twist in the light of the polemical situation. Nestorius distinguished between the Logos and the one from the seed of Abraham; Cyril rejects this distinction and offers instead the image of the heavenly man who is at once the divine Logos and from the seed of Abraham.

---

let him be anathema" (*ACO* 1:1,7,53,11–16; trans. T. H. Bindley, *The Ecumenical Documents of the Faith* [London, 1925], p. 270). Cyril also discusses the anathema elsewhere: *ACO* 1:1,7, 53 ff; 1:1,6, 135 ff; 1:1,15,24; 1:1,5,39–40.

20. *Nest.* 3.6 (p. 73, 24–36); see also *ACO* 1:1,5,24,20–21. Cyril has in mind the passage edited by Loofs: *Nestoriana,* p. 240, 6–9.

21. *Nest.* 3.6 (p. 74, 9 ff).

Christ is not ordinary man from the seed of Abraham, but the heavenly man come from God and now in the condition of man.

Nestorius, of course, did not claim that Christ was an ordinary man. The sermon on Hebrews 3 said quite the reverse. Christ was not like the prophets of ancient times, for they had been unable to act as mediators between God and man. But Nestorius' way of distinguishing Christ from the prophets was not Cyril's. Cyril saw red when Nestorius said that Christ offered the sacrifice for himself as well as for other men. This could only mean, says Cyril, that Christ was simply a man who was "like us but with the name of divinity plastered on." [22] Cyril brings a similar argument against Nestorius' view of the *theotokos*. Those who deny the *theotokos* make of Christ an "ordinary man having nothing more than we have." How could every knee bow and angels worship him if he were an ordinary man? Because Christ is the son become man "we were able to conquer in Christ and be stronger [κατευμεγεθῆσαι] than sin, put off corruption and escape death, so to speak, from the great joy in Christ 'O death, where is your victory? Where is your sting, O Hell?' As we fell in Adam, we have conquered in Christ. If Emmanuel was an *ordinary* man, how could the death of man benefit human nature? Although many holy prophets died in former times, the famous Abraham, Isaac and Jacob, Moses and Samuel, and the other holy successors, the death of these did not help the race of men on earth, but Christ delivered it. He offered his own flesh for us and giving it to death on account of us he delivered us from the bonds of sin." [23]

22. *Nest.* 3.1 (p. 55, 25–27).
23. *Arcad.* 7 (*ACO* 1:1,5, 63–64). On the *theotokos* see also *Nest.* 1.1: If the Virgin Mary is not *theotokos,* says Cyril, then Christ is merely a man and not the divine son from the father. There would be no freedom for mankind "from the blame contracted in Adam. . . . For in Adam mankind experienced 'dust you are and to dust you shall return,' but in Christ mankind has been enriched, being able to overcome [κατευμεγεθῆσαι] the snares of death and to dance in triumph over corruption . . . Christ has become a second firstfruits of our race." We are now enriched because "Immanuel the second Adam has appeared to us, not from the earth like the first but from heaven" (p. 17). Nestorius' opposition to *theotokos* is based on the same argument he used with respect to priesthood. For if the son is born

The term "ordinary man" enters Cyril's vocabulary through Athanasius, though it had been used much earlier. Justin, for example, had refused to acknowledge that Christ was an "ordinary man" for his blood did not come from man but from the power of God. This demonstrates, said Justin, that "Christ is not man of men and begotten in the ordinary course of humanity." [24] Athanasius also rejected it with respect to Christ. He thought that the Arians taught that Christ had a human origin and this was tantamount to saying that he is simply another man like us or an ordinary man. Christ is "not an ordinary man," wrote Athanasius, because he is the "true son of God by nature who has become man yet is not the less Lord and God and Savior." [25] In Athanasius the term was taken to be a denial of the divinity of the son.

In Cyril's argument with Nestorius, however, the divinity of Christ is not at issue; the phrase "ordinary man" or "simply a man" has a somewhat different connotation. In his treatise addressed to Emperor Theodosius' sister and wife on the teaching of Nestorius he writes: "Since human nature was sentenced to the curse and condemnation of death because of the deed of the first-formed, it was necessary to recover again that which it had in the beginning that there be a demonstration of unswerving obedience. But this was far beyond the measure of mankind. For there was no one free of sin. . . . But God the Father, skilfully recapitulating all things in Christ, laboring with great gentleness to return human nature to what it was in the beginning, sent his son born of a woman in order that by taking for himself the same body and making it his own, he might, as man on earth, be shown not to have known sin, and, therefore, being in every-

---

of Mary, he must be passible. Acknowledging the *theotokos* would only support the Arian argument (see Loofs, *Nestoriana*, pp. 174–75). In this connection Nestorius links Arianism and Apollinarism; both heresies make the Logos subject to human affections. This linking of Arianism and Apollinarism by Nestorius is important for understanding the Antiochene position vis-à-vis Alexandria, Cf. Loofs, *Nestoriana*, pp. 166, 19; 170,30; 179,4; 181,18.

24. *Dial. Trypho* 54.2. See *PGL*, pp. 761–62.

25. *Or.* 3.32; 3.51.

thing subject to the God and father, he might make human nature righteous in himself, free it from the bonds of death, crowned by the God and father with the decree of sinlessness." This could not have been done, says Cyril, by a "man simply" (ἄνθρωπον ἁπλῶς), but only by the "only son who had become man."[26]

Cyril's argument against Nestorius, then, is that the divine son, not a "mere man" from the seed of Abraham, became the apostle and high priest of our confession.[27] Christ cannot be divided into one from the seed of Abraham and one from the bosom of the Father. Christ is the one unique and extraordinary man, at once from God and born of man like us. Nestorius is really guilty of a Jewish interpretation of Christ, says Cyril, for he does not recognize how different Christ is from others. God had "given the law to men, Moses being the mediator. But the law was incapable of achieving good . . . for it brought nothing to perfection." Our redemption does not come through a "man like us but rather from God," for he that suffered in the flesh is God and he is our high priest.[28] The Jews sever Christ from God and make of him a mere man. "Why do you let yourself fall into the pedantries of the Jews? . . . Confess with us one Christ and do not sever him into two again." Jesus had to rebuke the Jews for not recognizing that he was the son come from God (John 10:34–36). For "he who was God has truly been made man that we too might be called offspring, no more of the first, i.e. of the earthy, to whom it was said by God, 'earth you are and to earth you shall return' and who leads us to death, but of the second, from above and out of heaven—Christ, I mean—who brings us again to the purest life, renders incorrupt that which is bound by death, and frees from sins that which was enchained by the bonds of sin." The result of Nestorius' thinking, says Cyril, is that there can be no new creation. "We have been deceived and are no less now in that situation in which we were of old before the coming. How

26. De recta fide ad Pulcheriam et Eudoxiam (*Pulch.*)20 (*ACO* 1:1,5,38). Cyril sometimes uses the phrase "simply a man" or a "mere man" as parallel to "ordinary man." See also *ACO* 1:1,5,25,23; 1:1,7,59–60; 1:1,6,145.

27. *Nest.* 3.2 (p. 60, 25).   28. *Nest.* 3.2 (p. 61).

then did 'old things pass away and how have they become new? What shall we say about the words 'if anyone is in Christ he is a new creature.' " [29]

Cyril has placed all his cards on the table. The argument of the book continues, but he has stated his chief criticism of Nestorius. Nestorius' view of Christ is inadequate on the following count: he believes that Christ is a mere man and therefore not the second Adam, the divine son come from heaven. Because he is an ordinary man he cannot be the initiator of a new covenant to take the place of the Mosaic covenant, and therefore there can be no new creation and beginning of a new way.

Cyril's reply to Nestorius represents a new stage in the development of the Christological discussion. Nestorius' discussion of the priesthood of Christ is part of the fourth-century discussion of the Trinity. Athanasius also had to give an answer to the Arians on the matter of Hebrews 3. The phrases "he became" and "he was made" must not be "understood as if the Word considered as Word was made, but that the Word, being Demiurge, afterwards was made high priest, by putting on a body which was originated and made, which he is able to offer for us; wherefore he is said to be made." [30] Both Nestorius and Athanasius were wrestling with the same problem—how to preserve the dignity of the son. Each believed that the Arians had perverted the Scripture and each proceeded in his own fashion to refute the arguments. What is striking about the parallel is that almost a hundred years separated Athanasius and Nestorius. Yet they were concerned with exactly the same problem!

Cyril devoted most of his early life to Trinitarian questions.[31] But in this first exchange with Nestorius the emphasis has shifted markedly. He still approaches the matter in the fashion of the Alexandrian tradition, but he is no longer worried about the

29. *Nest.* 3.3 (pp. 65–66); see also *Nest.* 4.5 (p. 86). For 2 Cor. 5:17 see also *Nest.* 5.3 (p. 99) and *Pulch.* 20 (*ACO* 1:1,5,42,33–35) where Cyril links together the inability of human nature to conquer death, new creation, and Christ as not simply a man.

30. Athanasius, *Or.* 1.53 ff. (*PG* 26:161d–164a; 169a–b).

31. See for example, his discussion of Heb. 3 in connection with the Trinitarian problems raised by the text (*Thes., PG* 75:361–63).

Arians and the divinity of the son. Cyril *does not* argue that the text from Hebrews gives no support to the Arian claim that the son is not equal to the father; rather he *assumes* that the son is equal to the father and seeks to show what it means that the Word was made man and became priest. Athanasius could never move on to this point because he was too pressed to defend the prior claim of the son's divinity. A similar situation existed with respect to the *theotokos*. Nestorius *denied* the *theotokos* because it suggested that the son was not truly God; Cyril *defended* it because it affirmed that the son was truly man and that it was the divine son, not an ordinary man, who underwent death and raised men to new life in the resurrection. Paradoxically Cyril's inability to recognize the polemical front Nestorius faced led him to put his finger on the distinctively Christological problem. The question is now: If the son is *homo-ousios* with the father, what is the relationship of the divine son to the Christ of the Gospels?

The use of 2 Corinthians 5:17 in the controversy also illustrates the shift in the *Fragestellung*. In the Trinitarian controversy 2 Corinthians 5:17 was used to defend the divinity of the son. Athanasius and others argued that Christ was "firstborn" because he was the beginning of a new creation. Firstborn of creation did not mean that he was the first to be created, but that he was the first of the new creation through the resurrection. But in the controversy with Nestorius, 2 Corinthians 5 is not used to defend the divinity of the son but to demonstrate that the divine son has truly become man and conquered death. "He will be called Jesus for he was in truth the one who underwent birth in the flesh from a woman. Thus he has saved his people, not as a man connected with God, but as God made in the likeness of those who are endangered, in order that in him first the human race might be re-formed to what it was in the beginning; for in him all things were new." [32] Similarly "firstborn" and "only begotten" were sharply distinguished from one another in the Trinitarian controversy. *Monogenes* referred to the relationship with the Father, and *prototokos* to the son as man. This distinction is still preserved, but now Cyril finds himself arguing that the two terms refer to one person. We say that "the one Lord and Christ . . .

32. *Chr. Un.* 744a.

the same is conceived of as only begotten and first begotten." [33]
Now the question is the unity of Christ and the reality of the
incarnation of the divine son.

In the controversy with Nestorius the Adam typology is used
frequently to show that the son underwent genuine human experience. The son did not come "simply to be seen by those on
earth and to live among men." If this is so, then he only *appeared*
to become man. No, he actually became man, "sharing in flesh
and blood and partaking of the same nature" (Heb. 2:14–15)
as man that he might destroy the power of the devil. God did
"what the law could not do" by sending his son. The only son
came among us as "a complete man to rescue us from the corruption which had been introduced into our earthly body, that
he might appear superior to sin, and that the stability and immutability of his own nature might color it [human nature] with
ink as in cotton." For this reason Christ is a unique and exceptional man. "Christ was the first and only man on earth who did
not know sin, nor was guile found in his mouth. He was established as the root and firstfruits of those being re-formed to newness of life in the Spirit and the incorruption of the body, and
receiving the firmness of divinity and transmitting it by participation and by grace to the whole human race. For knowing this the
divine Paul said: 'As we bore the image of the earthly, we will also
bear the image of the heavenly.' The image of the earthly has a
propensity toward sin and inclines us toward death. The image
of the heavenly, i.e. Christ, is set on sanctification and the return
and renewal of death and corruption to incorruption and life." [34]

To Cyril's way of thinking, the chief difficulty with Nestorius'
view of Christ was that it could not account for the uniqueness
of Christ. Nestorius could not show why this one man overcame
death when others did not. If Christ were an ordinary man linked
to God he would hardly be unique. He would have been like
other great men—Abraham, Moses, the prophets—who were incapable of meeting the challenge of death. The typology of the
second Adam establishes that Christ is the unique and extraordinary man, because he has come from heaven. He is God's

33. *Nest.* 3.5 (p. 72).
34. *Thd.* 20 (*ACO* 1:1,55, 3–13); see also *Pulch.* 5 (*ACO* 1:1,5,28, 10 ff).

son. In the controversy with Nestorius Cyril returns to this point
over and over again. Nestorius' Christology does not explain the
redemption of mankind, nor does it take into account the biblical
data concerning Christ. Thus in his most mature work on
Christology, the *Quod Unus Christus Sit,* Cyril's argument is almost wholly exegetical and soteriological. The book is little more
than an exegetical treatise on disputed texts raised by the controversy, and reminds the reader of Athanasius' orations against the
Arians. In the words of Durand, Cyril attempts to show that the
"dualistic Christology cannot do justice to the biblical data concerning Christ." [35] The Adam-Christ typology, and to a lesser
degree the Pauline idea of new creation, have a significant part in
the discussion.

The work opens with an attack on Nestorius' denial of the
theotokos. Cyril states at the outset that the central problem with
Nestorian Christology is that it does not take the incarnation
seriously. By denying the *theotokos* Nestorius refuses to recognize
that it is the divine son who has become incarnate, taken on
human flesh, and redeemed man. After the introductory comments Cyril turns to the first controverted texts.[36] "For our sake
he made him to be sin who knew no sin, so that in him we might
become the righteousness of God" (2 Cor. 5:24), and Christ
"was made a curse" (Gal. 3:13). The texts seem to suggest that
the son had been turned into a curse. Most exegetes met this
objection by claiming that Christ had not actually become a curse,
but that he appeared to have become one, or to have been cursed
on behalf of mankind. Cyril sets himself against this tradition
and offers another interpretation.[37] If Christ only appeared to
be made a curse, then the incarnation is denied. And if it is the
case that he only appeared to become a curse, then how can we
say that he became weary or hungry or was considered to be
among the transgressors?

"Was he not accursed that he might undo the curse and did
not the father make him sin that he might end sin?" He would

35. G. M. Durand, *Deux Dialogues Christologiques,* p. 116; *Chr. un.*
730a–c.
36. *Chr. Un.* 719 ff.
37. See Durand's note on the text, *Deux Dialogues,* pp. 318–19.

not render mankind incorruptible if he "had not achieved this in his own flesh first. For he did not allow it to remain mortal and under decay, Adam transmitting to us the punishment for the transgression, but rather as the flesh of the incorruptible God, his very own flesh, rendered it superior to death and decay." If Christ is not made a curse the "whole plan of the mystery is gone." For "how can God have raised him from the dead if he did not die? How would he have died if he had not been born according to flesh? How can there be a coming alive [ἀναβίωσις] from the dead bringing hope of everlasting life to the saints, if Christ was not raised?" [38] Cyril appeals to the Adam typology to show that the son underwent human suffering. As confirmation he cites Hebrews 2:14–17. "He himself likewise partook of the same nature, that through death he might destroy him who has the power of death." But the reference to 1 Corinthians 15:45 also accents the idea that the one who underwent genuine suffering was superior to other men, for through his death the way was prepared for resurrection and a "return for mankind to what is better." If Jesus had been simply another man like Adam, the human race would not have entered on a new way. How could Jesus cleanse men from sin, Cyril writes, "if he were a common man and was under sin? . . . He was not a common man with a nature like ours tyrannized over by sin. . . . We are transformed in Christ as a kind of firstfruits into what he is and superior to corruption and sin. As Paul says 'As we bore the image of the earthly, so we shall bear the image of the heavenly, i.e. of Christ.' For Christ is considered a heavenly man." [39]

An ordinary man cannot bring about the salvation of mankind. Only the second Adam, the man from heaven is capable of initiating a new creation. We fell into the snare of death through Adam, but "in Christ all things are new and there is a return to what we were in the beginning; it was necessary that the second Adam who is from heaven . . . should free mankind from the judgment and call upon it again the good favor from above."

38. *Chr. un.* 720b–e.
39. *Chr. un.* 722d–723d. See also 724d, 725c–e. For the Adam typology to show that the son was truly man and underwent suffering see *Ep. ad Succensum* 1 (*ACO* 1:1,6,155,17 ff).

Jesus has now become a "second beginning to those on earth," for he has conquered Satan. If Christ is the second Adam, says Cyril, then it is incongruous to say that the human experiences described in the Gospels refer to the "assumed man." In this instance Cyril is referring to Matthew 27:46, "My God, my God, why have you forsaken me?" This text provided exegetical problems, because it suggested that Jesus had been forsaken by God, or that the man Jesus was deserted by the Word. Cyril takes the text as an affirmation of the reality of the incarnation and appeals to the Adam imagery to support his view.[40] If there was to be a redemption of mankind there must be a new beginning, and the new beginning could only come about if the man from heaven actually underwent suffering and death and conquered death by his resurrection.

The argument of the dialogue, then, centers on one central point: only if Christ is a unique and uncommon man could he conquer death and be the beginning of a new life. Since we are earthly, the "curse and decay which came through the law was transmitted to us . . . but in Christ we have been made heavenly . . . grace coming down on us as from a second beginning and root, i.e. in him." For he "re-formed [$\dot{a}\nu a\sigma\tauοι\chi ει\acute{ω}\sigma\omega\nu$] us in himself for the first time to an admirable and marvelous birth and life," since we no longer belong to the first father Adam in whom we became corrupt. Only the divine son can conquer death and bring life, for only he is without sin and superior to other men. Is it the Word then who suffers? asks Cyril. Of course, it is the "image of the invisible God who endures the cross, despising the shame. For we do not say that simply a man honored by connection with him has been given for us, but it is the Lord of glory himself who was crucified for us." Therefore the "father has not given for us a *common man* taken aside to be in the rank of mediator . . . but him who is above the whole creation, the word which beamed forth from his being." Only God can bring salvation to men, says Cyril. "After all, this is a matter concerning the salvation of the whole world." [41]

Christ had to be different from other men if he was to do the

40. *Chr. un.* 756d ff. For 2 Cor. 5:17 see also *Chr. un.* 744a; 764a.
41. *Chr. un.* 725d–e; 724d; 765b–766c.

extraordinary thing for which he came. This conviction supported and informed Cyril's interpretation of the Scriptures in his commentaries and it supports and informs the argument against Nestorius. Even in the polemical writings it is seldom given simply a theological expression; more often it is stated in the language of the Bible, specifically the typology of Adam and Christ. Cyril's appeal to the Bible in the controversy did not arise out of an arsenal of proof texts stockpiled in Alexandria and ready for the occasion; nor was his exegesis simply conditioned by the demands of the controversy. The great themes developed over the years in the commentaries now appear in the controversy with Nestorius. In some cases Cyril resorts to a traditional interpretation, in other cases he sets out on his own course. But whether his interpretation of a specific text is traditional or untraditional, Cyril's distinctive mark can be seen in his handling of the controverted texts. There is an underlying unity between the earlier work of the commentaries and the controversy, and this unity can be seen in the exegetical motifs as well as the persistence of certain theological themes.

In his exegesis of the Gospels Cyril used the Adam-Christ typology to interpret the life of Jesus as the beginning of a new way. Following the lead of Irenaeus and others, he extended the parallel between Adam and Christ to include most of the major events in the life of Christ. In the controversy with Judaism he used the typology to support his view of the relationship between the way of life under the law and the new life of worship in spirit and in truth. It was used throughout the commentaries to express the significance of the redemptive work of Christ and to highlight the centrality of the resurrection; it was used in connection with the earth coming to life in springtime; it was used to underscore Cyril's conception of redemption as a new creation; it was used to express Cyril's idea of Christ as a superior and uncommon man; it was used to contrast Christ with Moses and the great saints of Judaism, and it was used against Julian to show the superiority of Christ over the gods of Greece and Rome.

The Adam-Christ typology also expressed Cyril's conception of the unity of Christ. In the *Quod Unus Christus Sit,* Cyril cites some texts more frequently (John 1:14, for example) than he

does 1 Corinthians 15 or Romans 5, but it is the Pauline conception of the second Adam which bears the weight of the argument.
Cyril's exegetical works are dominated by the conviction that
Christ is unique among men because he broke the bonds of death.
This one insight is now adapted to fit the requirements of the
polemical situation. The uniqueness of Christ now becomes the
basis for the unity of Christ. The imagery of the second Adam
expressed this conviction with imagination, clarity, and great
adaptability. The Adam imagery could be used to say that Christ
was man, yet it affirmed that as God's son he was more than
man. It said on the one hand that Christ was one with other
men, yet it said that he was unique and extraordinary. It showed
that Christ truly experienced suffering and death, yet it affirmed
that he had overcome them. By dying, Christ had trampled down
death. Within the limits of a biblical image the typology of the
second Adam expressed what patristic Christology would eventually confess in the formula of Chalcedon. "He is named the man
from heaven," wrote Cyril, "for he is conceived of as complete in
divinity and the same one complete in humanity and in one
person." [42]

42. *Ep. 39 ad Ioh. Ant. (ACO* 1:1,4,18,25–26).

Conclusion: The Bible, Judaism, and the Resurrection of Jesus

A polemicist of great skill and daring, Cyril of Alexandria was also an expositor of the Holy Scriptures. As a biblical theologian, he is a more interesting figure than he has been given credit for being. He did not have a great theological mind, but he drank more deeply of the biblical tradition than most theologians in the history of the Church. He did not have the subtle originality of Gregory of Nyssa nor the creative and expansive mind of Origen. Cyril was tedious, repetitious, and verbose, but he made imaginative use of the biblical materials, he handled the Bible with a high degree of theological sophistication, and he was kindled by the Spirit of the Scriptures.

Adolf von Harnack once wrote that "Cyril had no theological interest." His "belief in the Incarnation simply demanded a forcible and definite statement of the secret, nothing more. . . . This is why Cyril also stated his faith in what was essentially a polemical form only; he would not have taken long to have given a purely positive statement." [1] This assessment of Cyril is based almost wholly on his polemical and dogmatic writings—without reference to his commentaries. One can hardly resist the temptation: for Harnack Cyril's theology was primarily polemical because Harnack's sources were primarily Cyril's polemical writings!

The study of patristic theology has rested on two assumptions: that the fathers were primarily dogmatic or systematic theologians, and that they were Hellenists who developed their thinking with reference to Greek thought.

The dogmatic approach to the history of Christian thought has its roots in the late eighteenth and early nineteenth centuries, the very time when the study of the history of theology was emerging as a separate discipline within Church History. The first history of dogma was written by Johann Salomo Semler, the father of *Dogmengeschichte,* as a preface to the systematic theol-

1. Adolf von Harnack, *History of Dogma,* 4:174.

ogy of Sigmund Jacob Baumgarten. Semler's work was epoch-making, for he was the first to take seriously the factor of histori-cal change and diversity in theological development. At the same time it was not a little prophetic for the future of the discipline that the father of *Dogmengeschichte* wrote his major work as a preface for a *Glaubenslehre,* a dogmatics.[2] The assumption under-lying Semler's work was that theology is the rational attempt of Christian thinkers to find intellectual expression of Christian belief.

Semler's view that theology was an intellectual discipline carried on with the help of discursive reason shaped the great historical works on dogma in the nineteenth century. The histo-rians of dogma naturally turned to the categories of dogmatic theology in their interpretation of the historical material. The ar-rangement of the material in the histories of dogma followed the pattern of the *loci* of dogmatic theology. Each historical epoch was divided up along dogmatic lines and grouped under cate-gories such as the following: doctrine of God, doctrine of the Trinity, creation, anthropology, Christology, redemption, escha-tology. The history of dogma read like a systematic theology set up chronologically.

The result of this approach was twofold: it excluded as sources much material such as sermons, exegetical works, homilies, cate-chetical writings, ascetic and devotional works; it led to a pre-occupation with dogmatic questions. This method, wrote Albrecht Ritschl, sought "in each period the doctrines which emerged and placed them in the scheme and organization of the *loci,* which since the Reformation . . . were used to divide and order the material." This gave the impression, said Ritschl, that "the intel-lectual activity of each period turned on the same axis as that of the Melanchtonian Lutheran dogmatics."[3] Adolf von Harnack realized the weakness of this approach, and he was able to break out of the wooden ordering of the material characteristic of ear-

2. J. S. Semler, "Historische Einleitung in die dogmatische Gottesgelehr-samkeit von ihrem Ursprung und ihrer Beschaffenheit bis auf unsere Zeiten."
3. See Ritschl's review of Friedrich Nitzsch, *Grundrisz der christlichen Dogmengeschichte* (1870), published in 1871. See Albrecht Ritschl, *Gesam-melte Aufsaetze,* 1:147 ff.

lier writers. However, he still retained the earlier assumption about the character of patristic thought. "The dogmas of the Church . . . are the doctrines of the Christian faith logically formulated and expressed for scientific and apologetic purposes, the contents of which are a knowledge of God, of the world, and of the provisions made by God for each man's salvation." Harnack too assumed that theology was an intellectual discipline seeking appropriate philosophical categories to express the meaning of Christian faith. "Dogma is in its conception and development a work of the Greek spirit on the soil of the Gospel." Preoccupation with Hellenism and with dogmatic questions are really two sides of the same coin.[4]

Cyril of Alexandria was neither a Hellenist nor a dogmatic theologian. He does not live and move within the categories of medieval scholasticism or Protestant orthodoxy, nor does he breathe the air of philosophy. To be sure, like every thinker in Christian antiquity Cyril learned from the Greek tradition, but he did not find his spiritual home in Greek philosophy. He moves in what we today would call the world of religion—symbolism, metaphor, sacred scripture, tradition, liturgy, piety. His thinking is nurtured by a religious tradition and a sacred book; he is primarily a pastor, administrator, and exegete, not a university professor or schoolman. In the twentieth century we have grown to appreciate the role of symbolism in all human thought and especially in religious thought. We know that in dealing with religious questions the ordinary dimensions of language and life have always been considered inadequate. As Mircea Eliade once said, "Perhaps the most important function of religious symbolism . . . is its capacity for expressing paradoxical situations, or certain structures of ultimate reality, otherwise quite inexpressible."[5] The Scriptures are filled with such symbols and images and they

4. Harnack, *History of Dogma*, 1:1. I am quite aware that Harnack is speaking of dogma, not theology, and that he distinguishes dogma from theology. Nevertheless, Harnack's history of dogma is also history of patristic theology and his view of dogma is really of a piece with his view of theology.

5. Mircea Eliade, "Methodological Remarks on the Study of Religious Symbolism," p. 101.

have provided every Christian generation with a rich source from which they could ever draw fresh inspiration. The good shepherd, the light of the world, the way, the life, the vine and branches, the bread, the morning star, the city, the father and son, the paschal lamb, the new leaven. These and countless other symbols, drawn from the Bible and nurtured in Christian tradition, have formed the vehicle for Christian thought and reflection. They create a world of meaning and value which has no simple equivalent in nonsymbolic discourse and thought. Symbols have their own rationale—even logic,[6]—appropriate to the "odd" things they wish to express. Symbols cannot be simply translated; they must be seen on their own terms.

The second Adam is such a symbol. It was taken from St. Paul, but it provided Cyril with an image, at once particular and universal, to interpret the whole of the Scriptures. The Bible is the story of the one man who brought sin and evil to corrupt the original creation and the second man who brought restoration, transformation, and a new creation. The typology of the second Adam called attention to the *universal* significance of Christ and his unparalleled place in the history of redemption. In Adam all men died and in Christ, the second Adam, all men come to new life.

The concept of the second Adam, however, not only served Cyril's interpretation of the Scriptures and his understanding of redemption, but also expressed the central ideas of his Christology. It expressed for Cyril what a later generation would seek to express in the Formula of Chalcedon. "We confess one and the same our Lord Jesus Christ . . . made known in two natures . . . and concurring in one person and one hypostasis." Cyril did not oppose formulating ecclesiastical creeds or conciliar formulas —witness his participation in the Council of Ephesus—but his most original expression of the mystery of Christ does not lie in distinctions he makes between person or nature or any other formulations. As Adam, Christ was *like* other men and one with all men. He was "one of us." But as the second Adam or heavenly man he differed from the rest of mankind and was *unlike* other

6. See Ian T. Ramsey, *Religious Language.*

men. He alone had accomplished for the first time what no other man had been able to do. He had conquered death and shown himself to be an uncommon and extraordinary man. "He conquered death as man," said Cyril, but the victory over death set him apart from all other men. "The sign of the resurrection is mighty, for it is unambiguous proof that Jesus is God." [7]

The resurrection is the culmination of the life of Jesus. The son did not become man simply to join human nature to God by the union of divine and human in the incarnation. The son became man so that as man he might suffer, die, and rise from the dead, and thereby initiate a new way for mankind. The incarnation finds its meaning and fulfilment only in the death and resurrection of Jesus. The course of mankind had to be reversed, but this could not happen unless a second man undertook to undo the wicked deed of the first Adam. Deed had to be met by deed. Why did this one man conquer? He was not an ordinary man but one from heaven. "As the first was from the earth, the second was from heaven, although born of a woman . . . and though he became man, he is no less from heaven."

The great tragedy of Cyril's theology is that he developed this view of Christ not only through the exegesis of the Bible but also at the expense of Judaism. The beautiful things Cyril has to say about Christ are said by contrast to Moses and Judaism. The law kills and Christ brings life. It is true, of course, that Cyril's interpretation of Moses was not the only view available to patristic writers. Gregory of Nyssa, for example, presented quite a different view of Moses. For Gregory Moses was the symbol of the quest for perfection and the ascent of the soul to God. But Cyril was not Gregory, he had not learned as much from Origen, nor had he drunk as deeply of the Platonic and Philonic traditions. Cyril was, quite frankly, too biblical. His Achilles heel is the Bible, not Hellenism.

Gregory of Nyssa was also an exegete, but the scope and style of his exegesis differ markedly from Cyril's. Gregory wrote a philosophical and cosmological treatise on Genesis to complete Basil's work on the *Hexameron*. He also wrote a life of Moses, two essays on the Psalm titles, a series of homilies on Ecclesiastes,

7. *In Jo.* 8.28 (P 2:36, 6).

a work on the Song of Solomon, five sermons on the Lord's Prayer, a treatise on the Beatitudes, as well as several other exegetical works. In these works Gregory is chiefly interested in the ascent of the soul to God. Gregory did not attempt to expound the Bible book by book. He confined himself to a selected number of books and themes which were particularly suited to his theological and ascetic interests.

Cyril set out to expound almost every book of the Old and New Testaments; most he did chapter by chapter, and he was able to complete most of the works he had begun. No mean accomplishment, and it makes a difference in the way a man thinks. I do not wish to suggest that Cyril was a better theologian than Gregory because he was more biblical. But Cyril's exposure to the full sweep of the biblical witness led him to a theology which took seriously the history of redemption as it had unfolded in the Bible. The same God who freed Israel from Egypt, led her through the middle of the sea and gave nourishment in the desert, who brought water out of the rock—this same one in the same way is able to do wonders equal to what he did of old. This same God renews mankind through the resurrection of Jesus.[8]

It is precisely because Cyril was so deeply rooted in the biblical tradition that his points of reference were almost wholly Jewish, and it was because he was so preoccupied with Judaism that the Bible was the chief source of his theology. He knew no other way to interpret Christianity than in relation to Judaism, and Christian tradition knew no other way to view Judaism than as an inferior foreshadowing of Christianity. Cyril could compare Christ with Zeus or Apollo and other Greek gods, but he does this only when addressing Julian. Greek tradition seldom provided the context or inspiration for his thought. Familiar terrain for Cyril was not Greek antiquity but the antiquity of the Jews as presented in the Jewish scriptures. The most natural comparison was always between Christianity and Israel, Christ and Moses, Christ and the prophets, Christ and John the Baptizer. The Jews became the natural and inevitable foil for the development of his thought.

Paul provided the key to Cyril's reading of the Scriptures. Cyril

8. *In Is.* 48:20–22 (*PG* 70:1033a–b).

had no particular interest in the Paul of "justification by grace through faith"—though he discussed these texts. But it is the Paul of the "two covenants" and "true Israel," the Paul of Romans 5, 1 Corinthians 15, 2 Corinthians 4–5, the Paul who divided the history of mankind into two great eras (the time from Adam to Christ and the era after Christ) who fascinated Cyril. It is the Paul who himself got rid of the law in order to gain Christ, and who in Cyril's words, "considered it rubbish"; [9] it is the Paul who compared Christianity to Judaism and said that the "splendor that once was is no splendor at all; it is out-shone by a splendor greater still" who interested Cyril. It was from Paul that Cyril learned that the "law condemns to death, but the Spirit gives life." It was from him also, as he had been filtered through earlier Christian tradition, that he learned of the second Adam, the heavenly man, the new creation, and the centrality of the resurrection.

Cyril is part of a tradition which had its beginnings in the primitive Church. He was not an innovator in his attitude toward Judaism, though he refined and developed what he had received. Christian beliefs since earliest times had taken shape with reference to Judaism, and now the attitudes were hardening into a fixed mold. Now it is one thing to say that Christian theology developed by reference to Judaism, and it is quite another to say that Judaism became a foil for Christian theology. Unfortunately the two cannot be so neatly distinguished. For the claim that something radically new had happened in the resurrection of Jesus led Christians to the judgment that Judaism was somehow "old." Judaism had the patriarchs and the kings and the prophets. But Jesus was not a patriarch or a king, and he was more than a prophet.

The Christian claim of newness was bolstered by the experience of the Jews after the time of Jesus—defeat at the hands of the Romans, destruction of the temple and the holy city, persecution by the Roman populace. The Christian claim seemed to be vindicated by the history of Judaism. The old was growing older. Cyril's attitude toward the Jews is therefore shaped not only by the Bible but also by history. The constant references in his com-

9. *In Is.* 60:7 (*PG* 70:1341b).

mentaries to the Romans and the Jews attest to this. The fathers thought Judaism was dying, that the victory of the Church signified the demise of Judaism. They created a caricature to meet their expectations and refused to look at Judaism for what it really was. But the problem of Judaism arose as a theological issue because Judaism had not died. It had not come to an end in Jesus, and it was still a force to be reckoned with in the Roman empire.

Theology does not arise in a vacuum and Cyril's theology is no exception. The sheer historical fact of the continuation of Judaism after the rise of Christianity is a source of the theological difficulties Christians have had with Jews. If there had been no Jews in the fifth century in the Roman empire, Cyril's questions would be empty and hollow. But Judaism was still alive and Christians could not comprehend how this could be so. How could Judaism live on after it had found its fulfilment in Jesus? All things are new! Why has the old not passed away?

The problem then of the relationship between Christianity and Judaism is more far-reaching than it would first appear. For if Christian attitudes toward the Jews are nurtured on the Bible and supported by a Christian view of history, we are not dealing with a peripheral matter. The overwhelming impression from the study of Cyril is that Christian beliefs are so deeply rooted in attitudes toward Judaism that it is impossible to disentangle what Christians say about Christ and the Church from what they say about Judaism.

If we cannot disentangle Christian thinking from its historical and biblical context, can we create a new context? The answer must be yes and no. It is simply absurd to think that we can generate new points of reference for Christian faith which are divorced from the Jewish scriptures and the apostolic writings. Christians will give up neither the Jewish scriptures nor the apostolic writings. Christian theology would be inconceivable without Judaism, the Christian Bible, and the resurrection of Jesus. But the newness of the resurrection need not lead to a depreciation of Judaism, for the resurrection is a sign of the future, and the future is not the property of Christians alone. The irony of Christian theology is that its preoccupation with the uniqueness of Jesus not only blinded Christians to what takes place in Judaism, but it also blinded Christians to the future which lay even beyond Jesus. The Christians forgot that Jesus himself proclaimed a *coming* Kingdom of God. Even the resurrection of Jesus was not the *final* unfolding. There is more to come. The resurrection of Jesus was a signal of the end, but it is not the end itself. Both Judaism and Christianity will come to fulfilment only in the coming Kingdom of God.

Bibliography

Works of Cyril

Aubert, John, ed. *Cyrilli Alexandriae archiepiscopi opera.* 6 vols. Paris, 1638.

Chabot, I. B., ed. *S. Cyrilli Alexandrini commentarii in Lucam* I. Corpus scriptorum christianorum orientalium, Scriptores Syri 27, vol. 70. Paris, 1912.

Durand, G. M. de., ed. *Cyrille d'Alexandrie. Deux Dialogues christologiques. Sources chrétiennes,* vol. 97 Paris, 1964.

Migne, J.-P., ed. *Patrologiae cursus completus,* vols. 68–77. Paris: E. Typographeo Reipublicae, 1859–66.

Pusey, P.E., ed. *Sancti patris nostri Cyrilli archiepiscopi Alexandrini in d. Joannis evangelium. Accedunt fragmenta varia necnon tractatus ad Tiberium diaconum duo, edidit post Aubertum.* 3 vols. Oxford: Clarendon Press, 1872.

———. *Sancti patris nostri Cyrilli archiepiscopi Alexandrini in XII prophetas.* 2 vols. Oxford: Clarendon Press, 1868.

———. *Commentary on the Gospel according to S. John by S. Cyril Archbishop of Alexandria.* A Library of the Fathers of the Holy Catholic Church, vols. 43 and 68. Oxord: James Parker & Co., 1874, 1885.

Reuss, J., ed. *Matthaeus-Kommentare aus der griechischen Kirche.* Texte und Untersuchungen, vol. 61. Berlin: Akadamie Verlag, 1961.

———. *Johannes-Kommentare aus der griechischen Kirche.* Texte und Untersuchungen, vol. 89. Berlin: Akadamie Verlag, 1966.

Schwartz, Eduard. *Acta conciliorum oecumenicorum,* vol. 1. Berlin: Walter de Gruyter, 1914.

Sickenberger, J. *Fragmente der Homilien des Cyrill von Alexandrien zum Lukas-evangelium.* Texte und Untersuchungen, vol. 34, no. 1. Leipzig: J. C. Hinrische Buchhandlung, 1909.

Smith, R. Payne, ed. *A Commentary upon the Gospel according to St. Luke by S. Cyril Patriarch of Alexandria.* Oxford: University Press, 1859.

Tonneau, R. M., ed. *S. Cyrilli Alexandrini Commentarii in Lucam I.* Corpus scriptorum christianorum orientalium, Scriptores Syri 70, vol. 140. Louvain: L. Durbecq, 1953.

Other Primary Sources and Translations

Ammianus Marcellinus. Edited by John Rolfe. 3 vols. Loeb Classical Library. Cambridge, Mass., 1939.

Ante-Nicene Fathers. Buffalo and New York, 1884–86.

Apollinaris. *Apollinaris von Laodicea und seine Schule.* Edited by Hans Lietzmann. Tuebingen, 1904.

Athanasius. *Lettres festales et pastorales de S. Athanase en copte.* Edited by L. T. Lefort. Corpus scriptorum christianorum orientalium, vols. 150–51. Louvain, 1955. Other quotations from Athanasius are taken from *PG.*

Augustine. "In Answer to the Jews." In *Saint Augustine: Treatises on Marriage and Other Subjects.* Translated by Sister Marie Liguori, pp. 387–414. New York: Fathers of the Church, Inc., 1955. Other quotations from Augustine are taken from *CSEL* and *PL.*

Barnabas and Didache. Translated by Robert A. Kraft. New York, 1965.

Basil. *The Letters of Saint Basil.* Edited and translated by Roy J. Deferrari. 4 vols. Loeb Classical Library. Cambridge, Mass., 1926.

Brooke, A. E., ed. *The Fragments of Heracleon.* Texts and Studies, vol. 1, no. 4. Cambridge, 1891.

Clement of Alexandria. *Extraits de Théodote.* Edited by F. Sagnard. *Sources chrétiennes,* vol. 23. Paris, 1948. Other quotations from Clement are found in *GCS.*

Corpus christianorum. Series latina. Turnhout, 1953 ff.

Corpus scriptorum ecclesiasticorum latinorum. Vienna, 1866 ff.

Didymus. *Didyme l'Aveugle. Zur Zacharie.* Edited by Louis Doutreleau. *Sources chrétiennes,* vols. 83–85. Paris, 1958.

Eusebius. *Pamphili evangelicae praeparationis libri 15.* Translated by E. H. Gifford. Oxford, 1903. Other quotations from Eusebius are found in *GCS.*

Frey, J. B., ed. *Corpus inscriptionum judaicarum.* Rome, 1936–52.

Gregory of Nyssa. *Opera.* Edited by Werner Jaeger and Hermann Langerbeck. Leiden, 1960 ff.

Die Griechischen christlichen Schriftsteller der ersten drei Jahrhunderte. Leipzig, 1897 ff.

Hahn, August, ed. *Bibliothek der Symbole und Glaubensregeln der alten Kirche.* Hildesheim, 1962.

Hennecke-Schneemelcher-McL. Wilson. *New Testament Apocrypha.* 2 vols. Philadelphia, 1963.

Irenaeus. *Ep. Lugdunensis libros quinque adversus haereses*. Edited by W. W. Harvey. 2 vols. Cambridge, 1857.

Josephus. Edited and translated by H. St.-J. Thackeray; R. Marcus; A. Wilgren; and L. H. Feldman. Loeb Classical Library. Cambridge, Mass., 1961 ff.

Julian. *Works*. Edited by William Cave Wright. 3 vols. Loeb Classical Library. London, 1923.

Justin Martyr. *The Dialogue with Trypho*. Translated by A. Lukyn Williams. London, 1931.

Lampe, G. W. H. *A Patristic Greek Lexicon*. Oxford, 1961.

Landgraf, Gustav, and Weyman, C., ed. *Epistula de cibis judaicis*. Archiv fuer lateinische Lexicographie, vol. 11. Leipzig, 1898.

Loofs, Friedrich, ed. *Nestoriana. Die Fragmente des Nestorius*. Halle, 1905.

Méliton de Sardes. *Homélie sur la Pâque*. Edited by Michel Testuz. Cologny-Genève: Bibliothèque Bodmer, 1960.

Midrash Rabbah. London: Soncino Press, 1939.

Mommsen, Theodor. *Theodosiani libri XVI cum constitutionibus Sirmondianis et leges novellae ad Theodosianum pertinentes*. Berlin, 1905.

Nestorius. *The Bazaar of Heraclides*. Edited by G. R. Driver and Leonard Hodgson. Oxford, 1925.

Nicene and post-Nicene Fathers. Grand Rapids, 1952–56.

Origen. *Contra Celsum*. Translated by Henry Chadwick. Cambridge, 1953.

———. *On First Principles*. Translated by G. W. Butterworth. New York, 1966.

———. *The Song of Songs*. Translated by R. P. Lawson. London, 1957. Other references to Origen are to *GCS*.

Patrologiae cursus completus: series graeca. Edited by J.-P. Migne. Paris, 1857–66.

Patrologiae cursus completus: series latina. Edited by J.-P. Migne. Paris, 1944–55.

Patrologia orientalis. Edited by R. Graffin and F. Neu. Paris, 1903 ff.

Pharr, Clyde. *The Theodosian Code and Novels and the Sirmondian Constitutions*. Princeton, 1952.

Philo. Translated by F. H. Colson. Loeb Classical Library. Cambridge, Mass., 1958.

Socrates Scholasticus. *Ecclesiastical History*. Translated by A. C. Zenos. A Select Library of Nicene and Post-Nicene Fathers, ser. 2, vol. 2. Grand Rapids, 1957.

——. *Historia Ecclesiastica.* Edited by R. Hussey. Oxford, 1853.
Sources chrétiennes. Paris, 1942 ff.
Strabo. *Geography.* Edited and translated by H. L. Jones. Loeb Classi-
cal Library. London, 1917–32.
Tcherikover, Victor, and Fuks, Alexander, ed. *Corpus papyrorum
judaicarum.* 3 vols. Cambridge, 1957–67.
Tertullian. *Adversus Judaeos.* Edited by Herman Traenkle. Wiesbaden,
1964.
——. *De anima.* Edited by T. H. Waszink. Amsterdam, 1947.
Theodore of Mopsuestia. *Commentarius in Evangelium Johannis Apos-
toli.* Edited by J.-M. Vosté. Corpus scriptorum christianorum orien-
talium, Scriptores Syri, ser. 4 vol. 3. Louvain, 1940.
——. *Commentary on the Lord's Prayer.* Edited by A. Mingana.
Cambridge 1933.
Turner, C. H. *Ecclesiae occidentalis monumenta iuris antiquissima.*
Oxford, 1899.

Secondary Sources

Abel, F. M. "Parallélisme exégétique entre s. Jérôme et s. Cyrille
d'Alexandrie." *Vivre et penser* 1 (1941):94–119, 212–30.
Amann, E. "L'Affaire Nestorius vue de Rome." *Revue des sciences
religieuses* 23 (1949):5–37, 207–44; 24 (1950):28–52, 235–65.
Ambramowski, Luise. *Untersuchungen zum Liber Heraclides des
Nestorius.* Louvain, 1963.
Armendariz, Luis M. *El Nuevo Moisés. Dinámica christocéntrica en la
tipología de Cirilo Alejandrino.* Madrid, 1962.
Armstrong, Gregory. *Die Genesis in der Alten Kirche.* Tuebingen,
1962.
Arnou, R. "Nestorianisme et néoplatonisme: l'union du Christ et
l'union des intelligibles." *Gregorianum* 17 (1936):116–31.
Aubineau, M. "Incorruptibilité et divinisation selon saint Irénée." *Re-
cherches de science religieuse* 44 (1956):25–52.
Avi-Yonah, M. *Geschichte der Juden im Zeitalter des Talmud,* vol. 2.
Berlin, 1962.
Bacher, W. "The Church Father Origen, and Rabbi Hoshaya." *Jewish
Quarterly Review* 3 (1891):357–60.
Bardy, Gustave. *Didyme l'Aveugle. "Étude de théologie historique,*
no. 1. Paris, 1910.
——. "Les Débuts du Nestorianisme (428–33)." In *Histoire de*

l'Église, edited by Augustin Fliche and Victor Martin, 4:163–96. Paris, 1937.

———. "S. Jérôme et ses maîtres hébreux." *Revue bénédictine* 46 (1934):145–64.

———. "Les Traditions juives dans l'oeuvre d'Origène." *Revue biblique* 24 (1925):217–52.

Baron, Salo W. *A Social and Religious History of the Jews,* vol. 2. New York, 1958.

Barr, James. *Old and New in Interpretation. A Study of the Two Testaments.* London, 1966.

Bauer, Walter. *Das Leben Jesu im Zeitalter der neutestamentlichen Apokryphen.* Tuebingen, 1909.

———. *Rechtglaubigkeit und Ketzerei im aeltesten Christentum.* Tuebingen, 1934.

Bell, H. I. *Cults and Creeds.* Liverpool, 1953.

———. *Jews and Christians.* Oxford, 1924.

———. *Juden und Griechen im Roemischen Alexandreia.* Beihefte zum 'Alten Orient,' no. 9. Leipzig, 1926.

Benoît, André. *Saint Irénée.* Paris, 1960.

Béranger, R. "L'âme humaine de Jésus dans la christologie du *de Trinitate* attribué à Didyme l'Aveugle." *Revue des sciences religieuses* 36 (1962):1–47.

Bindley, T. H. *The Oecumenical Documents of the Faith.* London, 1925.

Blanchette, O. "Saint Cyril of Alexandria's Idea of the Redemption." *Sciences ecclésiastiques* 16 (1964):455–80.

Blumenkranz, Bernhard. *Die Judenpredigt Augustins. Ein Beitrag zur Geschichte der juedisch-christlichen Beziehungen in den ersten Jahrhunderten.* Basler Beitraege zur Geschichtswissenschaft, vol. 25. Basel, 1946.

Bornemann, Johannes. *Die Taufe Christi durch Joannes in der dogmatischen Beurteilung der christlichen Theologen der vier ersten Jahrhunderte.* Leipzig, 1896.

Brandenburger, Egon. *Adam und Christus. Exegetisch-Religionsgeschichtliche Untersuchung zu Rom. 5: 12–21 (I Cor. 15).* Wissenschaftliche Monographien zum Alten und Neuen Testament. Neukirchen, 1962.

Braun, Herbert. "Entscheidende Motive in den Berichten ueber die Taufe Jesu von Markus bis Justin." *Zeitschrift fuer Theologie und Kirche* 50 (1953):39–43.

Breccia, E. *Juifs et chrétiens de l'ancienne Egypte.* Alexandria, 1927.

Brok, M. "Un soi-disant fragment du traité *Contre les Juifs* de Théodoret de Cyr." *Revue d'histoire ecclésiastique* 45 (1950):490–94.

Brown, Raymond E. *The Gospel according to John,* vol. 1. New York, 1965.

Bultmann, Rudolf. *Das Evangelium des Johannes.* Gottingen, 1962.

Burghardt, W. J. *The Image of God in Man according to Cyril of Alexandria.* The Catholic University of America Studies in Christian Antiquity, no. 14. Washington, 1957.

Camelot, Thomas. "De Nestorius à Eutyches: l'opposition de deux christologies." *Das Konzil von Chalkedon.* Edited by Aloys Grillmeier and Heinrich Bacht, 1:213–42. Wuerzburg, 1951.

———. "La Théologie de l'image de Dieu." *Revue des sciences philosophiques et théologiques* 40 (1956):443–71.

Campenhausen, Hans Freiherr von. "Das Alte Testament als Bibel der Kirche vom Ausgang des Urchristentums bis zur Entstehung des Neuen Testaments." *Aus der Fruehzeit des Christentums,* pp. 152–96. Tuebingen, 1963.

Chadwick, Henry. "Eucharist and Christology in the Nestorian Controversy." *Journal of Theological Studies,* n.s. 2 (1951):145–64.

Charlier, N. "La doctrine sur le Saint-Esprit dans *le Thésaurus* de saint Cyrille d'Alexandrie." *Studia Patristica,* vol. 2. Texte und Untersuchungen, 64:187–93. Berlin, 1957.

———. *"Le Thésaurus de Trinitate* de Saint Cyrille d'Alexandrie. Questions de critique littéraire." *Revue d'histoire ecclésiastique* 45 (1950):56–65.

Chase, G. H. *Chrysostom: A Study in the History of Biblical Interpretation.* Cambridge, 1887.

Cross, F. L. "The Projected Lexicon of Patristic Greek." *Actes du VIe congrès international d'etudes byzantines,* pp. 389–92. Paris, 1950.

Cullman, Oscar. *The Christology of the New Testament.* Philadelphia, 1959.

Daniélou, Jean. *Bible and Liturgy.* South Bend: Notre Dame, 1956.

———. "Bulletin d'histoire des origines chrétiennes." *Recherches de science religieuse* 36 (1952):269–72.

———. *From Shadows to Reality.* Westminster, Maryland, 1960.

———. *Grégoire de Nysse. Contemplation sur la vie de Moïse.* Sources: chrétiennes, vol. 1. Paris, 1955.

———. *Histoire des doctrines chrétiennes avant Nicée.* Paris, 1958 ff.

———. *Origen.* New York, 1955.

————. *Platonisme et théologie mystique: Essai sur la doctrine spirit-uelle de saint Grégoire de Nysse.* Paris, 1944.

————. "The Problem of Symbolism." *Thought* 25(1950):422–44.

————. "L'unité des deux Testaments dans l'oeuvre d'Origène." *Revue de sciences religieuses* 22 (1948):27–56.

Daniélou, Jean and Musurillo, Herbert, ed. *From Glory to Glory. Texts from Gregory of Nyssa's Mystical Writings.* New York, 1961.

Deneffe, A. "Der dogmatische Wert der Anathematismen Cyrills." *Scholastik* 8 (1933):64–89.

Devreesse, Robert. "Les Actes du concile d'Éphèse." *Revue des sciences philosophiques et théologiques* 18 (1929):223–42; 408–31.

————. "Après le concile d'Éphèse. Le retour des Orientaux à l'unité." *Echos d'orient* 38 (1939):271–92.

————. "Chaines exégétiques grecques." In *Dictionnaire de la Bible,* supplementary volume edited by Louis Pirot, cols. 1084–234. Paris, 1928.

Dhôtel, J.-C. "La 'sanctification' du Christ d'après Hébreux 2,11." *Recherches de science religieuse* 47 (1959):515–43; 48 (1960):420–52.

Diepen, Dom H. M. *Aux Origines de l'anthropologie de Saint Cyrille d'Alexandrie.* Paris, 1957.

————. "La Christologie de S. Cyrille d'Alexandrie et l'anthropologie néoplatonicienne." *Euntes Docete* 9 (1956):20–63.

————. "Stratagèmes contre la théologie de l'Emmanuel: à propos d'une nouvelle comparison entre saint Cyrille et Appolinaire," *Divinitas* 1 (1957):444–78.

Diestel, Ludwig. *Geschichte des Alten Testaments in der christlichen Kirche.* Jena, 1869.

Dubarle, A. M. "Les conditions du salut avant la venue du Sauveur chez saint Cyrille d'Alexandrie." *Revue des sciences philosophiques et théologiques* 32 (1948):359–62.

————. "L'ignorance du Christ dans saint Cyrille d'Alexandrie." *Ephemerides theologicae lovaniensis* (1939), pp. 111–20.

du Manoir, H. "Cyrille d'Alexandrie (saint)." *Dictionnaire de spirit-ualité* 2 (1953):2672–83.

————. *Dogme et spiritualité chez saint Cyrille d'Alexandrie.* Paris, 1944.

————. "Le problème de Dieu chez Cyrille d'Alexandrie." *Recherches de science religieuse* 27 (1937):385–407; 549–96.

Duprè la Tour, Augustin. "La Doxa du Christ dans les oeuvres exégétiques de saint Cyrille d'Alexandrie." *Recherches de science religieuse* 68 (1960):521–43; 69 (1961):68–94.

Ebeling, Gerhard. *Kirchengeschichte als Geschichte der Auslegung der heiligen Schrift.* Tuebingen, 1947.

Elert, Werner. *Der Ausgang der altkirchlichen Christologie: Eine Untersuchung ueber Theodor von Pharan und seine Zeit als Einfuehrung in die alte Dogmengeschichte.* Edited by Wilhelm Maurer and Elisabeth Bergstraesser. Berlin, 1957.

Eliade, Mircea, "Methodological Remarks on the Study of Religious Symbolism," in *The History of Religions: Essays in Methodology,* edited by Mircea Eliade and Joseph Kitagawa. Chicago: University of Chicago Press, 1959.

Farrar, Frederic. *History of Interpretation.* Bampton Lecture, 1885. Grand Rapids: Baker Book House, 1961.

Faulhaber, M. *Die Prophetenkatenen nach roemischen Handschriften.* Paris, 1910.

Favale, Agostino. *Teofilo d'Alessandria. Scritti, Vita, et Dottrina.* Biblioteca del 'Salesianum,' no. 41. Torino, 1958.

Foerster, W. "ὀυχ ἁρπαδμὸν ἠδήσατο bei den griechischen Kirchenvaetern." *Zeitschrift fuer die Neuetestamentliche Wissenschaft* 29 (1930):115–28.

Freimann, M. "Die Wortfuehrer des Judentums in den aeltesten Kontroversen zwischen Juden und Christen." *Monatsschrift fuer Geschichte und Wissenschaft des Judentums* 55 (1911):554–85; 56 (1912):49–64; 164–70.

Galtier, Paul. "Les anathématismes de saint Cyrille et le concile de Chalcédoine." *Recherches de science religieuse* 23 (1933):43–57.

——. "Saint Cyrille et Apollinaire." *Gregorianum* 37 (1956):584–609.

Gavin, Frank. "Aphrates and the Jews." *Journal of the Society of Oriental Research* 7 (1923):95–166.

Gerber, Wolfgang E. "Exegese." In *Reallexikon fuer die Antike und Christentum,* 6:1211 ff. Stuttgart, 1966.

Gesché, Adolf. "L'Âme humain de Jésus dans la christologie du ivᵉs. Le témoignage du *Commentaire sur les Psaumes* découvert à Toura." *Revue d'histoire ecclésiastique* 54 (1959):385–425.

Ginzberg, Louis. *Die Haggada bei den Kirchenvaetern.* Amsterdam, 1899.

Goldin, Judah. "The Period of the Talmud (135 B.C.D.–1035 C.E.)." In *The Jews. Their History, Culture, and Religion,* edited by Louis Finkelstein. New York, 1949.

Goodenough, Erwin. *Jewish Symbols in the Graeco-Roman Period.* New York, 1964.

Goppelt, Leonhard. *Typos*. Guetersloh, 1939.

Grady, L. Augustine, S.J. "The History of the Exegesis of Matthew 27:25: A Study of Early Medieval Commentaries (630–1000) on Matthew's Gospel." Ph.D. dissertation, Fordham University, 1970.

Grant, Robert M. *The Bible in the Church*. New York, 1963.

———. *The Earliest Lives of Jesus*. New York, 1962.

———. "Greek Literature in the Treatise *De trinitate* and Cyril's *Contra Julianum*." *Journal of Theological Studies* 15 (1964):265–279.

———. *The Letter and the Spirit*. London, 1957.

Greer, Rowan A. *Theodore of Mopsuestia*. Westminster, Maryland, 1961.

Grillmeier, Aloys. *Christ in Christian Tradition*. New York, 1965.

———. "Das Scandalum oecumenicum des Nestorius in kirchlich-dogmatischer und theologiegeschichtlicher Sicht." *Scholastik* 36 (1961):321–56.

Grillmeier, Aloys, and Bacht, Heinrich, ed. *Das Konzil von Chalkedon*. 3 vols. Wuerzburg, 1951–54.

Gross, J. *La divinisation du chrétien d'après les Pères grecs*. Paris, 1938.

Guillet, J. "Les exégèses d'Alexandrie et d'Antioche. Conflict ou malentendu?" *Recherches de science religieuse* 34 (1947):257–302.

Hahn, Ferdinand. *Christologische Hoheitstitel*. Goettingen, 1963.

Haidacher, Sebastian. "Rede des Nestorius ueber Hebr. 3,1, ueberliefert unter dem Namen des hl. Chrysostomus." *Zeitschrift fuer katholische Theologie* 29 (1905):192–95.

Hanfman, George M. A. "News Letter from Sardis." *Bulletin of the American Schools of Oriental Research* (Aug. 10, 1965).

———. "Sardis Through the Ages." *Archaeology* 19 (1966):96–7.

Hanson, R. P. C. *Allegory and Event*. London, 1959.

Harnack, Adolf von. *Die Altercatio Simonis Judaei et Theophili Christiani, nebst Untersuchungen ueber die anti-juedische Polemik in der alten Kirche*. Berlin, 1883.

———. *Die Bezeichnung als "Knecht Gottes" und ihre Geschichte in der alten Kirche*. Sitzungsberichte der preussischen Akademie der Wissenschaften; Philosophisch historische Klasse, pp. 212–38. Berlin, 1882.

———. *History of Dogma*. Translated by Neil Buchanan. 7 vols. New York, 1961.

———. *Der Kirchengeschichtliche Ertrag der exegetischen Arbeiten des Origenes*. Leipzig, 1918.

———. *The Mission and Expansion of Christianity in the First Three Centuries*. London, 1908.

———. *Die Terminologie der Wiedergeburt und verwandter Erlebnisse in der aeltesten Kirche.* Leipzig, 1916.

Harrisville, Roy. *The Concept of Newness in the New Testament.* Minneapolis, 1960.

Hebensberger, J. N. *Die Denkwelt des heiligen Cyrill von Alexandrien. Eine Analyse ihres philosophischen Ertrags.* Augsburg, 1927.

Hefele, Charles J. *A History of the Councils of the Church,* vol. 2. Edinburgh, 1876.

Herford, R. Travers. *Christianity in the Talmud and Midrash.* London, 1903.

Hockel, Alfred. *Christus der Erstgeborene. Zur Geschichte der Exegese von Kol. 1,15.* Duesseldorf, 1965.

Hornschuh, Manfred. *Studien zur Epistula Apostolorum.* Berlin, 1965.

Houssiau, Albert. *La Christologie de Saint Irénée.* Louvain, 1955.

Hulen, A. B. "The 'Dialogues with the Jews' as source for the Early Jewish Argument against Christianity." *Journal of Biblical Literature* 51 (1932):68–70.

James, Wilhelm. *The Cruelest Month.* New Haven, 1965.

Janssens, L. "Notre filiation divine d'après saint Cyrille d'Alexandrie." *Ephemerides theologicae lovaniensis* 15 (1938):233–78.

Jeremias, Joachim. "Μωϋσῆς." In *Theologisches Woerterbuch zum Neuen Testament,* edited by G. Kittel, 6:852–79. Stuttgart, 1942.

Jones, A. J. M. *The Later Roman Empire: A Social, Economic, and Administrative Survey.* Oxford, 1964.

Jouassard, G. "L'Abandon du Christ en croix dans la tradition grecque des IVe et Ve siècles." *Revue des sciences religieuses* 5 (1925):609–33.

———. "L'Activité littéraire de saint Cyrille d'Alexandrie jusqu'à 428. Essai de chronologie et de synthèse." *Mélanges E. Podechard.* Lyons, 1945.

———. "Cyrill von Alexandrien." *Reallexicon fuer Antike und Christentum.* 3:499–516. Stuttgart, 1957.

———. "'Impassibilité' du Logos et 'Impassibilité' de l'âme humaine chez saint Cyrille d'Alexandrie." *Recherches de science religieuse* 45 (1957):209–44.

———. "Une intuition fondamentale de saint Cyrille d'Alexandrie en christologie dans les premières années de son épiscopat." *Revue des études byzantines; Mélanges Martin Jugie* 10 (1953):175–86.

———. "Saint Cyrille d'Alexandrie aux prises avec la communication des idiomes avant 428 dans les ouvrages antiariens.'" *Studia Patristica,* vol 6. Texte und Untersuchungun, 81:112–21. Berlin, 1962.

————. "Saint Cyrille d'Alexandrie et le schéma de l'incarnation verbe-chair." *Recherches de science religieuse* 44 (1956):234–42.

Juessen, Klaudius. "Die Christologie des Theodoret von Cyrus nach seinem neuveroeffentlichen Isaiaskommentar." *Theologie und Glaube* 27 (1935):438–51.

Juster, Jean. *Les Juifs dans l'empire romain*. 2 vols. Paris, 1914.

Kahle, P. E. *The Cairo Geniza*. Oxford, 1959.

Kerrigan, Alexander. *St. Cyril of Alexandria: Interpreter of the Old Testament*. Rome, 1952.

————. "The Objects of the Literal and Spiritual Sense of the New Testament according to St. Cyril of Alexandria." *Studia Patristica*, vol. 1. Texte und Untersuchungen, 63:354–74. Berlin, 1957.

King, N. Q. *The Emperor Theodosius and the Establishment of Christianity*. London, 1961.

Koeppen, Klaus P. *Die Auslegung der Versuchungsgeschichte unter besonderer Beruecksichtigung der Alten Kirche*. Tuebingen, 1961.

Kraeling, Carl. *The Excavations at Dura-Europos*, vol. 8. New Haven, 1956.

————. *The Synagogue*. New Haven, 1956.

Kuhn, K. G. "Se Siljonim und sifre minim." In *Judentum, Urchristentum, Kirche. Festschrift fuer Joachim Jeremias*. Berlin, 1960.

Kyrilliana. *Spicilegia edita Sancti Cyrilli Alexandrini XV recurrente saeculo*. Cairo, 1947.

Ladner, Gerhart B. *The Idea of Reform. Its Impact on Christian Thought and Action in the Age of the Fathers*. Cambridge, 1959.

Lampe, G. W. H. *The Seal of the Spirit*. London, 1951.

Langevin, G. "Le thème de l'incorruptibilité dans le commentaire de saint Cyrille d'Alexandrie sur l'Evangile selon saint Jean." *Sciences ecclésiastiques* 8 (1956):295–316.

Laubert, Friedrich. *Die Kanones der wichtigsten altkirchlichen Concilien*. Freiburg: J. C. B. Mohr, 1896.

Lebon, J. "Fragments arméniens du commentaire sur l'Epître aux Hébreux de Saint Cyrille d'Alexandrie." *Le Muséon* 44 (1931):69 ff; 46 (1933):237 ff.

Liébaert, Jacques. *La Doctrine christologique de Saint Cyrille d'Alexandrie avant la querelle nestorienne*. Lille, 1951.

Lieberman, Saul. "The Martyrs of Caesarea." *Annuaire de l'institut de philologie et d'histoire orientales et slaves* 7 (1939–44):395–446.

————. "Palestine in the Third and Fourth Centuries." *Jewish Quarterly Review* 36 (1945–46):329–70.

Loofs, Friedrich. "Das altkirchliche Zeugnis gegen die herrschende

Auffassung der kenosisstelle, Phil. 2:5–11." *Theologische Studien und Kritiken* 100 (1927–28):1–102.

Lubac, Henri de. *Histoire et esprit: L'intelligence de l'Ecriture d'après Origène.* Paris, 1950.

Lucas, Leopold. *Zur Geschichte der Juden im vierten Jahrhundert.* Berlin, 1910.

Lyonet, S. "Le sens de *eph hōi* en Rom. 5,12 et l'exégèse des pères grecs." *Biblica* 36 (1955):436–56.

Mahé, Joseph. "Les anathématismes de saint Cyrille d'Alexandrie et les évêques orientaux du patriarchat d'Antioche." *Revue d'histoire ecclésiastique* 7 (1906):505–48.

———. "Cyrille (saint), patriarche d'Alexandrie." *Dictionnaire de théologie catholique* 3 (1908):2476–527.

———. "La date du Commentaire de Saint Cyrille d'Alexandrie sur L'Evangile selon St. Jean." *Bulletin de littérature ecclésiastique* 9 (1907):41–45.

———. "L'Eucharistie d'après saint Cyrille d'Alexandrie." *Revue d'histoire ecclésiastique* 8 (1907):677–96.

———. "La sanctification d'après saint Cyrille d'Alexandrie." *Revue d'histoire ecclésiastique* 10 (1909):30–40; 469–92.

Mahien, L. "L'abandon du Christ sur la croix." *Mélanges de science religieuse* 2 (1945): 209–42.

Malevez, L. "L'Eglise dans le Christ: Étude de Théologie historique et théorique." *Recherches de science religieuse* 25 (1935):257–91; 418–40.

Manoir, H. du. "L'Argumentation patristique dans la controverse nestorienne." *Recherches de science religieuse* 25 (1935):441–61.

———. *Dogme et spiritualité chez saint Cyrille d'Alexandrie.* Études de théologie et d'histoire de la spiritualité, vol. 3. Paris, 1944.

———. "Le problème de Dieu chez Cyrille d'Alexandrie." *Recherches de science religieuse* 27 (1937):385–407; 549–96.

———. "Le Symbole de Nicée au concile d'Ephèse," *Gregorianum* 12 (1931):104–37.

Marrou, Henry-Irenée. *Saint Augustin et la fin de la culture antique.* Bibliothèque des ecoles françaises d'Athenes et de Rome, no. 145. Paris, 1938.

Merendino, Pius. *Paschale Sacramentum. Eine Untersuchung ueber die Osterkatechese des hl. Athanasius von Alexandrien in ihrer Beziehung zu den Fruechristlichen exegetisch-theologischen Ueberlieferungen.* Muenster, 1965.

Merki, H. ΟΜΟΙΩΣΙΣ ΘΕΩ: *Von der platonischen Angleichung an Gott zur Gottaehnlichkeit bei Gregor von Nyssa.* Fribourg, 1952.

Meyendorff, J. *"eph hōi* (Rom. 5,12) chez Cyrille d'Alexandrie et Théodoret." *Studia Patristica,* vol. 4. Texte und Untersuchungen, vol. 79. Berlin, 1961.

Milne, J. G. *A History of Egypt under Roman Rule.* London, 1898.

Mitten, David G. *Bulletin of the American Schools of Oriental Research* 170 (April, 1963):38–48.

Molari, Carlo. "La cristologia di S. Cirillo e l'antropologia neoplatonica." *Euntes docete* 12 (1959):223–29.

Monceaux, P. "Les Colonies juives dans l'Afrique romaine." *Revue des études juives* 44 (1902):1 ff.

Mondésert, Claude. *Clément d'Alexandrie.* Paris, 1944.

Montmasson, E. "L'Homme créé à l'image de Dieu d'après Théodoret de Cyr et Procope de Gaza." *Echos d'orient* 14 (1911):334–3; 15 (1912):154–62.

Moore, G. F. "Christian Writers on Judaism." *Harvard Theological Review* 14 (1921):198.

Moses In Schrift und Ueberlieferung. Duesseldorf, 1963.

Muehlenberg, Ekkehard. *Apollinaris von Laodicea.* Goettingen: Vandenhoeck and Ruprecht, 1969.

Musurillo, Herbert, trans. *Methodius: The Symposium.* Westminster, 1958.

———. *Symbolism and the Christian Imagination.* Baltimore, 1962.

Nau, F. "Saint Cyrille et Nestorius: contribution à l'histoire de l'origine des schismes monophysite et nestorien." *Revue de l'orient chrétien* 15 (1910):365–91.

Nautin, Pierre, ed. *Homélies pascales. Sources Chrétennes,* vols. 27, 36, 48. Paris, 1950.

Neusner, Jacob. *A History of the Jews in Babylonia.* 5 vols. Leiden, 1965 ff.

———. "The Religious Uses of History; Judaism in First Century A.D. Palestine and Third Century Babylonia." *History and Theory* 5 (1966):153–71.

Nielsen, J. T. *Adam and Christ in the Theology of Irenaeus of Lyons.* Assen, 1968.

Nikolasch, Franz. *Das Lamm als Christussymbol in den Schriften der Vaeter.* Wien, 1963.

Norris, R. A. *Manhood and Christ.* Oxford, 1963.

Pannenberg, Wolfhart. *Jesus: God and Man.* Philadelphia, 1968.

Parkes, James. *The Conflict of the Church and the Synagogue.* New York, 1934.

Pelikan, Jaroslav. *Luther the Expositor.* St. Louis, 1959.

Penna, Angelo. *Principi e carattere dell'esegesi di S. Gerólamo.* Scripta Pontificii Instituti Biblici, no. 102. Rome, 1950.

Philips, G. "La grâce des justes de l'Ancien Testament." *Ephemerides theologicae lovanienses* 23 (1947):521–56; 24 (1948):23–58.

Pollard, T. E. "The Exegesis of Scripture and the Arian Controversy." *Bulletin of the John Rylands Library* 41 (1958–59):414–29.

Prestige, G. L. *Fathers and Heretics.* London, 1940.

Quasten, Johannes. *Patrology,* vol. 3. Westminster, Maryland, 1960.

Quinn, Jerome D. "Saint John Chrysostom on History in the Synoptics." *Catholic Biblical Quarterly* 24 (1962):140–47.

———. "Oesterliche Freuhlingslyrik bei Kyrillos von Alexandreia." In *Paschatis Sollemnia* edited by Balthasar Fischer and Johannes Wagner. Basel, 1959.

Ramsey, Ian T. *Religious Language. An Empirical Placing of Theological Phrases.* London: SCM Press, 1957.

Recheis, P. Athanasius. "Sancti Athanasii Magni doctrina de primordiis seu quomodo explicaverit Gen. 1–3." *Antonianum* 28 (1953):219–60.

Renaudin, P. *La Théologie de saint Cyrille.* Tongerloo, 1937.

Reuss, Joseph. "Cyrill von Alexandrien und sein Kommentar zum Johannes Evangelium." *Biblica* 25 (1944):207–09.

———. *Matthaeus, Markus, und Johannes Katenen.* Neutestamentliche Abhandlungen, vol. 18. Muenster, 1941.

Richard, M. "L'introduction du mot 'Hypostase' dans la théologie de l'Incarnation." *Mélanges de science religieuse* 2 (1945):5–32; 243–71.

———. "Notes sur l'évolution doctrinale de Théodoret." *Revue des sciences philosophiques et théologiques* 25 (1936):459–81.

———. "Saint Athanase et la psychologie du Christ selon les ariens." *Mélanges de science religieuse* 4 (1947):5–45.

Richter, Gustav. "Ueber die aelteste Auseinandersetzung der syrischen Christen mit den Juden." *Zeitschrift fuer Neutestamentliche Wissenschaft* 35 (1936):101–14.

Riesenfeld, H. "The Mythological Background of New Testament Christology." In *Background of the New Testament and Its Eschatology,* edited by W. D. Davies and D. Daube, pp. 81–95. Cambridge, 1956.

Ritschl, Albrecht. *Gesammelte Aufsaetze.* Freiburg, 1893.

Robbins, F. E. *The Hexameral Literature.* Chicago, 1912.

Romanides, J. S. "St. Cyril's 'one physis or hypostasis of God the Logos incarnate' and Chalcedon." *Greek Orthodox Theological Review* 10 (1964–65):82–107.

Rosenmueller, J. G. *Historia interpretationis librorum sacrorum in ecclesia christiana.* Hildburghausen-Leipzig, 1795–1814.

Rucker, Ignaz. *Rund um das Recht der zwanzig ephesinischen Anklangezitate aus Nestorius wider Nestorius—im Lichte der syrischen Nestorius Apologie genannt Liber Heraclides.* Oxenbronn, 1930.

Ruecker, Adolf. *Die Lukas-Homilien des heiligen Cyrill von Alexandrien. Ein Beitrag zur Geschichte der Exegese.* Breslau, 1911.

Sagues, J. "El Espíritu Santo en la santificación del hombre según la doctrina de S. Cirilo de Alejandría." *Estudios eclesiásticos* 21 (1947):35–83.

Samuel, V. C. "One Incarnate Nature of God the Word." *Greek Orthodox Theological Review* 10 (1964):37–53.

Schelkle, Karl Hermann. *Paulus Lehrer der Vaeter. Die altkirchliche Auslegung von Roemer 1–11.* Duesseldorf, 1956.

Schluetz, Karl. *Isaias 11,2 in den ersten vier christlichen Jahrhunderten.* Muenster, 1932.

Schnakenburg, Rudolf. "Die 'Anbetung in Geist und Wahrheit' (Joh. 4,23) im Lichte von Qumram-Texten." *Biblische Zeitschrift* 3 (1959):88–94.

———. *Das Johannesevangelium.* Part 1. Freiburg, 1965.

Schubart, W. *Aegypten von Alexander der grosse bis auf Mohammed.* Berlin, 1922.

Schuerer, Emil. *A History of the Jewish People in the time of Jesus Christ.* New York, n.d.

Schulte, Elzear. *Die Entwicklung der Lehre vom menschlichen Wissen Christi bis zum Beginn der Scholastik.* Forschungen zur christlichen Literatur-und Dogmengeschichte, vol. 12. Paderborn, 1914.

Schwartz, Eduard. *Cyrill und der Moench Viktor.* Akademie der Wissenschaften in Wien, Philosophisch-historische Klasse, Sitzungsberichte, vol. 208, chap. 4. Vienna, 1928.

———. "Zur vorgeschichte der ephesinischen Konzils." *Historische Zeitschrift* 112 (1914):237–63.

Scipioni, Luigi I. *Ricerche sulla christologia del 'Libro di Eraclido' di Nestorio.* Paradosis: Studi di letteratura e teologia antica, vol. 11. Freiburg, 1956.

Scroggs, Robin. *The Last Adam.* Philadelphia, 1966.

Seaver, James Everett. *Persecution of the Jews in the Roman Empire.* Lawrence, Kansas, 1952.

Sellers, Robert. *Two Ancient Christologies.* London, 1940.

———. *The Council of Chalcedon.* London, 1953.

Semler, J. S. "Historische Einleitung in die dogmatische Gottesgelehr-samkeit von ihrem Ursprung und ihrer Beschaffenheit bis auf unsere Zeiten." In S. J. Baumgarten, ed., *Evanglische Glaubenslehre.* Halle, 1764.

Simon, M. "La polémique anti-juive de S. Jean-Chrysostome et le mouvement judaïsant d'Antioche." *Mélanges Cumont* (1936), pp. 403–29.

———. *Verus Israel: Étude sur les relations entre chrétiens et juifs dans l'empire romain (135–425).* Paris, 1964.

Simonetti, M. *Studi sull' Arianesimo.* Rome, 1965.

Souvay, Charles L. "The Twelve Anathemas of St. Cyril." *Catholic Historical Review,* n. s. 5 (1926):627–35.

Spannuet, M. *Recherches sur les écrits d'Eustache d'Antioche avec une édition nouvelle des fragments dogmatiques et exégétiques.* Lille, 1948.

Spicq, C. "L'Origine johannique de la conception du Christ-prêtre dans l'Epître aux Hébreux." In *Aux Sources de la tradition chrétienne: Mélanges offerts à M. Maurice Goguel,* pp. 258–96. Neuchatel, 1950.

Spindler, Aloysius. *Cur Verbum caro factum. Das Motif Menschenwerdung und das Verhaeltnis der Erloesung zur Menschenwerdung Gottes in den christologischen Glaubenskaempfen des vierten und fuenften Jahrhunderts.* Forschungen zur christlichen Literatur und Dogmengeschichte. Paderborn, 1938.

Staab, Karl. *Pauluskommentare aus der griechischen Kirche.* Neutestamentliche Abhandlungen, vol. 15. Muenster, 1933.

Staerk, W. "Anakephalaiosis." In *Reallexikon fuer Antike und Christentum,* 1:411–14. Stuttgart, 1950.

———. "Der escatologische Mythos in der altchristlichen Theologie." *Zeitschrift fuer Neutestamentliche Wissenschaft* 35 (1936):83–95.

Sullivan, Francis. *The Christology of Theodore of Mopsuestia.* Rome, 1956.

Theologisches Woerterbuch zum Neuen Testament. Edited by G. Kittel. Stuttgart, 1933 ff.

Turner, H. E. W. *The Patristic Doctrine of Redemption. A Study of the Development of Doctrine during the First Five Centuries.* London, 1952.

Urbina, I. Ortiz de. "Il dogma di Efeso." *Revue des études byzantines; Mélanges Martin Jugie* 11 (1953):233–40.

Vaccari, A. "La grecità di S. Cirillo d'Alessandria." *Studi dedicati alla memoria di Paolo Ubaldi.* Pubblicazioni della Università Cattólica del Sacro Cuore, ser. 5. Scienze Storiche, 16:27–40. Milan, 1937–45.

Vermes, Géza. *Scripture and Tradition in Judaism.* Leiden, 1961.

Voelker, W. *Das Vollkommenheitsideal des Origenes.* Tuebingen, 1931.

——. *Der wahre Gnostiker nach Clemens Alexandrinus.* Berlin and Leipzig, 1952.

Voobus, Arthur. *History of Asceticism in the Syrian Orient.* 2 vols. Louvain: Secrétariat du Corpus Scriptorum Christianorum Orientatium, 1958–60.

Walzer, R. *Galen on Jews and Christians.* Oxford, 1949.

Weigl, Eduard. *Die Heilslehre des heiligen Cyrill von Alexandrien.* Forschungen zur christlichen Literatur-und Dogmengeschichte, vol. 5, nos. 2 and 3. Mainz, 1905.

——. *Christologie vom Tode des Athanasius bis zum Ausbruch des Nestorianischen Streites.* Muenchen, 1925.

Wickert, Theodore. *Studien zu den Pauluskommentaren Theodors von Mopsuestia.* Berlin, 1962.

Wiesen, David S. *St. Jerome as a Satirist. A Study in Christian Latin Thought and Letters.* Ithaca: Cornell University Press, 1964.

Wilde, Robert. *The Treatment of the Jews in the Greek Christian Writers of the First Three Centuries.* Washington, 1949.

Wiles, Maurice F. *The Spiritual Gospel. The Interpretation of the Fourth Gospel in the Early Church.* Cambridge, 1960.

Wilken, Robert L. "The Interpretation of the Baptism of Jesus in the Later Fathers." *Studia Patristica,* vol. 11. Texte und Untersuchungen, vol. 108. Berlin: Akademie Verlag, 1970.

——. "Judaism in Roman and Christian Society." *Journal of Religion* 47 (1967):313–30.

——. "Tradition, Exegesis, and the Christological Controversies." *Church History* 34 (1965):123–45.

——. "Exegesis and the History of Theology: Reflections on the Adam-Christ Typology in Cyril of Alexandria." *Church History* 25 (1966):139–56.

Williams, A. Lukyn. *Adversus Judaeos. A Bird's Eye View of Christian Apologiae until the Renaissance.* Cambridge, 1935.

Wingren, Gustaf. *Man and the Incarnation.* Philadelphia, 1959.

General Index

'*Abodah Zarah,* 32

Adam, second, as symbol, 225. *See also* Adam typology

Adam typology, 91–92, 168; second Adam reforms to newness, 90; and new creation, 91; in Philo, 93; in ante-Nicene fathers, 95 ff.; in Irenaeus, 96–99; in Methodius, 99–101; in post-Nicene writers, 101 ff.; to show solidarity of Christ with mankind, 102–03; in Athanasius, 103–04; and uniqueness of Christ, 104–06, 110; used for Christ only after Incarnation, 108, 191; describes Christ as like other men, 108–09, 196; describes Christ as extraordinary man, 110, 141, 189, 196; to interpret events in life of Christ, 111–13; and Moses, 114, 121–22; and individuality of Christ, 121*n;* in Cyril's *Contra Julianum,* 193; and Christology, 199; in controversy with Nestorius, 210; shows Christ as undergoing human experiences, 216; in Cyril's *Quod Unus Christus Sit,* 217–19; expresses unity of Christ, 220–21

Adoption as sons of God, 117*n,* 159*n,* 160

Adoration in Spirit and in Truth: reason for title, 70, 76–77; and Cyril's exegetical-theological concerns, 83–84

Alexandria, synagogue at, 41

Alexandrian theology, 189, 214

Allegory, 45

Ambrose, 164

Ammianus Marcellinus, as source for Christian Jewish relations, 12

Anastasius, 202

Anti-Jewish polemic, not in a vacuum, 68

Aphrahat, 20–21

Apollinaris, 104–06

Archaeology, as source for Christian-Jewish relations, 11, 30–31

Arianism, 5, 107–08, 205–06; and baptism of Jesus, 130–33; *prototokos* interpreted by, 165

Arians, 201, 203–04, 214; Cyril and, 5; and Jews, 46

Aristobulus, 39

Armendariz, L., 151

Asceticism of Christians in Persia, 20

Asterius the Sophist, 166–67

Athanasius: distinguishes questions of Jews and Greeks, 24; and Jews, 46–47; answers Jewish interpretation of Bible, 48; Adam typology in, 103–04; *prototokos* in, 167–69; and Cyril, 170, 215; exegesis of of gospels, 206

Augustine: treatises against Jews, 18–19

Baptism of Jesus: interpreted in New Testament and in fathers, 127 ff.; Arian interpretation of, 130–33; interpreted by Cyril, 132 ff.

Barnabas, epistle of, 12–13

Baron, S., 66–67

Basil of Caesarea, 85

Baumgarten, S. J., 223

Bell, H. I., 40

Benoît, A., 98

Bible: Jewish interpretation of, 41, 48; Christian interpretation of, 45; and theological controversy, 201; and history of Christian thought, 222–24

Burghardt, W., 117*n*

Daniélou, J., 145
Death, victory over first accomplished by Christ, 113–14, 116, 161, 171, 184, 188, 195
Didymus, 48, 168
Discussions between Jews and Christians, 28–30
Dogmengeschichte, 223–24
Double scope of Scriptures, 130–31, 191
Dura-Europos, 30, 44–45
Durand, G. M., 217

Elert, W., 186*n*
Eliade, M., 224
Elvira, Council of, 25
Epiphanius, 29
Eudoxius of Constantinople, 205
Eusebius of Caesarea, 19, 23, 79–80, 169
Eustathius of Antioch, 206
Excerpta Valesiana, 12
Exile, as punishment for Jewish disobedience, 86
Ezechiel (Hellenistic poet), 38

Fayyum, 40
First-born (*prototokos*): interpreted by fathers, 165 ff.; in Cyril, 170 ff.; in Christological controversy, 215–16
First fruits, 115–16, 121, 123, 136–37, 139

Galen, 143
Gamaliel, 33
Genesis, interpretation in fathers, 85–86
Glory seen in passion of Christ, 185–87
Goodenough, E., 44–45
Gospels: interpretation of and Cyril's theology, 185; twofold scope, 130–31, 191
Greeks, arguments met with reason, 24

Gregory of Nyssa, 22, 102; first-born in, 169–70; exegesis contrasted with Cyril's, 226–27

Hagiographa, 34
Harnack, A., 35, 121*n*, 182, 199, 222–24
Heavenly man, 123, 103–06, 190, 216, 221. *See also* Adam typology; Christ
Hefele, C., 26
Hellenism and patristic thought, 2, 223–24
Hexapla, 42
Hilary of Poitiers, 101
Historians, ecclesiastical, as sources for Christian-Jewish relations, 11

Image of God, gradually lost, 134
Incarnation: and resurrection, 183; purpose of in Cyril, 188–89
Incorruption, 99
Innovation: victory over death as, 113, 116, 180
Inscriptions as sources for Christian-Jewish relations, 11
Irenaeus: Adam typology in, 96–99; and Cyril, 128*n*
Isidore of Pelusium, 29, 65; on Christian-Jewish discussions, 50–53

James, W., 177*n*
Janssens, L., 117*n*
Jerome, 29
Jerusalem, 20
Jewish arguments used by Greeks, 37
Jewish-Christian relations, sources for, 10–12
Jewish exegesis, 45–46
Jewish history. Cyril on, 63; supported Christian view of Judaism, 228–29
Jewish practices attractive to Christians, 19
Jewish questions: concerned chiefly

New creation: 90–92, 98–99, 115–17; resurrection as sign of, 117–18; Moses' birth seen as, 153; and sacraments, 164–65; relation of Christianity to Judaism seen as, 173; end of war as, 176; and Christ's suffering, 186; in Cyril's *Quod Unus Christus Sit,* 217–19

Newness: motif in early Christianity, 162–63; result of Christ's resurrection, 182–83

Nicene theology, 206–07

Old Testament (Jewish scriptures): relation to New Testament in Athanasius, 48; Christian use of, 66–67; relation between it and New Testament and in *Glaphyra,* 84

Only begotten (*monogenes*), 215–16

Ordinary or mere man, 138–39, 211–13, 214, 218–19

Origen, 2, 164, 166; on Jewish biblical interpretation, 15–16; his discussions with Jews, 28–29; on Jews, 42–43; Adam typology in, 96

Palladius, 69

Papyri as sources for Christian-Jewish relations, 11

Parkes, J., 25

Pasch, 33

Passion of Christ, seen as glory by Cyril, 184–85

Patristic theology, assumptions underlying study of, 222

Philo, 9, 38, 41, 143, 146, 151, 155; Adam typology in, 93

Prophecy, not literally fulfilled, 15–16

Quaestiones Veteris et Novi Testamenti, 30

Qumram, 71

Recapitulation, 97

Rejection of Judaism by God, 15

Resurrection: as topic disputed between Jews and Christians, 33–34; as unique accomplishment of Christ, 195. *See also* Christ, Resurrection of

Ritschl, A., 223

Rituals of the Jews, 15

Root, metaphor of, 120–21

Rosenmueller, J. G., 2

Sabbath, 12, 14, 16, 32, 34, 56, 60; kept by Christians, 19; Cyril on the, 62

Sanhedrin, Tractate, 33

Sardis, synagogue at, 30, 45

Scriptural interpretation, as topic in Christian writings on Judaism, 13

Semler, J. S., 222–23

Simon, Marcel, 32, 34

Socrates Scholasticus, 54–56, 58

Sozomen, 11

Spain, Jews in, 25

Spirit, God as, 71; spirit and truth contrasted with law of Moses, 72 ff.; not preserved by the first Adam, 109; descent of at Jesus's baptism, 128–40 passim; departs mankind after the fall, 135; in prophets of Israel, 137; returns to mankind at resurrection of Christ, 137; descent of on Jesus, 138–40; presence in Moses, 159–60

Spotless lamb, as image, and relation to second Adam, 181n

Spring, as new creation, 176–79

Synagogue: Christians forbidden to enter, 26; burning of, 27; at Sardis, 30, 45; at Alexandria, 41; at Dura Europos, 44–45

Syriac Christianity, 21

Talmud, 11

Tatian, 166

Tcherikover, V., 39, 40, 46

Temptation of Jesus, Adam typology and, 111

Tertullian, 16, 95, 163

Theodore of Mopsuestia, 23; Adam-
  Christ typology in, 107*n*
Theodoret (of Cyrus), 11, 29, 47
Theodosian Code, legislation on
  Jews in, 26–28
Theophilus of Alexandria, 48, 50
Theotokos, 210, 211, 215, 217
Torah, 33
Traenkle, H., 17*n*
Transformation: of Old Testament
  types into new revelation, 73–74;
  of Judaism through Christ, 88–89;
  Adam typology and, 114

Tutor, metaphor of, 83
Two times, 190–91
Types, 45, 47–48, 73–74, 78, 87;
  Old Testament types of Christ, 12,
  18; not understood by Jews, 60–
  62

Virgin birth, 22–23, 51
Vocabulary of Cyril, 89

War, end of as new creation, 179
Worship, in spirit and in truth, 3,
  61–62

Index of Scriptural References

Index of Greek Terms